THE SILENCE OF DARK WATER

An Inner Journey

Rabbi Wittenberg's publications include
Three Pillars of Judaism: A Search for Faith and Values (SCM Press);
*The Laws of Life: A Guide to Traditional Jewish Practice
at Times of Bereavement* (Masorti Publications);
The Eternal Journey: Meditations on the Jewish Year (Joseph's Bookstore)
and the *High Holiday* and *Pesach* Companions.

THE SILENCE OF DARK WATER

DARK WATER

An Inner Journey

Jonathan Wittenberg

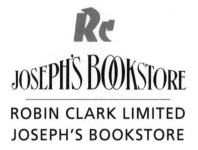

ROBIN CLARK LIMITED
JOSEPH'S BOOKSTORE

First published in Great Britain in 2008
by Robin Clark Limited and Joseph's Bookstore

The manufacture of the paper used in this
book was harmless to the environment and
came from forests replanted after harvesting

A catalogue record for this title is available
from the British Library

ISBN
Hardback: 978 0 7043 7133 0
Paperback: 978 0 7043 7162 0

Typeset by Antony Gray
Printed and bound in Great Britain by
T J International Ltd, Padstow, Cornwall

2

Dedicated to

the memory of my father

Adi Wittenberg

It has been told you what is good, and what God
seeks of you: only to do justice, love mercy
and walk humbly with your God.

Micah 6:8

and to my friends

Ronnie Cohen and

Leslie Lyndon

Always strive to be a human being.

Jack Cohen

Night descends in luminous darkness. The first stars are discernible among the intermittent clouds travelling beneath the immensity of the heavens. The bay is traversed by a seagull's cry. Again and again it calls across the vibrant silence of dark water. The outlines of the islands are blacker than the sky against the sea. The wash of the waves over the rocks and stones is like the rise and fall of a great breathing.

You are alive in us, you who outlive us a million million fold.

Contents

CHAPTER SEVEN
Struggles

CHAPTER EIGHT
Grief

CHAPTER 9
Onwards!

Preface

The path turned sharply between the pine trees and there lay the years before us.

It was such a simple meditation. My wife Nicky and I discovered it during a conference at Melk Abbey, which overlooks a curve in the Danube in Lower Austria. At the gate to the monastery gardens we were given a letter explaining that the way in front of us was lined with numbers representing the years of our life; we could already see them set on posts at a distance of five or six metres apart: 'Go to the age from which you have your earliest memories. Stop there, before continuing the journey through your life. Whenever a certain year prompts you, pause and consider: What have been the major upheavals and transitions, blows of fate, moments of happiness, changes and surprises in your life? Continue until you reach your present age, then open the second envelope.'

We all live with the pressures and constraints of our immediate concerns and only rarely find the stillness to savour the being and becoming of our life as a mystery and a privilege. This walk was such an opportunity. The gardens were really a woodland; mature trees and the winding path prevented us from seeing far ahead. But unexpected turns also allowed us to look forward, or glance back and see again a younger self whose dreams were now squandered, or realised, or changed with time, or still simply dreams.

We reached the years of our respective ages and opened the second letter: 'Now ask yourself what gives you a sense of purpose. Have you found meaning in your life? How do you hope to discover it in the future? What would you still like to achieve? How are you preparing for the end of your life? Consider these questions as you continue on your walk.'

It was strange to enter the future. Sixty, seventy, would these ages find us satisfied with our portion, if we lived so long? How would we encounter the task of relinquishing the capacities, possessions, loved ones of the years gone by? The woodland grew more open; suddenly eighty was not so far ahead, fifty only a glance behind.

Few experiences have ever presented me so simply but dramatically with the question: What does all this mean?

The present book was not prompted by that walk. I'd already been struggling with writing on those themes for over two years when we were privileged to be guests at that beautiful Austrian Abbey. But it does attempt to explore similar issues: To what does life's journey amount? What does it mean to have a mind, a heart, a soul and a conscience? Does God speak to us and, if so, what does God say? How does it feel to grow older? What gives life its depth and purpose? What might dying entail?

We all begin with our own experience, so this book uses the story of my life as a point of departure for its journey. But that is only the starting place for wider and independent explorations and contemplations. Where these lead will lie in the responses and reflections of different people; I hope they find a resonance there in the narratives of other lives and spirits.

JONATHAN WITTENBERG
January 2008; Shevat 5768

CHAPTER ONE

Setting Out

Security

I remember when I was six and we'd just moved down from Glasgow, and Isca, my mother's sister who became my second mother, was making cream for her guests. We were living in her flat, the upstairs of my grandparents' house, and I was ill. She was beating the cream by hand, and I was listening to the sound of the whisk and, most especially, for the pauses while she tested it to see if it was sufficiently thick. I heard her say to my brother in the other room, 'One mustn't beat it too much or it'll turn to butter.' And turn to butter it almost did. So at the last minute she added cocoa and sugar to give it a different flavour and, in spite of having been sick the day before, I was allowed to taste the tiniest half spoonful of the delicious mixture. That was over forty years ago, yet more than once I've heard myself telling my cake-loving children as they prepare the cream for the filling, 'Careful, it'll turn to butter if you beat it for too long.'

I must have been a couple of years older and we were in Switzerland. Those winter holidays, Isca's brainchild, were the highlight of the year; the cases being brought down, the boat train from Victoria Station, the sea, especially when it was rough, the lights of Calais from the ferry, walking down the platform alongside the huge dark green train to find the right compartment, choosing who would sleep on which couchette, secretly staying awake to watch the fields and towns of France fly past in the swaying darkness, waking in the morning to the sight of the Swiss mountains. My father invariably had to return early to go back to work, so Isca would bring us home a few days later. We relished those last few special days. Once, as we were getting on the local train to take us down from the resort to the main line station from which the sleeper departed, I climbed into the crowded carriage through different doors from Isca and my brother. At once I was surrounded by a wall of tall people; strangers swallowed me up. I had no idea where I was or where I had to go; I was convinced I would be lost forever. I despaired and started to cry. Isca found me immediately: 'Did you really think we would leave you behind?' she said. 'We would never ever abandon you.' Her words settled something more than my shaken feelings in the train that day.

One winter we went to Austria instead. We were in Innsbruck, having dinner at the station before the sleeper train arrived, when the waiter returned to our table with an enormous plate of chips: 'I don't think we gave you enough at the first serving, so here's another portion'. We thought this was wonderful. I remember, too, how earlier that day we'd gone shopping for winter clothes and Isca had bought me a black anorak decorated with pictures of flags from all around the world. 'It'll be warm for next year' she said, and with those words came her promise that, whatever might happen in the twelve months in between, we would surely return to the magic and the beauty of the snow.

It's strange which unexpected childhood scenes preserve their happiness.

I have at most a couple of dozen recollections of Lore, my late mother. I see her taking me into the shoe shop, telling the barber how to cut my hair. I remember her in those internal pictures in the way a small child recalls a parent. By the time I was conscious of my own growing up she was dead; I never knew her as her own person. I sometimes wonder who she was and what she was actually like. I'm grateful whenever I meet someone who can tell me more about her. I used to visit her grave quite regularly but that is less important to me now. I've realised that in my inner world new branches are still growing from her broken tree.

But it was Isca who brought my brother and me up, who looked after us, ran after us, worried for us and gave us her love.

When Nicky was expecting our first child, they asked us at the ante-natal classes to what we were most looking forward. 'To when the dog and the baby meet', I replied without hesitation, and immediately felt embarrassed for saying something so stupid. The fact that it was true only made me feel worse. I didn't want our beloved dog Safi, accustomed to our single-minded attention, to be jealous. He had, after all, a rather large nose to be put out of joint, to say nothing of his teeth. We took all available advice: 'Treat the dog like an older sibling', we were told, 'and make sure the baby brings him a decent present'. When the great day finally arrived and we brought our son Mossy home from the hospital, Safi behaved impeccably. But when Isca came round to help us, he promptly jumped into her car and adamantly refused to climb out. Understanding that he was in need of special attention, she took him away and spoilt him thoroughly for a day and half. Only then would he consent to return home.

I see now in my mind's eye how, when Isca and my father used to join us for the Friday night meal, bringing half the food with them, and Mossy was already two or three years old, he and Safi would run bounding up the road in the warmth of the summer evening to greet them, the dog jumping up to lick Isca's face, Mossy embracing her with the short arms of a toddler's unconditional hug.

My Father's Hands

My father's hands were broad and strong. When I was five we went for a walk together, just he and I. Our route took us through a garden centre somewhere near the Glasgow suburb where we lived. 'How's your wife?' the owner asked my father kindly. He offered some quiet explanation which I couldn't hear, whereupon the man went off for a moment and returned with a blue primrose in a small pot which he gave to me. I felt shy and drew back. 'You can take it,' said my father, 'It's for you.' All the time I never let go of his hand.

Sometimes when he woke me my father would ask me what I most wanted for my breakfast. 'Fried egg and apple,' I would always say, and he would bring it to me, the apple neatly cored and quartered at the side of the plate. My father helped the carpenter build the upstairs room in the bungalow where we lived; he knew how to handle all the tools, even the rotary saw with its roaring blade.

When I was young the grasp of my father's hands was the most trustworthy sensation in all the world. We would walk together to the synagogue and I would kick the brown and amber autumn leaves at his side. In my teens he taught me how to heat the soldering iron in the gas flame on the stove, then melt the special wire with the burning tip and manoeuvre the liquid metal into place to make a smooth, clean joint. The movements of his hands were precise, the veins on their backs full of vigour.

I was in my late twenties and we were working on some household job together, constructing shelves or repairing a cupboard in the kitchen. I was standing next to him in the scullery, looking over a piece of wood which he was holding. His hands seemed to me as strong as ever. But I noticed that the veins stood out and I could see their bluish purple colour. The skin, too, seemed slightly thinner and less taut, till he took the tools into his grasp with the old familiar skill.

Until I was in my mid-forties my father remained active and fit. He came round regularly and advised us how to mend broken toys and gadgets, how to strip the varnish off old oak furniture and restore the rich texture of the grain with proper beeswax polish, how to fit a large work surface into the bedroom which we were transforming into an office for Nicky.

But then his hands grew swiftly frailer. The purple veins seemed fragile and ran in high ridges above the skin, which looked almost translucent, as if it could easily be broken. His several stays in hospital resulted in blue and mauve blotches on the backs of his hands and on his arms where lines had been inserted to give him antibiotics and nutrients. I don't remember when I first became aware of that quiver, the faint, slight trembling of his hands which he couldn't control. His arm had to be held for the shortest of walks, from the hallway to the car, from the car to the door, from the door to the chair. Isca was looking after him all the time.

His hands shook above my head when he blessed me before the fast began, that final Yom Kippur of his life. It was hard for him to stand, so I crouched where he was sitting, in our old armchair by the kitchen door. His hands trembled terribly, and I wept.

In the weeks before he died my father held up his hands to us, the fingers facing outwards, their tips bent down either for our better grasp or because he simply couldn't uncurl them any more. He was calling, grasping, for our help, without which he had no strength either to stand up or to sit down. He was crying out, pleading, for life on which he didn't want to relinquish his final hold. The tenacious frailty of those last weeks was a torment to him, and, in a different way, to us, remembering how strong his hands had always been, how reassuring, how skilled in every craftsman's task.

During those days I often thought about Lear's response to Gloucester when they meet, both half crazy, both pushed beyond the edge of their endurance, above the cliffs at Dover. 'Let me kiss that hand', cries Gloucester, recognising the old king's voice. 'Let me wipe it first', replies Lear, 'It smells of mortality.'[1]

I sometimes wonder how my children see my hands. They take them often enough, for a pull up a long hill on a holiday walk, to direct them to the part of their back they want me to tickle or scratch. I can't exactly remember but I'm sure there must have been occasions when, holding my hand, one of them has turned it round to look at the back and commented on the markings of the skin: 'Daddy, where did you get that cut?' or, 'I can see all your veins, daddy, and they're a sort of purplish blue.' Children are curious about such matters.

My son is taller than me now, he runs faster; he also has many of his grandfather's skills. I've turned fifty, my father has died, so have many of my teachers and mentors. Time has earned me the equivocal privilege of entering the older generation.

My hands are still strong, I trust. I love working with wood, constructing bookshelves, repairing chairs, or, out in the garden, building ponds and rock gardens, digging and planting the vegetable bed. The skin on my hands hasn't, I think, begun to shrink or grow waxen or shiny. But my hands smell of mortality, just like everybody else's. The odour has got more intense of late and I'm puzzled about the meaning of getting older.

I Acknowledge

I acknowledge before you, Sovereign, living and
eternal God, that you have returned my soul
to me in mercy; great is your faithfulness.[2]

'*Modeh ani lefanecha, melech chai vekayyam* – I acknowledge before You, Sovereign, living and eternal God'; this is the first sentence a Jewish person is meant to say in the morning. With these words we are drawn to wakefulness from sleep; they stand above the gates through which our consciousness enters daily into this world. Often I say them in the middle of that strange transition, filled with the bewilderment of passage, still part possessed by something other, not yet fully cognizant of where I am, uncertain even about who this supposed 'I' who speaks them is.

'*Modeh*' means 'acknowledge' or 'give thanks'. This is a word I can readily say. Life is full of wonder. Rational thought has not yet suppressed the soul's affinities. I belong to that same consciousness which is coextensive with infinity.

The second word *ani*, 'I' – that I cannot say. 'I' am not yet; that person with height and mass, context and location, does not yet feel fully formulated, and the mind which will soon occupy it still clings to this other belonging, longing, until the daylight drives it from me.

'*Ani*', – what a strange word 'I' is. That single letter, that simple pronoun, differentiates us, names as separate our changing consciousness as if we truly were a single coherent entity, an independent being sufficient unto itself. But maybe that isn't entirely so. What if in the world of truth this 'I' by which I label myself doesn't actually exist? In the first moment of awakening my mind is inchoate as if it had until just now inhabited a quite different universe. Sometimes, on mornings filled with wonder, my soul in its first awareness is possessed with parting, as if I were struggling to force myself to leave the embrace of some being or some presence to whom I had been known with a great and accepting

7

love. My mind is still full of the warmth and mystery of this other belonging, though I cannot grasp its nature and it eludes me further with every second of conscious thought. I long to stay with it; I draw the focus of my thinking back from the objects and concerns which the daylight begins to lay bare before me in order to pursue the retreating intuition while my consciousness is still a cloud, shapeless, drifting, as if it could slip beneath the gates of the great barrier of forgetfulness and penetrate the memories of the spirit:

> Pay attention to the soul,
> Amber, agate, amethyst;
> Her light is like the sun's light,
> Seven times the light of the morning.[3]

If I do not follow it now, it will seem to me as if this knowledge has eluded me forever and I will mourn its escape until the memory of the memory fades and I forget that there was ever something I had lost. I look through the window and see the contours of the moon dissolving. Already the dark sky is luminescent; soon it will have engulfed everything in its invasive brightness. If I could only push my awareness back down into those spaces where it still knows that it belongs to something else.

On what will my consciousness settle? This is the moment before the borders between the worlds are sealed. There, in that other domain, everything and everyone exists at once: parents, children, paths of childhood, tracks across the mountains, down into the pine woods, down beneath the clouds. A few seconds, one more opening of the eyes, and all the crossing points will be closed; access will be denied and there will be no recourse to appeal. The world within my heart vanishes; the knowledge of it withdraws to a painful point of yearning. I begin to think, and am again as ever, and all the tarnished and familiar thoughts of the day before rush back home to seize my mind. I am like I always was. I yield to the old coherence.

Now I can truly say '*ani*', I am. What was illusion, is; what was has become as elusive as the vanishing moment which even now just fled.

And yet I know. I know that there is something which I know, though what that something is I do not understand. Except for this, that there

8

exists another world, or at least another perception of the world, and that the rational mind alone will never find its entrance. That is why I prize those moments of half-sleep before the dawn, when understanding holds me like a child on its lap and all I have to do is be and think of nothing at all. Maybe there is a path back there. Maybe if I cover my head in prayer and strive to travel down until the contours of this world dissolve, I shall recover an awareness of that place where I once was.

Therefore I'm wary of believing only in what is capable of measurement and proof and am doubtful of the absolute truth of exclusive definitions of what is and what is not. Right now I appear to be this and you appear to be that. But maybe there other forms of perception in which things might not be that way. Isn't all matter in a constant process of transition and becoming? We all belong together to the great totality of what is; into this great reservoir 'you' and 'I' dissolve; from it we are resolved, who you are and who I am. Moved by countless and unfathomable causes, neither 'you' nor 'I' is static but constantly susceptible to change. For, though we are responsible for our conduct and answerable for our actions, we do not belong to ourselves, we are not ultimately our own.

The sky is liquid blue. It's time to throw off the covers and get up, time to say the whole of the prayer: '*Modeh ani lefanecha*, I acknowledge before you, Sovereign, living and eternal God, that you have returned my soul to me in mercy; great is your faithfulness'. Your faithfulness to me may indeed be great, but even as I say the words I feel that I am losing you. Will I be able to remember? What about my faithfulness to you? Will you stay with me and help me, you who made me conscious of your presence only now, just these two minutes previously, and whose withdrawal is accompanied by a forgetfulness so absolute that I often refuse to believe that there's anything I've forgotten?

Make me faithful to you through the living of this day. Make me realise that you are present in the places where I walk, that you speak with all the people whom I meet. So let reverence for life pervade me, lest I break the twigs of its branches.

Life, to whom I belong, talk to me throughout this day, in moments of kindness, thoughtfulness, beauty. Fill me with the love of you and do not let me wrong you. Great is your faithfulness.

Horse's Breath

In me are people without names,
Children, stay-at-homes, trees.
I am conquered by them all
And this is my only victory.

Boris Pasternak[4]

In my dream I was with my father. I wasn't helping him into the car, as I often did in the last months of his life, but walking with him along the pavement outside the railway station to the row of waiting horse-drawn carriages. It was very cold; there were patches of ice over the cobbled street. My father had on the warm grey and blue felt jacket he used to wear when we were young and which he later passed down to me. The breath from the horses rose in a comforting mist.

We were back in Zermatt where we went for our first winter holiday when I was six and my father younger than I am now. We got off the train and entered the world of fairy tales. No cars were allowed in the village, only sleds. Every morning we fed the horses sugar as they stood between the shafts waiting for passengers. I can still see them standing there patiently, the blankets over their backs. I still sense Isca taking my hand and carefully showing me how to stretch my fingers flat so that the big horses could feel for the sugar with their lips and gently take the lumps.

I remember how, when I was just four, my father pulled me along on my tricycle all the way home from Hoyse, the sweet shop where they sold the toy dried flowers which uncurled as soon as you put them into water. I loved those flowers and for years wanted them for my birthday, long after we'd all forgotten where they came from. If you were to ask me today what happiness and security mean, I would go back in my mind to that scene: sitting on the tricycle while my daddy pulled me along by the rope attached to its handlebars, green fields and trees all around and not an alien thought in my head. This inner picture of my father towing me along the pavement still serves today as the touchstone of my love for him.

10

Love is stored in memories like these. Even the great passions which fill the heart with yearning are distilled over time into specific recollections, how my wife and I drove that night up into the mountains and suddenly there was snow on the road, how we disembarked from the tiny ferry and clambered down into the cove where the beds of oysters lay uncovered in the low tide and the setting sun flung at the water a brilliant, radiant red.

All day that dream has hung over my mind and burned in my heart, making it raw, exposing a tenderness which is often callused over. I'm aware of everyone I see. Often I just want to hurry past the people in the street and get to where I'm supposed to be going, but today I'm glad of every greeting. This lady is just getting out of her car and has a kind word for my dog as he runs sniffing up to her. This man has put his shopping down for a moment and I'm happy to stop and say 'Good morning'.

Later, I hesitate as I leave the hospital where I'd gone to visit a child who was very ill, then turn back to speak to a family huddled in the courtyard with their mobile phones. I don't know them; I've never even spoken to them before, but I saw them earlier outside the same ward and know that they too are waiting for news of a sick child. They welcome my greeting. 'May God bless you', we say to each other, touched by this moment of companionship between Muslim and Jew, and a brief warmth displaces our respective anxieties.

Everything matters; nothing has no value. For a while I'm transformed by the vital awareness of this obvious truth.

All kinds of motivation run dry. My head generally tells me what to do and I usually, though not always, have the will-power to follow its directions. Judgment and will-power are necessary; there is no morality which is not dependent on them. But in those moments when we live from the heart they resume their secondary place. Love and its intuitions direct our path.

In times of darkness, when the sky is like a vast tarpaulin closing off the day, I look up at those bright points where love has pierced the dark fabric and allowed a pin's breadth of light from the boundless radiance beyond to travel through, and my half a dozen stars are sufficient to show me the way.

A memory accosts me like a presence. We had been driving north across the border into Scotland and had passed Dunblane when our son Mossy, who was just eighteen months old, woke up hungry and began to cry. We stopped the car and searched for a sandwich or a biscuit, anything, but the bags were empty. Then my wife saw a sign, 'Deliveries', with an arrow pointing down a lane; surely that must lead us somewhere. Rabbits hopped in every direction as we followed the winding drive. When I returned to the family after letting the dog out onto the grass, the ladies who were polishing the brass fittings on the hotel door had interrupted their work to help Mossy play with a jumble of gumboots.

After we'd eaten we went rowing on a small loch, then stood for a while looking north towards the hills. Suddenly it was as if my mother was beside me. 'Were you ever here?' I asked her in my mind, 'When you were young and just married and beautiful before you became ill, did my father bring you here?' I saw her, not from the power of memory, but as she looks in the small picture that has always stood on the piano.

'I am here', she says, standing on the grass with the low hills towards the north and the mild sky behind her.

For a moment it is as if there were, garnered in my heart as the gift of many people, sufficient love to defy even time itself.

A Missing World

I grew up with a world which wasn't there. The absence is immeasurable; I don't even know all the names.

My cousin and I were sitting in the flat in Jerusalem where the family had lived since 1940. I have only one cousin, although my mother had two sisters and my father had three. With seven siblings in my parent's generation, the laws of continuity suggest that there should be at least fourteen in mine. But it is not so; we're only three: my brother Raphael, my cousin Michal and myself. Such, even if one survives, are the effects of flight and war. Families are scattered across the face of the earth; it takes a generation to settle, people die young, they don't find partners. Refugees and survivors often end up losing much of their future as well as their past.

Our aunt Steffi died recently. She never married and she had no children, so it fell to my cousin to sort out her affairs. We sat together and looked through her photograph albums. There were pictures of her as a child, with friends, as a nurse, among colleagues. But there was also an older generation of photographs, presumably gathered together in a hurry and slipped into her bag when the family fled Nazi Germany. They packed their suitcases in a single evening. They laid the table for tea to make it look as though they were off on holiday and would be back a few days later, then they departed that very night, never to return. My father's father owned a timber mill in Europe; he never really found his place in Israel. He died just months before my older brother was born; my cousin thinks it was from a broken heart. I never met him and, to my sorrow, know almost nothing about him. Apparently the mill, carrying the name Wittenberg, still stands in the town.

All photographers should take this lesson to heart: put the names of the people and the place and date where the picture was taken on the back of every single photograph as soon as it's printed out, because, however obvious this information may seem at the time, fifty, eighty or a hundred years later there won't be anybody left to remember. My cousin and I could recognise almost none of the faces.

My surviving aunt Hella was in the room with us. (She too has since died, and my father has joined them.) She was very ill at the time and could no longer say for certain who all her visitors were, but there were three faces in the photographs which she recognised at once: her father and her two aunts on her mother's side, Sophie and Trude.

Sophie Redlich, Trude Paiser, from time to time I had heard my father mention their names but never until now had I seen their faces. They perished in the Shoah. I remember my father telling me how the rest of the family had tried in vain to persuade them to leave. I looked carefully at the pictures. Sophie had a soft and beautiful face; she was sitting with her husband on a bench in the garden of a villa. Trude was smiling and holding her baby close to her face so that their cheeks touched. The child was called Arnold: Arnold Paiser, he will scarcely have been old enough when it all happened even to know why he and his family were being hounded and murdered.

Who were these people, my very own family? Was it too late to redeem anything of their lives except their names and these photographs, or to honour them with anything more than the passing dignity of a memorial prayer? We have a card, written by my great grandmother Regina Freimann in Theresienstadt and dated November 1943, but postmarked February 1944, sending her last, brief greetings to her family. Any more detailed form of communication was forbidden them by the censor.

My father's eldest sister Eva died in Palestine in 1944. My father told me how the doctor said that she needed to have red wine and chicken soup, but it was war time and they simply didn't have the money for such luxuries. Though she couldn't have known it, she perished at about the same time her grandmother was being deported to Auschwitz. Her two aunts who had stayed in Europe were probably already dead.

Eva was buried in a beautiful location on the Mount of Olives overlooking the Old City of Jerusalem, almost directly opposite the golden gates. At that time the cemetery was still under British control; from 1948 until 1967 it was ruled by the Jordanians, making it inaccessible to Jews. Later, the family decided to add to the inscription on Eva's gravestone the name of her grandmother and the fact that she had perished in the Holocaust. I read these words myself for the first time last summer when my aunt Steffi was buried in the same section of the cemetery. Extraordinarily, the plot the burial society found for her proved to be adjacent to her sister's. There they lie together head to foot, Steffi reunited with the sister for whom she, a young nurse, had cared throughout her last illness over sixty years before.

I dreamt last night of a huge Passover gathering. So many members of the family came to join us and the food was so plentiful that boxes of unleavened bread were piled high outside the back door of my parent's house. On top of them were vegetables in every shade of green, orange and red, together with great plates of eggs, fish and cakes. Ever more dishes were brought from the oven as one group after another of aunts and cousins requisitioned the kitchen in threesomes and foursomes and contributed their unique heirloom recipes for the Passover. The children had gathered around the growing mountain of food and were staring in wonder and anticipation. Then they rushed off to the house next door which we had rented so that all the many branches of the family could celebrate the festival together.

There's little I love more than listening to family stories. I've often heard Isca describing with great fondness how before the war the family would assemble for birthdays and holidays in Frankfurt, where my grandfather served as rabbi until 1939. There would be poems and plays, happiness and celebrations. Whenever I visit my aunt Ruth, my mother's sister, I ask her to tell me about different members of the family. She has a wonderful memory for all the branches of the far flung clan and a gift for recounting their stories. I always try to take one of my children with me when I go; I want them to hear and I need them to remember.

My brother and I grew up in London, children of refugees. Our grandparents lived five minutes away; on the short walk round to their house which we made every few days Raphael and I used to count the paving stones and guess exactly how many there would be on that particular occasion. Almost all our grandparents' guests spoke German. If every single member of our family was present for Passover, the New Year or a special birthday, and even this didn't happen all that often, there would be precisely seven of us around the table. At the time, seven seemed to me an extremely large number of people. It was a long time afterwards before I began to realise that this simply wasn't so.

The Meaning of 'Was'

Alles vergeht und alles wird vergessen
Everything passes and all is forgotten

Before dawn, when I was still half asleep, someone's voice slipped into my mind a line from a poem: 'Alles vergeht und alles wird vergessen – Everything passes and all is forgotten'. I think it must have been my grandfather speaking but I couldn't be sure, nor, on waking, could I recall from whose work he was quoting, or whether the words were simply the product of a dream. But they drew me after them through my misty semi-consciousness with a great compulsion, as if they held a secret, as if, in contrast to their apparent meaning, they marked a gateway between life and death. All that day they haunted me, weaving together places, lines of poetry, voices. Yet they say that everything is destined to oblivion. Can that really be the truth?

The question holds me ever more unrelentingly in its grasp as I grow older: What is the meaning of 'was'? What's the ontological status of what has been? Where, if at all, does it continue to reside, or has it really departed forever? What has become of the love and the hate, the presence and the voices, of those who are now dead?

After a person has gone, is it still possible to trace the pattern of how she loved the interweaving branches through which she looked up at the stars? Are the great connections still present which her consciousness made, between heaven and earth, between her heart and the hearts of her children? If so, is this an act of remembering only, an intuitive reconstruction, the effect of a still hovering, still vital love? Or is it some hidden current emanating from the person herself, she as she actually is, still preserved in a dimension of existence unconfined by the limitations of time as mortals measure it? Or is everything obliterated, so that a life leaves no remnant of itself, no record of its presence, except memory?

Perhaps the world retains more traces of previous lives than we think. It makes every sense to regard the earth as haunted. Terror can still be sensed above the altar at Stonehenge two thousand years after human sacrifice ceased. When Nicky was three or four years old her parents placed her on the stone; she still remembers how she screamed. They say that no birds ever sing in Glen Coe where the Campbells murdered the Macdonalds and that the land which covers the vast mass graves in Lithuania and the Ukraine, Ponar, Babi-Yar and countless other sites of genocide, testifies to the sin which was committed there. The very earth refuses to be fruitful.

Sometimes it seems to me that even our thoughts leave traces of themselves behind. At times, if I've been angry, I stop and try to gather them back into myself lest they should reify behind me, affecting, perhaps, the growth of the tree underneath which I was passing, occasioning some invisible damage inflicted who knows where. Maybe that is why certain houses transmit from the very walls and ceilings a sense of warmth and family love, while others communicate a feeling of solitary misery and dysfunction. This cannot simply be attributed to memory, because when the relevant events occurred we weren't there, we never even knew the dramatis personae of the place.

As time passes, more and more of what I think and feel relates to an invisible world. I recently visited the cemetery where my synagogue buries its dead; before I left I stopped by at least a dozen graves of friends, saluting them and asking their blessings for their families. Though my thoughts are still mainly occupied with the present and the future, I experience these dimensions ever more in their continuity with what has been, with the hearts and faces which gave them birth. Often I follow the web of what used to be, trusting that it will lead me into the spirit of what now is. Do all these events and persons really no longer exist, just because it so happens that when they occurred was yesterday, not today? The impetus to investigate them becomes more assertive as I grow older. It wakes me up more frequently in the night, it addresses me less and less from the periphery and ever more from the centre of my being. It tells me that without them I can neither know who I myself am nor what life truly is.

I feel myself called to trace the lives of the family dead. I listen in my mind to my parents talking about how they reread the old letters which they and my grandparents so carefully preserved. I look up at the picture of my grandfather when I study a verse he especially loved. At times I hear him intone a phrase or comment on a prayer. Under stress I turn to him in my thoughts and ask him what he would have done in such a situation. Once I was on a flight diverted to Frankfurt and found myself with a whole unanticipated day to wander round the neighbourhood where my mother and her sisters grew up. I phoned my aunt from a booth outside the Palmengarten (in her old age my grandmother used to confuse it with Hampstead Heath) and said to her, 'Can you guess where I'm standing right now?' The Westend-Synagogue where my grandfather officiated has been reconstructed and I imagine him standing on the steps outside it with my beautiful and elegant grandmother, greeting the guests after a wedding.

They're dead and gone. At least they're definitely dead, but I don't entirely know if they're gone or what precisely that would mean. I fantasise that somewhere in the library of infinity each day's reality is stacked side by side next to its yesterday and its tomorrow, from the beginning to the end of time. Who knows which one of them is most real? Who's to say that our spirit doesn't sometimes slip through the bars of time on the wings of longing and experience the presence of what was?

Of course, in this world of chairs and tables and buying and selling the dead have no participation. They feature mainly as that great absence in our lives, the emptiness beside the widow which forced the woman, after her husband had died, to learn how to walk all over again before she could dare to cross the street. She was afraid she would simply lose her balance and fall over.

Yet the love of those who have died still adheres to everything around us. I feel it when I lift up my grandfather's Kiddush cup, or see a pear tree blossom like the wonderful specimen which grew in the centre of their garden. I am sure my mother must be there on that path by the chestnut trees wearing that muff I once saw in the photograph, to protect her hands from the snow.

God's Dreams

– O what made fatuous sunbeams toil
To break earth's sleep at all?

Wilfred Owen[5]

I arrived at just the wrong moment and became an embarrassed witness to a furious family quarrel. My friend's father lost his temper and, marching out of the house, slammed the door behind him with such force that the glass flew out and shattered across the floor. There followed a long silence, filled with fear. Then I heard the sound of weeping. My friend's mother was saying to her children between sobs, 'I didn't want it to be like this for you; I didn't want it to be this way at all'. Though I was only ten or eleven at the time, I've never forgotten the scene.

I think that's exactly what God must be feeling when the world's destroyed, when tens of thousands of people drown in the Asian Tsunami, among them many children, or when killers blow people up on the bus or in the market, or when rockets are dropped on innocent people, or bombs fall on them, turning them into shreds of flesh and bringing grief to all who know them. I imagine God is weeping and thinking: 'I didn't mean it to be like this; I hadn't wanted it to be that way at all'.

When children are born, parents dream about how they'll grow up and who they'll become. I fantasize that God must have had such dreams for the world, dreams for the seas and forests, dreams for the birds and animals, and above all, dreams and hopes for human beings, created in God's own image. I imagine that God sometimes thinks about those dreams.

It isn't difficult to reconfigure what God's dreams must have been. After, all, what kind of dreams would you and I have had if we'd created the world?

The world will be beautiful, from the first fashioned light to the last made human being. In spring the sunshine will glow in the bright new grass and in winter the evening twilight will burn between the trees. The fur of young animals will be soft, arousing mercy. The form of all living things, how the heart beats, how the breath animates the body, will be intricate, awakening wonder. The immensity of the universe, how sound travels, how light bends, will humble the mind, inspiring awe.

The world will be shared. There will be differentiation, but no domination. No one will have a greater right than anyone else to find work, seek companionship, raise children and pursue understanding. Everyone will respect the rhythm of the earth together, the rotations which form its days and months, the celebration of its seasons and years.

The world will be ruled by the laws of love and respect. All people will recognise the humanity of everyone else. Through awareness of their own vulnerability they will perceive the necessity of others for protection. Through the joy of partnership they will understand the universal need for fellowship and love.

The world will be a place of honesty and justice. The fulfilment of creation will be peace.

Such must have been God's dreams, and God weeps because their broken fragments lie scattered all about us throughout the world.

Of course I don't literally believe that God cries. But the rabbis weren't shy of the image when imagining God's response to the great catastrophes of history. God weeps, and the angel Metatron, as upset as any child who sees for the first time the face of his ever stoical father crumple in tears, says in distress, 'Let me weep, but you, God, you mustn't weep.'[6] Yet God, in the ferocity of pain, insists, declaring, 'If you don't let me weep now, I'll go to a place where you have no permission to enter', and there in secret God will weep alone.

But God really does cry. If God is present in us all, then God is crying whenever parents bury their slaughtered child, whenever a man looks out at his ravaged fields planted with patient hope, whenever a little girl opens the door to the room where her mother used to comfort her and finds it empty because she's dead and gone.

We, too, weep with God. We weep for the destruction of beauty and the murder of hope. We weep for the violence which afflicts so much of the body of humankind and nature; we weep for the violence performed against us and we weep for the violence performed, if not directly by us, then in our name. We weep because hatred and violence should exist at all to afflict a beautiful world. We weep because of the rapacious and competitive way of living to which we've allowed ourselves to become enslaved.

A friend, whose life is dedicated to the documentation of suffering, showed me pictures of homes and hospitals he'd taken in Iraq soon after the invasion. Parents and grandparents stood watch over their offspring; there were no medicines to treat their children, they had nothing to offer except their helpless presence. One pretty girl of three or four lay on her side protected by her mother's hand; the hand was half the size of the child. 'By now', he said to me, 'All these children are almost certainly dead.'

We weep, too, for something greater than individual pain, we weep for hope itself. We weep because of that waste which Wilfred Owen so devastatingly described in his account of the death of a soldier in the First World War:

> Move him into the sun –
> Gently its touch awoke him once . . .
>
> Think how it wakes the seeds, –
> Woke, once, the clays of a cold star.
> Are limbs, so dear-achieved, are sides,
> Full-nerved – still warm – too hard to stir?
> Was it for this the clay grew tall?
> – O what made fatuous sunbeams toil
> To break earth's sleep at all?[5]

Perhaps we shouldn't be so upset, but tougher and more cynical. Isn't life inevitably selfish, competitive, bloody and cruel? Isn't love self-interest and beauty chance, equality a fantasy longed for by the weak and peace an interlude maintained by the strong? Why bother with dreams?

Yet we cannot help ourselves. We persist in hoping and continue with our dreaming. After nineteen hundred years of exile, when it finally appeared that the Jewish people might have the opportunity to return to their homeland, two choices were put forward for the new national anthem, *Hatikvah*, 'The Hope', and Psalm 126, containing the words 'When God returned the captivity of Zion we were as in a dream'.[7] Amidst the shock and ashes of the eleventh of September 2001, according to one radio survey the most popular song in America was John Lennon's *Imagine*: 'You may say I'm a dreamer, but I'm not the only one'.

We inherit the ineradicable legacy of being dreamers; dreaming cannot be uprooted from our souls.

Our life should be an affirmation that we still believe in God's dreams. Broken dreams are not necessarily irredeemable.

Two summers ago I was climbing up the narrow road which traverses the southern peninsula of the Isle of Skye. The view behind me across the sea was clear and brilliant. Ahead, however, the light was dull and the prospect of the steep hills sombre. Suddenly there came into sight above them the crowns and ridges of the distant Cuillin mountains, blue-grey through the mist, radiant in a far off flash of sunlight. At once the horizon was transformed. I stood still in spontaneous reverence; the world is full of beauty.

In spite of so much manifest hatred, the world is full of love as well.

There are countless individuals who strive for justice, peace and understanding, like the woman I met who devotes her existence to the care of refugee children traumatised by the loss of their parents who were either killed or separated from their offspring as entire families fled for their lives. Such people are my inspiration and the ground rock of my faith.

We are the custodians of God's dreams. Just as it rests within our capacity to destroy them, so it lies within our power to bring them closer to fulfilment.

We live permanently at the intersection between realisation and desecration. There, at those crossroads, God's dreams are our signposts, pointing toward the path of responsibility which stretches through the unknown years ahead.

CHAPTER TWO

Learning

Lech Lecha – The Journey

And the Lord said to Abram, Get you gone from your country, from your family and from your father's house, to the land which I will show you

Genesis 12:1

Sometimes I think it isn't God who says to Abraham, 'Go forth!' but simply life. For life is ruthless to us all, harrying us from the moment of conception until the breath departs from our body at death. We are all subject to the radical equality of time, which commands every one of us, saying 'Get you gone!'

Therefore it cannot be those words themselves, but rather how we hear them, which determines whether or not they come from God. This was the view of Rebbe Yehudah Aryeh Lev of Ger, who taught that what was special about Abraham was not that God spoke to him. God speaks to everyone. It was that Abraham heard.[1] He understood that God was there in that demand to go forth. God is a presence which transforms the nature of the journey. It's no longer only a form of wandering, of following a path half-plotted and half-stumbled upon amidst the exigencies of time. It has become a quest between the human and the other, between the transient and the transcendent. It's the talking and the listening between them, the arguments, the long silences, and the singing on the way.

Thus the imperative 'Go!' doesn't stand alone. Attached to it is '*lecha* – to you', yielding the familiar '*lech lecha* – go to yourself'. These two words are composed of the same consonants, a fact clearly apparent in the unvocalised, vowel-free text of the Torah, so that, although they are read as lech lecha, the going and the self which we become may also be pronounced as the same. Hence what we are is our life's journey and to become ourselves we have to go. Maybe that's why, according to one interpretation, the country to which God promises to lead Abraham is not 'the land which I will show you' but 'the land where I will show you you'.[2]

> As you set out for Ithaka
> Hope that your road is a long one,

wrote C. P. Cavafy, reflecting on one of the other great foundational journeys of western literature, the Odyssey.[3] But the archetypal Jewish journey is not a treasury of islands and sirens; it's the discovery of that 'you', 'you' the inner self, 'you' the other, 'You' God, towards whom all life travels. It's a ceaseless process; there's no homecoming, only a further setting out. For as the 'you' which I discern changes the person I become, so the 'I' who sets out is no longer the same traveller going forth. I am constantly in my journey, my new departure, lech lecha until the end. Thus there is no final answer to the question 'Who am I?', only the process of discovery, a constant becoming, until death.

Even the Torah ends en route, not with an arrival but with an unfinished journey. Go up the mountain, says God to Moses, and look at the land I promised you; see it from afar and resign yourself to the fact that you're never going to get there. According to rabbinic legend, God orders Moses to visit the burial place of Abraham, Isaac and Jacob in the cave of Machpelah as soon as he's died and tell them that the divine promise has been fulfilled; God has brought their children's children to the promised destination.[4] But it isn't true. The people have not yet entered the land. However, what God has indeed given, and what God always gives, is 'the land where I will show you you'.

So the question becomes: How do I travel through my life? What must I become and how do I discover who is, or are, the 'you' who form the dramatis personae of my life?

New horizons, new depths constantly restore our ignorance and create fresh opportunities to make discoveries.

The only true way to gain knowledge is to offer our heart and soul to life along the path of our journey. They are our *olat tammid*, the daily offering which life requires of us. In the Temple the *olat tammid* was the only sacrifice entirely consumed upon the altar; if we truly want life to be our teacher, we cannot withhold the heart.

The soul is a mystery. But when on an autumn morning the sunshine makes the raindrops gleam on the cold grass I sometimes feel as if there is a kind of joy I share with everything, as if we were pervaded not only by the same light but by the same quickening, the same consciousness, the grass, the birds and the 'I' which intimates its own participation, the secret of its eventual transformation. For the consciousness is like the sea and life a rock pool as the tide sweeps in. It fills it and recedes, fills it and recedes, until one day that 'I' which had thought itself discrete and independent is embraced completely and entirely rejoined to the sea.

Meanwhile, I'm grateful to you, companions on the journey, whether or not we're as yet acquainted. Our world is shaped by how well we care for one another. Already you've transformed me many times with your attention. We're fashioned by many millions of interactions and no one can unravel the strands of love and anguish which knit together a life. Nor will we ever fully know the sum of what our own actions engender in other people or how their effects are to be valued, for good and for bad.

Thus we greet each other, people of our lives, and accompany one another on the way.

Lech lecha! May our journeys lead to the land where we discover the humanity which is both you and me, the country where God shows us who we truly are.

My Teachers

For many years my brother and I shared a room. Sometimes, when our eagerness to continue reading was cut short by our parents switching off the lights, we would defy the instruction to 'go to sleep' by talking and telling stories for hours, sufficiently quietly, of course, to ensure that we wouldn't be overheard. Once, for some unknown reason, (our grandfather was a rabbi but there was nothing pious about us as children) the conversation turned to God. I don't remember exactly how old we were, but I must have been nine or ten and Raphael twelve or thirteen. I said something like, 'But that's not such an important subject to worry about', whereupon Raphael replied philosophically, 'But what else is there which could possibly be more important?' Clearly, it was this conversation which set us on course for our future destinies, he to become an economist, I to enter the rabbinate. I'm sure I've got the precise words wrong, but I definitely recall how I thought at the time, and have done ever since, that my brother was absolutely right.

Raphael and I would visit our grandparents at least once each week. When I was small, I would play games with my grandmother while Raphael would receive a lesson on Judaism from my grandfather in preparation for his Bar Mitzvah. In summer we would pick the raspberries and blackberries which grew in abandon in the semi-wilderness towards the back of their large garden. In autumn we would go out to harvest the pears and cooking apples which were carefully stored on the tops of cupboards and wardrobes, where they slowly ripened, or rotted, before those which still passed reasonable muster were turned into *compotes* and pies. All this changed over the years as our grandparents grew older and frailer. Our visits became more frequent; we would sit and talk with them, check on their food supplies and make sure that they had everything they required. Sometimes I went straight from school to their house. A mutuality of interests emerged when I found that I could practise for my exams by reading to them in German, while they, in spite of my mistakes, seemed to have enjoyed the entertainment.

Those visits also gave me the opportunity to ask my grandfather serious questions. Once he started to talk to me about the Talmud. He had first studied Talmud with his own father who had been the rabbi of Erfurt, in Germany, then later and in more depth at rabbinical college in Berlin. I can still remember how he said in German: 'Das verlangt eine besondere Schärfe, – it's a discipline which demands a particular mental acuity.' I hadn't yet studied any Talmud at that time, though I knew of the existence of the work, represented by the row of heavy volumes on my grandparents' shelves. I can't remember what else my grandfather said, but I often reflect on the impact of that short conversation. How could I be so lazy as to remain ignorant of this subject, so central to Jewish life? If I didn't study Talmud, who would teach it to my children? How could I possibly justify the failure to take responsibility for its transmission?

Later I spent a year in Israel after completing my degree. I'd intended to work in forestry, but my plans fell through and matters turned out far differently from how I'd imagined. I found myself looking after an elderly relative, accompanying him to prayers every Friday night and Shabbat morning. He worshipped in a small upstairs synagogue in a very orthodox quarter of Jerusalem. I came to love that service, the men in their favourite corners, the hum of Yiddish voices studying Torah, the clash of an emphatic phrase or insistent exclamation, the spartan melodies chanted with deep feeling, the silence during the most important prayers. Everyone else wore black, except for one elderly man who had a golden gabardine; I didn't know what, if any, his status was in the community, but it was usually he who read from the Torah. He had an habitual smile; his face reflected an inner radiance, which, from afar, I respected and liked. One day quite unexpectedly he called me over and said: 'I don't know who you are but I can see that in life you will have great opportunities for practising kindness.' Then and afterwards I received his words, which he bestowed on me like a blessing, with a deep sense of privilege and responsibility.

Not long ago a friend, whose illness had so far defied diagnosis, asked me to come over for a talk. She spoke about her terror of being smitten by some sudden attack which might leave her paralysed and unable to speak. The doctors, she said, had been reassuring, but only to a degree. They had pointedly refused to go so far as to say that she had nothing to fear. Sometimes, when she had to stay overnight in hospital for tests, she would lie awake for hours petrified at the thought of what might happen to her and what would then become of her family. So far, the worst hadn't come to pass; in fact, the signs were that the threat was receding. But anything might still happen, and at any time. Would I come, if she needed me? Would I sit with her there in the hospital for an hour or two during the long, engulfing night if she became really afraid?

I gave her what reassurance I was able. I couldn't know if I'd be available at the right time, should I be asked, or even which of us might need whom, or who of us would in the end live the longer. But if called, I will go, so long as I can. My friend's words have made me think more deeply about all the people who are alone, afraid and dependent on the good faith of others. Which of us would consider ourselves invulnerable? How then can we fail to answer, should we be needed?

I've been privileged to have many wonderful teachers at school, university, rabbinical college, among my colleagues and in my congregation. At school, the woodwork master screamed at me for chiselling a grove which was so wide that the pieces intended to fit together could literally be shaken like a rattle. But he gave me warm praise for redoing the work so snugly that neither length of timber would budge in the joint at all. I've never forgotten the lesson. I had a succession of brilliant English teachers. I've never lacked for rabbis and lecturers to inspire me. I meet people all the time whose conduct in the field of spiritual care or social justice, or whose daily courage or kindness, leaves me filled with admiration. They set humbling and inspiring examples. I learn from the insights and observations of my community in every *shiur*, or class of study and discussion, which we conduct together. I learn from my family and from the direct and fearless questions which the children ask. They stop me from taking anything for granted. There are also countless opportunities from which I fail to learn.

But now I see that it is the quiet, unintended and unanswerable challenges which have really directed my life.

Never Bored

Her mind is a palace. She moves through history with the
fluency of a spirit, mourns the burning of the library
in Alexandria as if it happened yesterday.[5]

My friend's uncle lived to be over a hundred. He was a wonderful, generous-hearted man and whenever I was in Jerusalem I used to visit him in his flat full of beautiful pictures and ask him for his blessing. I felt it would protect me not only from misfortune but, no less importantly, from the aspects of myself I mistrusted. He was a scientist, a doctor and a lover of the fine arts, especially music. 'Boredom!' he said to me one day in horror, 'Boredom! I don't understand what the word means. The world is so fascinating and there's so much to be interested in that it's incomprehensible to me how anyone can possibly be bored.' He'd never in his whole life, he told me, been bored for one single hour. He reminded me of the way my grandfather used to say that it was ignoble to have no time. How often in moments of ungracious haste I recall this genial observation

There's joy and vitality in a mind absorbed and engaged. Maybe that's why adults love watching children explore the world, how they jump up and down with excitement about travelling on a bus, observe the frost with puzzlement and ask what the moon and stars are made of. I can still visualize our son's first bath. Holding him with anxious care we hesitantly lowered him into the warm water; to our great relief he seemed to enjoy it and extended his arms in a slow gesture of tactile exploration. I recall the great excitement the first time we took the children on the night train to Scotland (we were in the Midlands before they went to sleep) and their exuberance on finding that there was enough snow in the morning to try out a toboggan. I even remember the dog's first discoveries, how he ran eagerly down to the sea to drink and jumped backwards in horror when a wave rose up and soaked him; how he refused to get off the train in the Cairngorms because the platform

30

was covered in snow, which he'd never seen before and so wouldn't budge till I climbed down first, whereupon he descended gingerly, placing his paws with the greatest of care not on the ground but on my shoes.

Surely we were born for the happiness and adventure of discovery. That so many children should grow up in wretchedness and servitude is an unspeakable disgrace. Young hands and eyes should encounter life and beauty, and, encouraged by facilitative love, create the paradigms for the mind's eagerness. But innumerable children enter a universe of misery, hunger and neglect and the early sounds and sights which confront them must make them want to roll up into a ball and protect themselves from the suffering and brutality of this earth.

Maimonides teaches that there's a natural link between curiosity, wonder and the love of God: 'When a person contemplates God's great and wondrous works and creatures and from them obtains a glimpse of God's wisdom which is incomparable and infinite, he will straightway love God, praise God, glorify God, and long with an exceeding longing to know God's great name; even as David said, "My soul thirsts for God, the living God" (Psalm 42:3).'[6] The world, according to the daily morning prayers, is renewed by God every day; nothing is the same as it always was. Therefore life should constantly elicit our attention and evoke our sense of awe.

Yet few of us find it so simple. Again and again I'm struck by what I've failed to notice. I may perceive it in the neurological sense, but I properly observe only a fraction of what lies before my very eyes. I go into the garden and realise that some of my favourite plants have been flowering for days. Even though I love them, I've almost missed them. How could I have been paying so little attention? Yet I do it all the time. When I was a child my parents would chastise me for looking down at the pavement as I walked along. Now I regret everything I failed to see, or almost everything.

There are three short prayers said each morning which I wished I would take more to heart. The first is the simplest, a blessing to God for opening the eyes of the blind. Only, the Hebrew means rather more than such a translation suggests. The natural choice of verb to express the physical act of opening, be it of the eyes or of a door, would have been *poteach*, whereas the word actually used is *pokeach*. This term signifies a change in the level of our awareness, an inner opening as well. We thank God not only for the gift of sight, but, equally, for the capacity for insight. 'I once was blind, but now I see', runs the refrain from *Amazing Grace*. That morning blessing implies that our blindness is never a thing of the past. It is recurrent, and the opportunity for greater discernment and deeper perception lies constantly within us and before us.

The second prayer asks God to open the heart: '*Petach libbi betoratecha*, – Open my heart', it says, but then the translation once again becomes problematic. Does *betoratecha* mean 'in your Torah', in which case what we are asking for is greater knowledge of Torah? Or does *betoratecha* also mean 'through your Torah', implying that even knowledge of the Torah is only the gateway to something deeper, a more comprehensive empathy, a more intuitive heart? In fact, it's not so easy to translate the word *libbi*, 'my heart', either. In the Bible and early rabbinic literature the more modern distinction between heart as seat of emotion and mind as centre of thought is not apparent. *Libbi* probably therefore includes both. Thus what the prayer really means is: open my heart and mind, arouse my consciousness. We all recognise the difference in quality between hours lived dimly and indifferently and those experienced from the centre of our being. Everything about us is sharper and more finely attuned, our mind, our feelings and our spirit. In those moments we truly live.

The third prayer takes, like the first, the form of a blessing; we thank God for teaching us Torah. As for the question of precisely how God achieves this, that is an issue which the prayer itself does not address. One can take a limited, academic view of what learning involves. Torah consists of texts and commentaries, therefore studying Torah means paying attention to those same texts and commentaries. This is certainly the case. But at a more profound level the meaning of Torah is revealed in its interconnections with life. Thus the whole of life becomes the scope of Torah and life itself our teacher. There is no encounter from which we do not have something to learn. It's in this sense that God can truly be described as teaching Torah, through God's presence in every interaction. Such teaching must be as frustrating to God as it is to any member of the profession returning dejected to the staff room at the end of a maddening day. Except that for God it must often be even more painful to watch human beings ruin, through egotism and violence, the beauty of a world which isn't even theirs. Still, there must also be moments of great joy, as when a child picks up a shell on the beach and runs across the sand to her friends crying out, 'Look, what I've found', then stops still and hugs the treasure to her chest before disclosing the magic of its pink and white patterns to their scrutiny; or as when an old man sits by the river and it flows through his mind and the sparkling water is the only consciousness.

If God is our teacher, there isn't a moment which cannot become a time of learning, provided we have sufficient humility and sensitivity. For wisdom doesn't consist in accumulating information, but in selfless and compassionate attentiveness to the present. As the second century sage Ben Azzai famously said: 'Who is wise? The person who learns from everyone'.[7]

Humility

I came home at eleven that night to find the old man in whose flat I was living, and for whom I was entrusted to care, waiting anxiously at the front door. When I'd left a couple of hours earlier he'd been preparing for bed but now he was fully dressed and even had his coat on. 'Where've you been?' he asked me, 'It's time for morning prayers'.

For months I'd walked by his side every Sabbath to the small synagogue half a mile away; he was too frail to manage even that short distance on his own. But what should I say to him now? He was strong willed and wouldn't easily be dissuaded. I explained to him that it was late at night and suggested that we should both go to bed. This only made him more impatient. He led me to the window and, pointing to the moon, declared, 'Can't you see, the sun's already up in the sky!' To collude with him would have been impossible; he simply wasn't strong enough to endure a pointless tour of the local streets at such an inhospitable hour. Furthermore, I was directly responsible for his well-being, especially now that his wife was in hospital. I had no other choice than to insist. How was I to persuade this venerable but obstinate man to go back to bed without subjecting him to the most pathetic humiliation? I had no idea what to do, nor can I remember for sure, twenty-five years later, how the situation was resolved, though I fear that in plain amazement I must have contradicted him before I even knew what I was doing: 'That's not the sun, that's the moon'.

Since that time I've seen much worse. I've watched as parents have asked to be reminded of the names of their children and grand-children; I've listened as children have told me how their mothers no longer seem to recognise them at all. Closer to home, I've observed myself struggle to hunt down in some temporarily inaccessible corner of my own mind a familiar name or a recalcitrant adjective. I'm cheered when I hear that it happens to others and when someone makes the banal comment that everyone has 'senior moments' like that. But I'm comforted only to a degree; in some part of myself I'm afraid and am already wondering how to read these first possible signs of my own disintegration.

The Talmud teaches that we should have particular respect for old people who've forgotten their knowledge because 'Both the whole tablets and the fragments of the tablets were placed in the ark'.[8] Moses was instructed to take not only the second, replacement, set of tablets engraved with the Ten Commandments but the smashed pieces of the first tables which he'd broken when he saw the golden calf, and to put them all together in the ark. I often think of that saying and of the pity and mercy it embodies. The few remembered embers of Torah are as precious to God as the entire sacred canon and the vessels which contain them must be treated with the same reverence as the Ark of the Covenant itself.

The other day a friend told me how his father kept asking to be reminded of his wife's name and it struck me forcibly how great a reason this is for humility. There's no cause to let the contents of our mind make us proud. All our knowledge is provisional, it slips away unnoticed; one day we may search for it and find it gone, remembering nothing.

All we know is next to nothing anyway. The greatest minds have always been impelled not by the desire to vaunt their discoveries, but to follow the quest for the unknown. 'The most beautiful thing we can experience,' wrote Albert Einstein, 'is the mysterious. It is the source of all true art and science. He to whom this emotion is a stranger, who can no longer pause to wonder and stand wrapt in awe, is as good as dead: his eyes are closed.'[9] At such moments of potential discovery our words, familiar descriptions and previously rehearsed theories function as shadows, as a hovering fog between us and the world, preventing us from perceiving accurately. We have to let them go in favour of a deeper intuition, a more compelling consciousness of what we truly apprehend, to which our old assumptions and articulations only present a barrier. Afterwards we will have need of explanations; then there will be time for words. We can't avoid them: How else can we describe the experience to ourselves, in what other way integrate something new and different into the patterns with which our mind is familiar? But in the moment of apprehension there must be silence and attention; anything else is sacrilege.

Not knowing is an essential part of the journey towards God. One should be distrustful of those who know too much, especially of those who are quick to declare who's saved and who's damned, whom God favours and whom God hates. Their very certainty is evidence of their ignorance. But the person who has true knowledge understands this above all else: that what we discover in the experience of encounter transcends all knowing, that, at least in the moment of intuition, our self consciousness is overwhelmed and nullified, and that then and thereafter our most integral and relentless commitment is not to define or judge, but simply to be faithful in thought and action to this 'life of all life' which has poured through us and cleansed us and to which we belong.

I often yearn for that state in which my mind is free of its burdens and preconceptions and I can descend to the well which entices my consciousness down to below my heart. There I hear water gushing and flowing, filled from a source which is quite other than my own, a gift from life itself. From here my nourishment comes; all I have to do is be attentive. All words which attempt to describe the sound of this water are inadequate descriptions, obfuscations of its music.

The Gaps Between the Letters

The Talmud contains an abstruse and almost certainly theoretical discussion about which scriptures may be saved in various circumstances should one's home or synagogue go up in flames during the holy sabbath. Needless to say, a complete Torah scroll should be rescued if at all possible, though, of course, human life and safety take precedence. But what about an incomplete scroll? How many letters must it still retain in order to be considered sacred? What of a scroll which has entirely faded? What, finally, about the empty parchment itself, the blank columns before the beginning of Genesis and after the end of Deuteronomy, as well as the margins above, below and between the writing and the spaces for the *petuchot* and *setumot*, the open and closed paragraphs into which the text has traditionally to be divided? After all, without the gaps between them there can be no words, just as without silence there is no speech. Has the blank parchment acquired holiness by virtue of its proximity to the text or is there nothing in it worthy of saving? The Talmud leaves the question unresolved.[10]

The eloquence of empty spaces often presents a greater challenge to our hearts and minds than the most articulate discourse. I was recently sent the following poem:

> I read of a man who stood to speak at a funeral of a friend.
> He referred to the dates on her tombstone from the beginning
>   . . . to the end.
> He noted that first came her date of birth and spoke of the
>   second with tears.
> But he said what mattered most of all was the dash between
>   those years,
> For that dash represents all the time that she spent alive
>   on earth
> And now only those who loved her know what that little line
>   is worth . . . [11]

I've sat on numerous occasions with mourners pondering how to convey, in the limited number of letters the stone masons allow, the essence of an entire life and its relationships. It simply can't be done. The words are suggestions only, pointers towards the unending silence in which the heart is traversed by memories which all the years of survival can neither fathom nor exhaust.

I've often thought about the gaps between the words of Torah. For it's precisely there in that open, undetermined space that the interpreter's imagination flourishes, that explanations, possibilities and entire hypothetical dramas seize their stage. The unspoken invites fantasy even more than does the stated word: Why did God suddenly decide to speak to Abraham? What thoughts filled the three silent days while he and Isaac walked towards their sacrifice at that fateful place which God would show them? What happened to make Moses leave the Egyptian palace and set out to find his brothers?

But I only recently came across a remarkable and compelling observation; it concerns the gap at the very centre of Torah. While teaching my son Mossy for his Bar Mitzvah I noticed a footnote in tiny print[12] informing the curious student that if one counts the sum of all the words in the entire Torah it emerges that those in the very middle, with an equal number before and after them, occur in the Book of Leviticus, chapter 10, verse 16. That is the traditional computation, though its accuracy is disputed. But what is so striking about this calculation is that the relevant words are *darosh darash*, meaning 'He emphatically enquired'. They have of course a specific context. Moses wanted to discover exactly what had happened to the sin offering, key portions of which Aaron and his sons were supposed to have eaten as an essential part of the ceremony to dedicate the Sanctuary. But when his older children Nadav and Avihu were consumed by fire, Aaron and his remaining sons failed to do so. Moses was angry and wanted to know why they had ignored God's command, (though as soon as he heard Aaron's explanation he let the matter drop).

But the words *darosh darash* transcend their place in the narrative. The root *d.r.sh.* means to search, enquire, expound; it gives its name, through the noun *Midrash*, to the whole inexhaustible rabbinic process of exploration, probing, asking, challenging and imagining, that endless endeavour to uncover at least some of the 'seventy faces of Torah' understood to be implicit in each and every one of its words. The emphatic doubling of the word, *darosh darash*, known grammatically as the infinitive absolute, seems here to reach out into the before and after. There are, at least according to this footnote, exactly the same number of words from the start of the Torah at *Bereshit*, 'In the beginning', up to and including the first *darosh*, as there are from and including the second *darash* until the Torah ends with its final words, *Be'einei chol Yisrael*, 'In the eyes of all Israel'. Thus the two verbs at its centre summon the entire contents of the Torah and draw them into an unceasing process of exploration.

But on further reflection I realised that it isn't true that the words *darosh darash* constitute the precise centre of the Torah. What is actually in the middle is the blank space between them, the silence which transcends articulation, from which every endeavour to discover knowledge proceeds and to which all interpretation must return. However brilliant the idea, however inspiring the insight, that little gap swallows it back up and restores the Torah to its pristine potential in which it awaits the next moment of perception, the next flare of the spiritual imagination.

Rabbinic thought contains no suggestion that the process of interpretation is ever complete, that the final answers have been uncovered and that we know what the Torah truly means. Of course, there is such a thing as authoritative exegesis, especially in the domain of legal extrapolation. After all, there has to be a consensus about how we understand what the Torah actually requires us to do. Even here, though, there are differences and it is the pride of the Talmudic process that it records debate rather than decision and seeks to ascribe an author to every minority view. But the Torah is inexhaustible, the search for meaning endless. To present even the best and most inspiring of interpretations as the exclusive and immutable truth is to subvert Torah. Another age, another spirit, will have something else to say. *Davar acher*, notes the Midrash time and again, 'Another matter, another interpretation', allowing the student to chose from a list of alternative possibilities none of which is definitively right or absolutely wrong. For preceding them all, in between them all and following after them all is the gap, the blank space between searching and searching which swallows up all answers. It is there, in the ignorance and unknowing just beyond the boundaries of our thought, that discovery lies, just as God always awaits us in the silence beyond all formulations.

A friend once once told me about a particularly mean book review; it stated simply: 'This volume fills a much needed gap in the literature on the subject'. It took me a minute to get the point. This caustic comment has a certain profundity in relation to the interpretation of Torah. What we often have to transcend is not so much our ignorance, as what we think we know.

A vital mind may momentarily be full, but soon it becomes empty and attentive again; in its emptiness lies its capacity for fullness. The fire of creativity burns in the passion of discovery, God's presence drawing us over and again into the space beyond our knowledge where our jaded understanding is consumed and the excitement of communion is restored.

Truth

The seal of the Holy Blessed One is truth[13]

Even today it bothers me. I still think about that moment almost thirty years ago in Cambridge when we were talking about the Middle East. I don't remember the name of my fellow student and I can't recall exactly how the conversation reached this stage, but at some point, rejecting my attempt to put across a different perspective, he declared: 'I'd rather you didn't tell me; I'm comfortable with my position'. I may have been wrong, he may have been right. But that's not the point. It was his calm rejection, his self-possessed assertion that he didn't even want to hear what I had to say which irritated me then and which vexes me even now. Who says that any of us has the right to be comfortable with our position? Isn't the search for truth more often propelled by the feeling of being uncomfortable with our position? Isn't it precisely those phenomena which refuse to conform to our patterns and prejudices which we ought to pursue?

In some circles truth itself is close to becoming a dirty word. I recall another debate and the inevitable analysis which followed: 'The trouble with that rabbi's contribution', said one lady, referring to a colleague of mine, 'is that he used the words "the truth"'. In some circumstances I might have agreed with her. There's little more dangerous than the claim that one's own perspective, story, ideology or sacred cannon expresses the absolute and only truth. But there's also a price to be paid for saying with a patient sigh, 'You have your truth and I have mine. There is no real truth. All versions are of equal value.' This post-modernist *laissez-faire* attitude turns tolerance into negligence and offers an open invitation to intellectual laziness and moral relativism. Not every story is equally valid and some are definitely false. 'The seal of God is truth', teaches the Talmud.[13] This doesn't mean that we can know truth in any complete and final sense, the truth, the absolute, total truth. But neither are we free to desist from pursuing it with all the means at our disposal.

'Acquire truth, and sell it not', states the Book of Proverbs, making it clear that the process requires persistent effort and application.[14] There is such a thing as evidence and such a process as enquiry. The empirical method cannot simply be ignored because certain premises, or prejudices, are too sacred to be challenged. Some propositions, including sometimes ancient and hard-held beliefs, are contradicted by evidence. But the fact that we care deeply about them cannot be turned into a reason for protecting them from the rigours of investigative analysis. We are commanded to be intellectually vigilant just as much as we are required to be morally engaged. Ultimately, thinking is a moral obligation; to explore truth is right, to perpetuate falsehood wrong.

The pursuit of truth is exciting. When the mind is on fire with an idea, the whole personality is subsumed in an experience no less absorbing than any other form of passion. For a while, nothing else exists except the issue in question. Those minutes when the whole world disappears before a poem, before a single line or image, before their magic and their fire, are among the most joyous in our lives. I remember enthralled debates; if someone watching from the outside should have questioned in perplexity, 'What was all that fuss about a mere few words?' I would have retorted, 'But the heavens were open and the very meaning of creation was at stake!' I recall solitary moments when I've said to myself in the silence, 'Now I understand', as a phrase from Shakespeare or a commentary on the Torah penetrated to a new depth in my heart thirty years after I first began to think about them. But, of course, I was wrong. I hadn't understood, and I never will, because all our comprehension is always provisional, compelling at the time but ultimately only an interstice of stillness on the unending path of exploration. Make too much of it, worship it, and it becomes an idol, a barrier to the pursuit of the endless and elusive possibilities of truth. The real wonder lies in the experience of discovery itself, when the mystery of knowledge engages us and we feel that we've been touched by the very energy which animates creation and makes it breathe. Surely that's the meaning of the expression *chiddushei Torah*, new insights into Torah. Their value lies less in the resultant interpretation, important as that may be, than in the moment of insight itself, the joy and wonder of communion.

This is why Jewish wisdom has always praised learning more than knowledge. The mind that sits still at the centre of its conquests soon grows stale amidst the prejudice of habituated opinions. But, questioning and searching, it is renewed and humbled all the time.

However, the pursuit of truth is also painful and challenging. It requires us to forgo the security of familiar assumptions and forsake what seemed like certainties. Few of us are prepared to do so with anything other than great reluctance. From a very early age we form pictures of what the world is like and narratives of how it functions. We hear stories, and quickly develop our own, which tell us what's just and what's unjust, who's right and who's wrong. Judgments formulate themselves in us without our even being conscious of the process. Almost involuntarily we come to see them as the 'truths' by which all things are to be measured, when in fact they may, at worst, be little more than accumulated prejudice.

There is never a greater need to be aware of this process than in situations of enduring tension and conflict. In telling ourselves our own history we inevitably generate a counter-narrative of the other; the two together become an all-inclusive myth, encompassing 'who we are' and 'who they are'. In this dynamic, the most basic principles of our humanity are liable to be swallowed up; some people emerge as more equal than others and only the right kind of neighbours end up meriting our love.

Both ancient and modern systems of thought have proved themselves well suited to the perpetuation of such myths. If they follow the narratives of religion, they frame their other as heretic, unbeliever, unredeemed. So-called 'religious' hate-mongers can always find sources with which to prove their 'truths' and assert them as God-given facts. But it must not be forgotten that secular ideologies frequently function in similar ways, demonising and denouncing those who are different, those who fail to conform, those who challenge tyranny and lies, while the organs of the modern state, from the media to the secret police, propagate their stereotypes and intimidate everyone else.

I had much opportunity to ponder these matters during many hours of participation in live debate on an Arabic television network. Most of the programmes included ample time for viewers' challenges and questions. I came to realise that the roots of what I frequently experienced as hostility were nourished by something deeper than antipathy to the policies of particular Israeli governments. They fed on a different myth, on a version of history in which the entire perception of Judaism, as well as of much of the Christian and secular western world, diverged sharply from what I believed to be the case. I could have limited myself to arguing over the facts; sometimes I did. But I also couldn't help but ask myself what my own myths might be and how they were structuring my view of the world without my even being conscious of the fact. This realization, that we are made to march by different myths, has been a profoundly unsettling and often downright frightening experience. It has also been an invaluable lesson.

But it hasn't made me into a relativist. I'm not willing simply to say 'You have your truth and I have mine; both are equally valid'. Different perceptions are by no means necessarily of equivalent worth. I've listened to many outrageous claims about Judaism, Israel, America and the West as a whole which I categorically reject, just as I repudiate ignorant and bigoted assertions about Islam and the East. Some things are, after all, simply untrue. The value of the experience has been in making me think far more carefully about the power of our myths and what they prevent us from seeing. One viewer evidently experienced a similar realization and her words moved me greatly. She phoned in to say that she now understood that Israelis were human beings too, just like Palestinians. For myself, I never for a moment thought that Palestinians were not human beings. It's just that their humanity wasn't as real to me; it had never been part of my own story. They represented the danger at the margins, the terror invading across the border. They didn't really have voices and faces. That lasted until I began to visit Palestinian homes and meet Palestinian people, until I started to listen.

We have to hold our myths in check by testing them against reality. I firmly believe that people shouldn't be considered truly educated in the modern world unless they've learnt to be attentive to alternative stories and allowed themselves to be challenged by them. This applies above all to leaders, especially in the powerful field of religion. That is not because the other version may prove better, or because it necessarily will, or should, oust our most precious assumptions. It's rather because the very fact of listening to differing perceptions engenders self questioning. It makes us more circumspect and more humble; we are far less likely to fail to notice the humanity of the person in front of us, whatever their race or faith.

There is no form of idolatry more powerful and pervasive than the unchallenged myth. People kill in its name all the time.

But 'the seal of God is truth', truth for the sake of which we are called upon to step beyond the circle of what we presume to know, and listen.

In the Dark

By day God will command his love
And by night his song is with me [15]

At night a world of wonder is revealed and at dawn a world of love.

For years I've had a passion for walking at night, on my own or with the dog, kept on the lead for safety, trotting along beside me. But there's little need to be afraid of cars here; they're extremely few along these tiny backways at this hour and anyway their headlights make all the fields and hedgerows gleam from half a mile away. There's plenty of time to climb a bank or press into the bushes by the edge of the road. I like to walk steadily and fast, as if I were gliding and the fields were slipping by me and the whole of my consciousness and all of my body were intent upon this movement.

A secret nourishment takes place at night. Maybe it's because of the withdrawal of human endeavour, the suspension of the sounds of building and transportation, that constant activity of aeroplanes, trucks and tractors which it's almost impossible to evade for long. At night there aren't people everywhere. The world is not for use by night; the fields and woodlands wake and breath, their roots drink in the rain, and in the absence of the all intrusive light the leaves and branches, still or moving with the wind, transmit their silent prayers. They surround me, include me and transform me.

I walk fast. I pass the trees which mark the field's edge, tall and dark against the blackness of the night. The road slopes upwards and leaves the shadows behind; one light still burns in the house across the valley. The road turns down into a forest and I can see neither the dog beside me nor the ground in front of my feet. The woods surround me. The woods embrace me and fill my mind with their great meditation. I emerge into the open and look upward to the skies.

I don't stop. Life compels me to walk; I walk in search of it, often I walk in love with it. Sometimes an owl's cry pierces the night and the darkness is transfixed by its sharp vitality. All at once, a bird passes by me only a few feet away, born on slowly beating wings as it swoops from tree to tree. Sometimes a deer's eyes glow in the black lane ahead, before the animal turns and runs back into the night.

I'm rarely tired when I'm walking at this hour. I go back only because I remember that the morning will bring another day for which I have to prepare with sleep. My feet carry me home where the magic of the night world deposits me at my door and forsakes me.

Whenever we stay near the forest I cajole the children to come out with me into the dark. We set off around eleven o'clock or midnight. At their age and at this hour I can't always expect them to walk. I stop the car in the middle of nowhere and we open the windows and listen. We catch a rabbit, a pony, a group of deer in the dim glow of the sidelights. We watch in reverence until the animals turn and go. We get out and listen to the silent woodlands breathing. We stand on the bridge over the river and see the gleaming ripples eddy and vanish on the water.

What wonder! I long to walk a path of wonder with them. We go home to bed and when we close our eyes images of the trees and branches become our prayers and their silent contemplations accompany us in our sleep.

CHAPTER THREE

The Heart's Education

Bright Moon in the Sky

I kiss my hand
To the stars, lovely-asunder . . .
Kiss my hand to the dappled-with-damson west;
Since, tho' he is under the world's splendour and wonder,
His mystery must be instressed, stressed;
For I greet him the days I meet him, and bless when I understand.

Gerald Manley Hopkins[1]

When I awoke it was if the moon which illumined the frosty paths in the forest of my dream now shone over the whole of my life, purifying everything in a gentle and harmonious light. I felt the restoration of a lost but unforgotten joy and was filled with resurgent energy and love.

All things were present; nothing was lost. Here were the frozen brambles and the sodden ditches rimmed with ice along the lanes where I used to walk for hours at night to catch the vitality of the trees and fields. Here is where I cycled through the falling snow and she turned off into the white Cambridge lane, through the white darkness, and I knew that we would never talk like that again, recognising in the December cold the fact of our parting ways. Here is the door where I stood entranced in the Jerusalem Sabbath night, afraid to knock because the house where she lived was holy ground and I didn't want to disturb its sanctity with so abrupt a noise. Here is the girl who became my wife, standing in the doorway, waiting and smiling. Here is the field with the verge full of bluebells where I went on the fortieth anniversary of VE Day to sit and ponder, thinking about the planes which flew overhead in the Battle of Britain, and flew, obscuring the sky, to Normandy on D-Day, never imagining I would ever see the place again, or that it would prove to lie just off the road to my wife's childhood home. This is the inn in the forest as we first saw it in the frosty twilight one winter day some fifteen years ago, the gables covered in snow, logs in the great fireplace. Here we are once again with our three small children holding out their hands to the ponies in the woodland opposite, testing the depth of the muddy water in the puddles and drains against the height of their boots. Nothing is lost; nothing is gone forever.

Everything is neglected and forgotten in the merciless displacement of one moment by the next and one reality by another. Unable to touch what is even a single second past, we mourn for it all our days. But our inner life is capable of a strange simultaneity in which nothing is ever irretrievably lost, no word or sight or smell beyond the reach of evocation. The heart has the capacity to reawaken everything. Does this mean that those experiences still exist? Or are they merely recollections? What is their ontological status? These questions tease and trouble me. But I know that one day in my death, when all I am is memories full of love and yearning, I shall be compelled to yield up everything like a water drop when it meets the sea and there at once both ceases to exist and becomes what it most truly is. My whole life will be embraced by all life and will in that moment be both present and complete and nothing whatsoever, both fulfilled and destroyed, and part of all that is.

Here, in the meantime, I am included, a separate yet, in my best moments, conscious partner in the bond of life, in the unity of God's infinitely differentiated consciousness which constitutes creation. This must be the meaning of God's name *Chei Ha'olamim*, Life of all the worlds, that vitality which includes the stone, the river, the butterfly and the human heart.

Most of the time I forget this truth. The failure to remember isn't an inevitable consequence of being composed of matter, because matter too is part of the transmigration of form into form. Nor does my seeming separateness invariably mean that I experience myself as this distinct, independent, isolated 'I'. For at any instant life may call and the resurgent spirit return to the home where it belongs.

At such moments I greet you most warmly, partners, anonymous companions in the forest, ponies and deer, squirrels and rabbits. I appreciate you, friends in the garden, robins, finches, snowdrops. One life traverses us; one consciousness transcends us all.

I greet you in the street this morning, lady on your way to work so early in this bitter cold, cat by the pillar at the end of the driveway, leaf on the paving stone. We're bound together by virtue of this hour and this place which, out of all eternity and infinity, we occupy together.

The moon is fading, a translucent blue is dissolving the darkness and the power of *hesed* is awake, the love which signifies our partnership in God's sacred bond.

At such moments I can live with joy and I'm not afraid; at such moments, and only then, I imagine I'm ready for my death, and not afraid.

An Open Heart

'And the Lord your God will open your heart.'

Deuteronomy 30:6

The heart is the source of love. Therefore we have to strive our whole life long to keep an open heart.

There are many reasons why the heart may be closed.

Maybe it was never open in the first place. Maybe it never received love and encouragement in childhood. Maybe it was born into a world of neglect, where its parents communicated their own starvation through indifference, preoccupation with themselves, or anger at the very existence of a child with its constant demands and requirements. Maybe its parents died young, with the result that the joy and curiosity of childhood perished with them and there wasn't a loving aunt or grandmother to care for the sad, bewildered infant. Maybe the family became separated in their flight from war or persecution and their child was left alone in an unfamiliar land. Where then is the love to bring the heart to life? Where is the hope which the heart needs to explore its world?

Or other afflictions came later, teaching the heart to curl up, protect itself and close. Maybe it was abandoned by the person with whom it fell in love and no one helped it rediscover the courage to dare a second time. Or years of attrition in a lonely marriage shrunk it to a scarcely breathing mass. Or it suffered the loss of a child, and all the happiness and laughter fell silent about the house.

Sometimes the heart itself is responsible for its own eclipse. As with every living organism, the right environment is necessary for it to flourish: honesty, warmth of feeling, courage and compassion. A life with too many distractions or careless and debasing habits separates a person from the heart. The squandering of its integrity drives the heart into semi-permanent hiding from where the main indications of its survival are signals of distress, engendering more discomfort.

51

Or maybe the heart has betrayed itself by doing wrong to others and has become hardened by its own insensitivities. It's as if the world then says to it, 'I can't talk to you any more. Be greedy, vengeful, lustful or envious if you must. But until you change you'll never again live a life of beauty, grace and love.' The worst punishment of all is when the heart no longer knows what it has lost; the very capacity to listen is forfeit, it simply cannot hear.

Yet nothing is irrevocable until death. Until the final hour the heart can still revive; whole realms of perception can be regained in moments. When the heart awakes, new horizons unfold around it; the sensations it experiences are at once a revelation and as natural as playing at the seashore to a child. 'This', it says as it breathes in the sharp new air, 'this is what life really means. This is who I truly am.'

Many qualities have the power to wake up the heart: joy, love, truth, beauty, pain, remorse, pity and understanding.

Joy is the heart's exuberance, the brilliance of light on the crest of the wave, the sound of the rain after long months of drought, gyrating shadows under the sunlit beech trees in the wind, the touch of a trusted hand, the presence of the person with whom we're in love, the sound of the voice for which, in our loneliness, we've longed and prayed.

Love makes the paralysed heart feel. Love pierces the layers of fear and distrust which cling to the anxious core of our consciousness. Love unclenches the heart. Love breathes into us a second breath of life and makes the heart its instrument of happiness.

Beauty is the heart's delight and consolation. Beauty has the power to embody pain itself in healing form, as if the spirit of a higher and more harmonious realm had embraced even the cruelty and caprice of our world. Beauty renders the unbearable amenable to feeling and breaks the heart. Beauty, in the very same moment, is joy articulate.

Truth pierces the heart with knowledge. The mind may try to deceive itself, rehearsing the lies of which it seeks to be convinced. But the heart's awareness can't be feigned. Truth is not always for our comfort; it may burn us like hot metal with remorse. But it may also bring us consolation, like the brightness of pebbles on a day of calm water, still and luminous on the floor of the sea.

Pity is the sign by which the heart is known; pitilessness is the signature of a hardened, buried heart.

The heart which rediscovers itself after years of concealment will suffer. Like the pain of unused muscles, the power of overwhelming experience will make it ache. But this is as nothing to the glory it discovers, entering a different world, more beautiful, more merciful and full of far deeper, richer love.

Partnership

Before I married Nicky I didn't know what partnership could mean.

Nicky, kind, attractive, grounded, sharply intelligent, sensible, thoughtful, fair-minded and loving, has shared her life with me for approaching twenty years. Her family have lived in the same house in Kent for two generations; her mother knows who planted every flower and tree in the garden. Her family are close, loyal and unpretentious. Not long after we'd met, her mother realised that her daughter's incipient relationship with a rabbi could prove useful. 'Ask him what my Hebrew name means,' she requested of Nicky, who promptly relayed the message to me. 'She'll first have to tell me what it is,' I replied. 'It's *Azmah*,' she informed me. 'You'll have to tell your mother, then,' I said with some hesitation, 'that her Hebrew name means "so what"'. They thought it was hilarious; I doubt my own family would have found it quite so funny.

Before we got married I was worried, as well as excited. I was frightened of losing my private space. I thought: what'll we do with all this time we're going to have together? What'll we have to say to each other through all those years ahead? It never occurred to me then that daily life would prove such a rush, with work, the children, the congregation, the dog, the garden and all the other assorted animals and responsibilities; that time, just time for only her and me together, just time for us to breathe, would be something of which we would want more and more and risk having less and less; that time was our most precious commodity and that there would never be enough of it simply to sit down and appreciate the world and be still.

Before we got married I didn't understand the relationship between time and love. Family friends since my childhood in Glasgow, who were like parents to me during the periods when I lived for several months in Israel, told me, sensing my uncertainties, 'Love is a thing which grows'. But I didn't know then how deeply love sends down its roots to drink from the waters of memory or how, like a familiar and protective tree, it forms the reliable canopy of shade.

I didn't know then that silence could be more powerful than passion, just quietly keeping company, with a cup of coffee and each our own book, looking up at one another periodically, merely to check that we're both here, together, without the phone to answer or the shopping to fetch, simply being, next to one another in the world.

I didn't know then that in between the rushing, planning, worrying, hoping and aspiring, the ferrying, cleaning, washing-up and repairing, there would be moments of calm like those in the kitchen and garden, she preparing the vegetables for an enormous soup, I cutting up the apples for a cake, she holding aloft the falling branches of a shrub, I trying to tie in the recalcitrant greenery.

I didn't know that we would live to see the trees we planted flower for the tenth season, or is it the eleventh, or twelfth? I didn't know that we would be together long enough to have forgotten what we did, 'Was it here we stopped when we came to Somerset fifteen years ago?' and to share the sudden restoration of our memories, as we travelled the road become familiar once again: 'Yes, definitely it was here. I remember that gate and the way the path cuts diagonally across that field.'

I didn't know then that we would develop an intuition for that most private of all matters, how another person finds their God, or that sometimes I would know, just know, that when Nicky was looking at a favourite plant or watching the children in a certain manner she was at one with her God in silent appreciation and prayer.

I hadn't realised then how permanent it would all seem, our home, the books and papers on the table, the children's socks dumped in the corner on the floor (always a different pair, invariably dumped in a corner), the missing piece of homework, the phone call saying 'I'll be home a little late; can you check that the children actually are where they're supposed to be?'; or how I, coming quietly back into the house after another endless meeting would find them safe in their beds, our daughter's tape-recorder still playing long after she had drifted off, and Nicky fast asleep.

I hadn't realised then how fragile it all would feel, walking through the park together behind the dog's swiftly vanishing paws, packing the bags for a short holiday and thinking, 'Soon the children will be grown up and won't want to come with us any more', while searching for their missing walking boots.

No doubt everybody says, 'Where did it all go?'; no doubt every couple looks at their teenage children and thinks, 'Only yesterday they were babies'. The years have gone where time always goes, into the vast library of eternity from where no one will ever retrieve it. But at least a part of that time has been catalogued in our hearts, impermanently but firmly, and has become what they now are, transformed into their very cells. Part of it, too, is garnered in our children, much of it, I trust, where, mixed with vivid memories of our foibles and regretful recollections of our bad jokes, it now belongs to a different, but hopefully no less loving story.

Love's Power

*Many waters cannot quench love, neither can floods
drown it; if a person were to give all the wealth of his
house for love, they would scorn him utterly.*

Song of Songs 8:7

Without love, what would be the point of getting up in the morning? To care for whom or hope for what? If there were no one I loved I wouldn't want to live. That's why many people inwardly choose to die and I doubt if I would have the strength to be any different. Only recently a man said to me, 'It would be better if I were dead'. He'd been lonely for so long that he'd become habituated to misery and had lost all hope that he could ever feel different any more.

All over the world innumerable lives begin in deprivation. A famous film about orphanages in China showed two- and three-year-old children tied to their chairs, aimlessly rocking backwards and forwards. According to the film, no activity was arranged for them save the minimal maintenance of feeding them and dealing with their defecation. They were shown no affection, there appeared to be no emotional engagement with them at all. The hopelessness of these children was so comprehensive that craving itself had turned numb.

In moments of bleakness even the most buoyant heart remembers the hours of its abandonment, because no life passes entirely without them, and the very recollection of such utter desolation fills it with helplessness and fear.

How lucky we are if we're wanted on this earth, if nurture and affection, joy and attentiveness surround us:

> Thus day by day,
> Subjected to the discipline of love,
> His organs and recipient faculties
> Are quickened . . .
> No outcast he, bewildered and depressed

wrote Wordsworth, describing how from babyhood we grow not only physically but intellectually, emotionally and spiritually through our mother's love.[2] Otherwise the world around us would remain implacably alien and confusion and misery would suffuse us.

'These I have loved,' declared Rupert Brooke, celebrating those favourite objects we treasure from our earliest childhood because they signify happiness and security:

> Wet roofs, beneath the lamp-light; the strong crust
> Of friendly bread; and many tasting food;
> Rainbows; and the bitter smoke of wood . . . [3]

But during the years between childhood and adulthood the nature of our loving changes. It grows into longing, at once physical and spiritual, into dreams of desire and yearning. Eyes, hair, a smile, the invitation of a gesture, the excitement of the proximity of a whole other person, alive, intimate; worlds of adventure become possible. 'By night on my bed I sought him whom my soul loves; I sought him, but I found him not'.[4]

Because of you the universe makes sense. Wonder has settled over everything like the first sight of frost to a child when all the earth is silver and white. What's your name? Where do you live? Here, sitting on these steps at one o'clock in the morning waiting for the coach to take us home, is it only chance that unites us in this conversation, an accidental meeting in the eternity of time and the endless possibility of space? Because of you this night is burnt into my consciousness forever with an engraver's pen of fire. Twenty-five years later I think of it and my heart still remembers.

Sometimes love begins to grow unnoticed, as the roots develop in the soil before the stem grows into the light. Sometimes love flames up in the first moment as if a fire had been ignited in some element of the spirit incapable of burning out. Then the soul perceives with an intuition in which the sweep of the future is revealed until the very hour of death itself. 'Jacob kissed Rachel and he lifted up his voice and wept': Why did he kiss her when he'd never even seen her before? Because he'd fallen hopelessly in love. Then why did he weep? Because, say the rabbis strangely, he saw that she would not lie next to him in death.[5] What they meant was that their meeting, here by the well in Paddan Aram among the shepherds and the sheep, had opened the depths of his heart and the knowledge of their eventual inevitable separation had filled those depths with tears.

A man says to a woman: 'You're so beautiful to me that you are revelation; the beauty of everything which exists is made known to me through you. Again and again you repeat for me the moment when longing embraces form. I love you because of who you are; I love you because you transform the world. God's presence rests on your hair, in your eyes, upon your face.'

When God completed the work of creation, God blessed it and God's first commandment was love.[6] When passion floods the consciousness the entire force of the vast unending ocean pours into the cove; only when the tide has abated does the world with its shadows return.

'Do you remember how it was when we first met? I never imagined the first time I saw you that a day would come when life would be inconceivable without you.' We become interdependent, absorbed into the structure of each other's hours and seasons. Planning is unimaginable alone. Often the very ordinariness of their context leaves the most basic bonds invisible until one of the partners dies: 'She used to deal with all of that and now I haven't a clue', the widower says, pushing away a pile of bills. But this only reflects how dependent we grow. We come to exist in a perpetual dialogue of which we're often scarcely conscious and whose subjects include shopping, eating, quarrelling and innumerable hours exchanging banalities over the phone, a dialogue which rests upon the assumption of a continuous partnership where the notion of absolute and independent identity has long ago been absorbed and reconfigured. We are, because we love. We are, because of how we love and are loved. This is our ontological secret from the beginning.

The man stood at the side of the grave in which his wife was about to be buried and said: 'I'm not simply bereft; I don't feel as if it's another person whom I've lost. I've been cut in half; I've been torn asunder. It's as if a part of my own self is simply no longer there. I'm standing here and I'm still alive but the feeling is insupportable.'

The woman said: 'He was my friend, my mentor, my partner, my counsel, my consoler and my beloved. How can I now go outdoors into the street?'

Of what use are the words of the comforters? It's questionable whether the Bible really says 'Love is stronger than death'. A meticulous translation would be more even-handed: 'Love is as strong as death'.[7] How terrible, when both of them have us in their grasp and tear at us in irreconcilable directions.

But even if it's only death's mere equal, we can still defy everything else through love. When the nature of the place to which they'd been taken had become clear to Viktor Frankl, he turned to his friend and said:

> Listen, Otto, if I don't get back home to my wife, and if you should see her again, then tell her that I talked of her daily, hourly. You remember. Secondly, I have loved her more than anyone. Thirdly, the short time I have been married to her outweighs everything, even all we have gone through here.[8]

Not even the final silence can put an end to love. Death does not extinguish it; to imagine it does so is mistaken. Love escaped death's reaches long ago.

Heart's Treasures

Never seek to tell thy love,
Love that never told can be
For the silent wind doth move
Secretly, invisibly.

William Blake[9]

All the love we ever feel is treasured in the heart; there, like a great secret, it lies garnered all our lives.

I recently participated in a series of discussions to which we were invited to bring something special, an object, poem, picture or piece of music, which was spiritually important to us. At first I was sceptical: would people really have the confidence to share anything so personal? But what followed was intensely moving. We listened to one another with great respect and attention; we all realised that what we were being offered was the privilege of glimpsing for a moment some of the treasures stored in each other's hearts.

'My father was a diplomat; he used to travel a great deal. Most of the time my mother couldn't accompany him; she was busy looking after us. But when we children were a little older our aunt would sometimes move in and our mother would go off with my father to the most exotic places. Twice she was away for a whole month. To calm us down she promised to keep a diary of all the special places she visited and the interesting things she saw. I was always so excited when she came home that I paid little attention to those notebooks full of sketches and jottings. It wasn't until after she'd died that I began to look at them properly. Now I turn to them all the time. I keep them near my bed and read them whenever I can't sleep. I hear her voice speaking the words; often the extracts make me cry. But they also bring me comfort and help me to feel that I can cope.'

'It's just a very ordinary picture. You'll probably think I'm silly. There's a lantern in the window of an old stone cottage. I don't even know where that cottage is. It could be down any country lane with a field on one side and houses on the other. But it's as if I'm stopping by that lantern and the light is drawing me in. The space inside is safe and welcoming. I could be on my own there, but I wouldn't feel alone. I could pray there. I think I could even talk to my brother there; he died when he was only seventeen. But once I showed it to a friend, it's only an ordinary picture, and he just looked at me as if to say "So what?" I found that really hard.'

My own turn comes. I struggle to select one single concrete object. My memory is full of pictures. My heart is filled with people and voices, places and absences. I suddenly remember the view onto the golf course and a field with horses from the room I shared with my brother when we were small. I recall how I went back with my wife to look at that house, the house where I was born. We played a tape of Moira Kerr singing *The Lord's my Shepherd* over and over again and I wept as I drove. When I saw the little garden and the steps up to the porch I was overcome by an overwhelming sense of gratitude; I felt that I had never wanted for anything all my life. And in some dimension protected from time's devastation, it was all still there.

My heart is replete with other images and sensations: the smell of jasmine in Jerusalem, of dry pine needles in the Galilee; the lights of Tiberias from across the Kinneret at dusk; the clanking and groaning of the night train as it passes over the points, the sweet scent of air off the fields and forests; the crown of the tree underneath which I prayed, at five o'clock on the Sabbath morning, when sent to walk the dog before taking my wife into hospital to give birth to our son; – the love attached to all these memories is garnered in my heart.

Yet the heart also holds secrets which it never yields.

I found a photograph recently while sorting through the papers of a lady who'd lived all her life alone. It was a picture of a young and handsome man; on the back he'd written simply, 'When you look at this, remember'.

I once overheard two nurses talking about an old man who was dying on their ward. He'd been married for many years and his wife had looked after him devotedly until she herself had died. Now this man had one last wish. He desperately wanted to trace the girl who'd been his first love and to see her once again before he died. He was certain she was still alive. She was somewhere in South Africa; friends of his had bumped into her there a couple of years ago and, remembering that she was an old flame, had casually passed the information on to him. That was all he knew, except that he wouldn't be able to die in peace until he had set eyes on her one final time. The nurses didn't know what to make of this request. It brought to my mind Zhivago's poem about the terrible day on which he and Lara were parted forever:

> Till dusk he roams about
> Putting back into the drawers
> The scattered scraps of stuff,
> The patterns used for cutting out,
>
> And pricking himself on a needle
> Still stuck in a piece of sewing, .
> Suddenly he sees her
> And cries quietly.[10]

That needle will still be stuck in Zhivago's heart ten years later, so that seeing a similar piece of sewing, he will weep even then.

Sometimes it's the mourning within love which carves, with slow attrition and passionate longing, the deepest pools inside the heart.

Few of us would be able to recount the story of our own heart's growth. How much less, then, do we understand the history, the inner dynamic, of the development of other people's hearts. However deeply, however unselfishly we love them, we are almost certainly unaware of anything more than a fraction of the events and encounters which have stirred and challenged the hearts of our brothers and sisters, our partner, our own children.

These are the secrets, never to be told.

'But My Heart is Awake'

On your part my heart says, 'Seek my face'.
Your face, God, shall I seek.

Psalm 27:8

'I sleep, but my heart is awake', says the beloved in *The Song of Songs*.[11] But what if it's the other way round, what if we're awake, but it's the heart which is asleep? Isn't this the reality of so much of our life, that we cannot find the pathway back to our own heart?

The water is almost still, only the smallest ripples travel towards the shore; the unbroken surface of the sea reflects the red clouds of dawn. A seagull cries above the bay, a heron takes a watchful step across the sand. In the steep banks of the cove the woodland birds are waking. My heart wakes with them.

Virtually everyone lives large parts of their life in a state of semi distraction. One functions reasonably well, one does what one's supposed to do. Often one doesn't even notice. For a while it seems to matter little if the consciousness is far away from the centre of the self. Busy and battling, preoccupied with a thousand interactions, the mind is engaged, content even, at the periphery of who we are. But sooner or later we begin to hear a stifled call, an obscure 'Where am I?' at the core of our being. The half awareness of living as an absentee from who we are, caught up in the corners of our consciousness, comes to weigh like a lustreless sky, dulling all we do:

> . . . I am, and live like vapours tost
>
> > Into the nothingness of scorn and noise,
> > Into the living sea of waking dreams,
> > Where there is neither sense of life or joys,
> > But the vast shipwreck of my life's esteems . . . [12]

Perhaps it's too much pain which shuts the pathway to the heart, though pain itself can open it once more. 'I can't feel anything; it's as if my insides have gone numb', says the woman whose husband died without warning of a heart attack. There must be some somatic mechanism which prevents the sheer power of our feelings from overwhelming us. For, were we truly alert to every perception, the most ordinary day could provide sensations which would simply overwhelm us. 'If we had a keen vision and feeling of all ordinary human life', wrote George Eliot, 'it would be like hearing the grass grow and the squirrel's heart beat, and we should die of that roar which lies on the other side of silence.'[13]

Or we dare not visit our heart because we're afraid to hear its voice. Several times I've heard people say, 'I knew for years before I left him that the relationship wasn't right'. There are many things we know; but the awareness is too painful, the implications are too complicated, to act on them would turn our existence inside out. For what the heart is actually saying is 'Stop lying to yourself and change your life.' Or it says, 'What are you so frightened for? You're betraying nobody except yourself.' Or it says, 'Why do you always keep this distance? Allow life to embrace you.' We hear and know. Then we turn back to the familiar pattern of the daily round and pay for our self protection the price of living with half a heart.

These defences develop a reality of their own. Slowly, like callus, they grow. They become, with time, a barrier against feeling itself; neither grief nor happiness fully animate us any more. We don't perceive from the heart; after a while we cease even to be aware that we're no longer aware. An invisible and almost impermeable membrane mediates between us and the world, which neither joy nor sorrow can pierce.

Then our mood changes. Since childhood I remember welcoming tears with grateful relief as a sign of finding my way back home. I am myself once more; once again I really feel. I throw myself down on the grass and worship life in a great embrace.

For the heart doesn't sleep forever. Though we may be unaware of them for months or even years, it harbours sensations like an underground lake, gathering waters from the rains and streams which feed it. At last the river emerges and there its great nourishment awaits us.

Heart's Light

At the raw centre of being the heart cries out. It says to the consciousness, 'Come back. We need each other. Your neglect is hurting me and the pain calling to you from inside your ribs is me. Why have you been so preoccupied with other things? Why do you constantly yield to distraction? Have you forgotten how you used to shelter in my darkness until we made each other whole? You'll go mad if you ignore me; you won't know who you are any more. If you don't came back, you won't be able to love, or sing, or dance or play like a child. You'll be restless and frustrated; your life will feel futile. I'll hide myself from you; you'll have no more access to me then, you'll forget I ever existed. That's why I'm calling out to you now: Come back before you lose the very memory of your yearning.'

This soreness calls from the heart like an appeal to homecoming. Sometimes one says to oneself, 'I wish the world would leave me alone. I wish I could pull a thick blanket over my head and, hidden in the warm darkness, recede to the inviolable place where I am and where I know. I wish I could enter that chamber and rest, concealed from invasive light and persecuting speech. Leave me alone to breathe for a few moments. Let me be. For I recognise this space; I curl my hands around the wick of who I am and see. The fretfulness in my consciousness dissolves. Here I can weep and no one will find me out. Here I can be silent and no one will force me to speak. I shall stay here secure in the chamber of my heart until anguish becomes peace and hopelessness is transformed into sorrow.'

Here we are again, together now, at one in this safe darkness. I've found you again, core of my life. I'd dried out like a desiccated plain, but now my life is soluble in tears. I cry for the dog because he's getting older. 'What'll happen when he dies?' my little daughter asks. I don't want the dog to die. Here in this place he won't die. My childhood hasn't died here. Here, I can still walk to school. I can see the primroses in the ditch that runs along the lane. I can stand by the small loch and watch the low hills; my son is only one-and-a-half year's old, my mother will return from the dead and she too will be here.

Of course I know that all this isn't true. But I also know that it's absolutely so. Here in this unassailable place it's permitted to be present with the absent, and the absent is permitted to be present, and my heart is a miniature eternity where it's permitted to keep company with everything that was and always is, but out there in the ignorant world, is not any more. I shall stay here until the darkness becomes light.

> I said: Surely the darkness shall cover me, the light shall be
>   night about me.
> But even the darkness is not dark from you;
> the night shines like the day, the darkness is as the light. [14]

A strange illumination has discovered me even here, where I went to escape the all-invasive light. Gently it envelops me, it shines on me and warms me. Some ancient love lies here curled up, a root which like the desert rose has withdrawn its sap into a dehydrated ball and waits. Here it has been preserved in safety. Life flows back through my consciousness like a river, like a song, like the very spring itself. I love you, flower, dog, child, friend, field, sky. Only keep me company, do not desert me, in the bright world to which you now return me.

I'm nervous of going back outside. I'd wandered so far from my house that I hadn't even known that I was lost, forgetting that I ever had a home. In my ignorance I'd become a stranger even to myself. I must make a vow before I leave this place: I will never allow myself to become this lost again.

Yet even as I say these words I know that it will not be so; I shall forget. But afterwards I'll return and once more beg like an outcast to be let in. I can make my heart no promises that we'll never be parted again.

For the heart is hidden in the darkness of our being; yet in the heart shines the eternal light. The heart is the bare nerve of our vulnerability; yet in the heart is music inviolable.

The heart is where the consciousness is repossessed by life.

What's Really Ours

Lech lecha, says the Torah, 'Go!' But when our life's journey is over, what do we really have at the end of it all?

We've probably acquired possessions. It would be hypocritical and foolish to claim that they aren't important. I love my books, my plants, my mug for tea and my favourite coffee cup.

If we're fortunate, we've made a home. Almost everyone changes residence during the course of a life; we may choose to leave, we may be forced to relinquish our dwelling place. But if we stay anywhere reasonably safe and pleasant for any length of time we develop a connection to the place, the gruff and often unacknowledged affection of habit. We become familiar with the view out of the window, we grow accustomed to our stretch of street.

We have attainments. We each have our skills and somewhere in our memory is the game won, the job done, the successful conversation on which our confidence relies. What we do matters, not only because we often succeed in being helpful and inventive but because we are vulnerable and need achievements to re-establish our sense of self worth.

But by far the most important part of our journey isn't connected to what we own or attain. After all, no one, not even Moses, reaches the promised land. The most significant part of our life is summed up in the small word which follows the order to go: '*lecha*, to you'. Commentators are divided on what those two syllables actually mean: they're merely an emphatic particle to stress the urgency of God's command; they tell us that the journey will only be genuine if it reveals our potential; they point to the ultimate purpose of human life, to know one's own true self. But the fact remains that, plainly translated, *lecha* means 'to you'. The true destination of all our travels and the ultimate value of our existence is summed up in those words: 'to you'. This is the significance of our life's journey; that, in the end, is all we have: the you, the others alongside whom we've travelled and the impact of our relationships with them.

That means love; except that this monosyllabic word must be expanded to its full capacity to include everything such partnership entails. It's the companionship, the mundane history of our lives experienced in parallel with each other, the memories, associations, hours of intimacy, discoveries, moments of wonder; the daily rituals and routines, bringing the tea upstairs in the morning, dividing the news-paper, sorting the unpaired socks, walking down the street, matters so ordinary that they're effectively forgotten, except when some sudden sight or smell restores their context and they come to the fore in the mind and haunt it as if yesterday were no longer unreachable but demanded only the stretching out of our hands and they would touch again as they did when we sat by that very table, in that same village, overlooking that stream. If this is what love means, then love is indeed all we have.

Our poor, beloved dog Safi died. The children were terribly upset; so were their parents. The question is asked: what was the point of having him at all, seeing that he had in the end to die? The answer lies in the intangible, unquantifiable meaning of companionship. We loved him and this love remains part of our experience until we too die, when it will continue to assert its importance as part of other people's experience of us, and so onwards, in diminishing measure, until all who knew us, and all who knew them too, are also gone.

All we have is 'you', the others in our life whom we've loved and for whom we've cared.

Yet even this statement is untrue. We don't 'have' them either; we don't have anybody. Nothing belongs to us. The significance of our life passes beyond ownership; it's already out there, travelling on its own journey, beyond our control, past our knowledge, dissolving beyond recognition into a greater existence in which the pronouns 'I' and 'you' and the possessive adjectives 'mine' and 'yours' have no more place.

All that remains is the love.

The Heart's Prayer on the Day of Atonement

The Day of Atonement should be the time above all others when God and the heart meet. It is hard to hear our own heart, difficult to listen to the heart of another person. Life distracts and harries us. But on Yom Kippur there is stillness, time in the presence of God.

What does the heart say when it meets God and God tries to enter? What are its prayers at *Kol Nidrei*, the meditation about vows with which the fast commences, during the great confessions, in the memorial hour of *Yizkor*, and at *Ne'ilah*, the closing of the gates?

Kol Nidrei is the prayer of undefeated hope. When the great cellist Jacqueline du Pré developed multiple sclerosis and was no longer able to play, she would listen each year, before *Yom Kippur*, to her own recording of Bruch's *Kol Nidrei*. The thought of this brilliant lady seeking comfort in the profound beauty of that music moves me greatly. It speaks of the truth that even though the body may be dying, we do not relinquish our deepest dreams. The soul still needs to soar and the heart still yearns for what it loves. Perhaps that is the meaning of the *Kol Nidrei* itself: 'In the past we made vows, but we broke them. We will make them again in the future, and no doubt break them again. For this, God, forgive us in advance. But what we will never do is give up; nothing will make us abandon our dreams.' That is why over two thousand, seven hundred years ago the prophet Isaiah, watching the Assyrian armies occupy the heights around Jerusalem, spoke of the day when no one would hurt or destroy in all God's holy mountain. That is how Nelson Mandela, through twenty-seven years in prison, maintained his faith that the bonds of tyranny would be broken and that not only his own people, but also their oppressors, would one day live together in justice and in freedom.

Therefore let this be the heart's *Kol Nidrei* prayer: I've wanted to be kind and generous; but I've often been selfish and mean. I've wanted to be guided by my heart and spirit, but too often I've followed my nerves and temper. I've dreamt of a world of peace and fellowship, but I've felt

70

fear, suspicion and hatred. Yet for all my failings, for all the failures of humanity, don't harden my heart, don't shrink my soul. Don't make me cynical. Let me strive to be truly human till my dying day. God of infinite spaces, though life and my faults constrict me, don't deprive me of your dreams.

In the *Viddui*, or confession, we acknowledge the wrongs we have done and the pain we have inflicted. Judaism teaches that we all together share responsibility for our society as a whole. Our world is full of violence and injustice. How many children have had their limbs torn off by bombs and land mines, the legacy of one violent, hating generation to the innocence of the next? How many children have died in hospital because there is no medication for the despairing staff to give them? How many children spend their days by rubbish bins searching for food? How much of this earth have we destroyed? Sometimes, full of fear, I have a presentiment of the world as desert, the trees dead, the bird song silent, while there lie randomly by the roadside the dehydrated corpses of animals. Then the ceaseless violence of modern life, its roads, power stations and bombs, seems like a deranged assailant, pounding its bleeding victims over and again.

Judaism teaches that we are specifically responsible as individuals. A friend once told me about a nightmare in which he was holding a raw and aching heart. It was his own. It spoke to him and said: 'This wound was made when you screamed at your father while he stood there in silent sufferance. This is the scar created when for months on end you never once said, "I care about you", to your wife. And this hole here represents your child waiting, waiting for you to notice.' Were we able to fathom to their depths the souls of those near to us, we would be happy for the good we had brought them, but also profoundly ashamed for the hurts we had, often in ignorance, inflicted.

Therefore let this be the heart's *Viddui* prayer: Let me never be unfeeling. Drive indifference out of me; make me a person who cares for others and for the world. Don't burden me with fruitless guilt but, where it is right and just, purify me with remorse. Where I've been driven by anger, jealousy, greed or hate, stop me; then, in the stillness, bring me home to the person I truly can be. Where I've damaged life, give me the honesty to say sorry and the courage to make good. I know the past is beyond my reach, but prove to me that it is not entirely irredeemable. Help me to understand it differently; make it my teacher, to do good.

Yizkor is the remembrance of all the people we have known, loved and lost throughout our life. 'The shock goes, but the sadness stays', a lady told me recently. 'It's not just that my parents are dead; they were the last of their generation, so there's no one left to talk to. I'm learning to live with holes.' The holes come early. The child can no longer lie down next to the dog and say everything into its ear. A person cannot sleep, weeping, struggling to comprehend the absence next to them in the bed. How many there are who loved us, encouraged us, joked with us, who have gone! The *Yizkor* meditations ask us to bear witness to them, and to the hole itself. There are no panaceas, no perfect words. Rachel Remen relates how a medical colleague remembered what happened when she was a little girl and her kitten died. Everyone had something philosophical to say and none of it helped. But her grandmother simply held her close and explained that when grandpa died she had felt the same. Sobbing, she looked up and saw that her grandmother was crying too; somehow this companionship was consoling.[15]

Let this be the heart's *Yizkor* prayer: I remember you, and your love still speaks to me today. I've walked on, even through days when I feared I could not. What choice did I have? I've seen horizons I longed to share with you. How many years is it? Sometimes it feels as if we're only half a moment apart; surely we could touch across that small gap. Yet in the incomprehensible distance between life and death, a moment and forever seem the same. Many times my heart has been numb and I haven't known if it's like a bud closing at night or a light going out forever. God, protect me from loneliness and desolation. Don't let my heart contract and shrivel; don't let fear and sorrow destroy me. If life is the carrying of love from generation to generation, from person to person, let me bear love faithfully and humbly. If life is the distillation by the soul of the sorrow and the beauty of your world into compassion and generosity, into tenderness and love, make me generous, make me loving!

Ne'ilah is the song at the closing of the gates, the song of the final possibility: 'Open unto us the gate, at the hour of the closing of the gate.' Everyone knows: life is short and passes swiftly. Yet the word *zeman*, time, also hints at opportunity. We have a choice. We all struggle between the part of us which says 'Have courage!' and the part which says 'Why bother?' But life is a brief privilege and the moment of its beauty is now; the glory of the western sky, the racing clouds beneath the moon. If something is good and worthwhile, do it. If something is right and the conscience dictates it, commit yourself to it. If something brings comfort, hope and joy, give it. Don't think it doesn't matter: No word is lost and no deed goes to waste. Somewhere it bears fruit, maybe in the mind of a person we don't even know. Don't think the moment is not worthwhile because, lost in eternity, a single moment amounts to nothing. For eternity is present in every moment, and our life is the privilege of sharing it – now!

Let this be the heart's *Ne'ilah* prayer: May I not go through life ignorant and unused. May all things be my teachers, challenging me, searching me, awakening tenderness in me. May life speak to me and within me, as the birds sing in the clearing, the whales in the depths of the sea. When I'm frightened, when I'm empty, restore me with your spirit as rain brings life to the roots. And when I have to die, may life's immensity console me in the joy of life's abundance.

But for now, the task is to return to life and use it to the full. Therefore, so long as I'm privileged to be here, let me say: 'I shall sing to the Lord with my life; make music with all my being to my God'.[16]

CHAPTER FOUR

Becoming a Rabbi

Service

'Let your breath do the work,' he said.

I was downstairs in the synagogue office with my friend Harold and the beautiful black shofar I'd bought many years ago in Jerusalem. A shofar is a hollowed out, unadorned ram's horn. Blown well, it produces a wild, haunting and powerful sound. My grandfather used to blow the shofar in the synagogue on the New Year, my father blew the shofar wonderfully, my son has inherited the gift. So I'm one in a chain of generations. But, as all who've tried it know, blowing the shofar is an art which isn't easy. It was only a few days before *Rosh Hashanah* and I was taking a short lesson.

'Think of yourself as a vessel through which the breath travels. Then simply let it flow from you into the shofar.'

Harold moved to New Zealand several years ago and I miss him greatly. A cranial osteopath by vocation, he's a gentle man with a quiet, understated wisdom, a true healer of body and spirit. I always feel safer in his presence. 'When you give your sermons,' he added, 'you don't always need to put so much personal effort into the expression of the words. If they're good words and they come from the heart, just let them go. They'll do their work.'

His presence beside me in the synagogue that New Year reassured me and I blew the shofar well.

Although our short conversation took place several years ago, Harold's simple counsel has stayed with me and I often reflect on what he said. 'It's an act of service': nothing sums up the task of being a rabbi, or a human being, more aptly or succinctly.

The clergy has become more and more like a business. There's constant pressure to consider marketing, publicity, popularity and competition. Nothing can be taken for granted. Especially in a metropolis like London, churches and synagogues have to fight for their sliver of people's most precious commodity – time. This isn't necessarily an entirely bad thing; it needn't turn rabbis and priests into 'purveyors of religion' in the same way as others market fashionable brands of footwear. It forces one to focus carefully on the quality and relevance of what one has to offer. I've seen some wonderful examples of how religion can be presented in a beautiful and compelling, but unobtrusive manner. I was recently privileged to visit the cathedral in Dunkeld; guests were made welcome in the readiest and most gracious of ways. A lady with a kind smile handed us a simple leaflet which explained: 'Here the casual visitor involuntarily becomes a worshipper'. Well might this be said of such a house of God, standing between the Scottish hills and the River Tay, surrounded by verdant lawns among majestic pines.

But the persistent demand to define success in terms of numbers, to cultivate one's personality and aim for impact as if one were competing with the media, and then to go off and raise the money to upgrade all one's projects, risks becoming not only an outer but an inner distraction, eclipsing the spirit.

For at the heart of ministry is service. If one were to ask, 'service of what?' the traditional religious answer would be 'service of God'. But a fuller response might be 'service of life' because life is immeasurably precious in its own right, and all life is ultimately a manifestation of God. It's an act of service to feed the birds, rescue an abandoned animal, look in on a sick neighbour who lives alone and needs someone to do the shopping, care for the destitute poor or keep company with a dying man. Any vocation is a form of service and the religious vocation is the service of God through the service of all life, the smallest part of which belongs indivisibly to the divine.

A religious leader's greatest sin is to promulgate hatred; his or her greatest virtue, to deepen our reverence for life. Mercifully, in this regard life itself is a constant teacher. Just as Harold instructed me to let the breath flow from myself into the shofar, so I learn over and over again that it's not my own breath in the first place, that nothing is ultimately mine, and that to feel the breath enter me – life's simplest, most essential gift – is at once a privilege and a source of obligation.

I sometimes think it's strange that one can earn the title rabbi, or priest or imam, through a course of study. It goes without saying that learning is important; in Judaism studying, teaching and rendering ritual and legal decisions are at the core of the rabbi's task. A rabbi has to be part of the living continuum of Jewish knowledge.

But I'm not sure that this is sufficient to merit the title of religious leader. That depends on how a person lives, on how a person serves. It can only really be decided after death, when our pilgrimage is complete and all our deeds are known. Did we serve life faithfully? Did we serve life with love?

Between Love and Fear

At this time a special emissary goes out towards the south.
His name is Raphael and he possesses all kinds of healing.

Zohar III 204a

There are days when one comes awake full of anguish, days when one wakes filled with love.

When I was a teacher, before I studied to become a rabbi, I always liked to arrive in school early. I would walk across the empty hall and look through the half-open doors of the classrooms. In those few minutes before the children came I would feel like a sponge, absorbing anxiety and desolation. It was as if anguish and hunger were falling from the walls and pouring into me, the feelings of so many tens of children wondering what awaited them this day. Who would feed them, who would look after them and protect them from the torment of exposure to their fear and loneliness? Only very slowly, as we began to talk to one another, to teach and to learn, would these troubled sensations yield to the merry conviviality of children who know that they are cherished and protected.

The vestiges of those feeling have never entirely left me, the terror of the cupboard which is bare, the empty shelves of an inner world devoid of nurture. Maybe there is in birth itself an abandonment so severe, echoed and repeated in every subsequent change and loss, that the heart is haunted all its life by a pain from which there can be distraction and release, but never cure.

The Torah contains a terrifying curse: 'You shall be afraid by day and by night; you will have no confidence in your own life. In the morning you will say, "I wish it was evening", and in the evening you will say, "I wish it was morning", because of the fear in your heart which makes you afraid.'[1] No doubt those words were composed as a response to a physical reality, a state of persecution and deprivation so harsh that they invariably bring to mind images of skeletal beings struggling not to

77

succumb to famine, exhaustion and despair. But they describe, too, an internal world of helplessness and loss, which, for those once sensitised to it, all the wealth in the world can camouflage, but never take away. One can even feel it sometimes in the street, a dizziness, a sensation of having no weight, as if all around were a vacuum which prevented the inner cry from traversing the silence. 'Hello', one says, 'How are you?' as if everything were fine. But what one feels inside is that one could, should, must disappear forever between the cracks in the paving stones.

Most of the time one doesn't think about how much courage it can take to face the morning. How much cold, fear, hunger, hunger for food, hunger for warmth, hunger for a hug, hunger for harmony, hunger for true, loving attention is being kept at bay by the sum of these children's spirits in this classroom? The truth is that in this world there isn't enough love to go round. At some point in life the great whirlpool of misery sucks at almost every heart and down we go into the place of our most primitive wounds.

But we are not helpless. Only very rarely is there nothing whatsoever we can do. Many attitudes and actions have the power to preserve us from the terror within: routine, discipline, work, humour, curiosity, cheerfulness, friendship, engagement with the world. But the greatest cure of all is love; only love is the heart's true healer. With all else, anguish still haunts the margins of our consciousness, the awareness of the precipice at the edge of the steep and twisting path, the knowledge that there is no fence.

Sometimes one wakes up in the morning filled with love. The songs of the birds, the transformation of the light, stir intuitions of a world in which there is an invisible but all pervading consciousness which is indeed love. That is what the Zohar teaches: 'At this time the sound of birds can be heard making their nests, as it is written, "There the birds make their nests" (Psalm 104:17). These birds thank and praise the Holy Blessed One and the hind of dawn bestirs herself in the world and says, "How great is your goodness which you have stored up for those who fear you" (Psalm 31:20). The emissary then goes forth and does what he is commanded . . . His name is Raphael and he possesses all kinds of healing . . . '[2] This 'emissary' touches the still dormant consciousness with tenderness and we wake in the excitement of joy and the embrace of compassion. Beauty becomes articulate; everything speaks to us, the world and its phenomena, the man sweeping the street, the snowdrops under the hedgerow, the child on her way to school. Healing permeates us.

Love sutures the heart. It prevents the life-blood from draining through the holes of myriad wounds down into the void. It fosters the very organism of the body, as if the invisible corpuscles were producing more blood cells and the interconnecting signals of the brain were more alert. The soul rejoices: 'My God, the soul which you have given me is pure. You created it, you fashioned it, you breathed it into me', and through it I am breathing in your world.[3] I am bound to every form of consciousness within it, born on the breath of a great love.

If only that love would never depart; if only we would never experience abandonment again. I wish that love would pour down like moonlight when the wind drives a rift through the clouds to illumine the dark path. I want that love to enter the sore heart between the scabs of its wounds. I want us not to be afraid of loneliness anymore.

Fear will not overcome us; the consciousness of love is too pervasive and too simple, it enters beneath all barriers and, while the watchmen search to keep it out, it's already there, within. Love will not forsake us; though at times it seems to burn in isolation in the heart, its fire comes from horizons far beyond. Should it ever be extinguished, something greater will re-kindle it.

We must tell ourselves that we need not be afraid.

Kindness

These are things to which there is no upper limit,
. . . acts of faithful kindness.

Mishnah Peah 1:1

. . . that best portion of a good man's life;
His little, nameless, unremembered acts
Of kindness and of love.

William Wordsworth [4]

'I've got the most wonderful neighbour,' the lady explained to me. 'When my husband was in hospital she knocked on my door every evening, just after I got back, to see if I was all right. She always had something hot for me to eat, a soup or a pasta dish, something she'd cooked herself. It made such a difference to how I felt when I came home to the empty house.'

I've witnessed countless examples of kindness. Most of them are so natural that it's easy to overlook how special they are because they're so simply integrated into the texture of people's daily lives. Many years ago my wife and I stopped at a small family-run nursery; the plants were arranged on a stall by the roadside but you had to go into the house to pay. As we left, the lady said, 'I must take you to meet my daughter; everyone who comes here says hello'. She led us into the living room where the girl, who obviously suffered from major disabilities, was lying on the couch. I'm not sure she was able to speak, but she gave us a beaming smile. 'I bring everyone in to say hello,' her mother repeated with great affection, and her daughter gave us another brimming smile before we left.

The greatest human quality is kindness which comes from the heart.

A favour is best done gladly, but one can grit one's teeth and still do it. A kind deed brings welcome as well as the act itself, because kindness is always generous. But true loving-kindness includes the heart, which is why genuinely kind people have a gift for making others feel safe in their presence and for spreading love wherever they go.

Kindness has a timetable all of its own. The hour over tea at the kitchen table belongs to it, as do the twenty minutes at the bedside, at the school gate, on the phone. Its tasks are shopping, cooking, washing, fetching, taking a friend to a doctor's appointment, helping a sick person from the bed to the bathroom, remembering birthdays, dates and anniversaries in the diary of other people's anguish and hope. Its appurtenances are milk-jugs, walking-sticks, warm gloves, flowers and the dog's lead. Its landscape is the vulnerability of human flesh, its nakedness before accident, illness and aging. It's at home with the soreness of the human heart, people's worries about their children, parents, partners, friends, themselves and the meaning and purpose of their lives. Its skills are listening, presence, patience, understanding and being slow to judge. Its achievements lie in making the ordinary cheerful and the painful bearable.

Kindness has many resources, but first and foremost it gives of itself. That's why kindness is also redemptive for the person who practises it. More than fame, achievement, excitement, travel, hobbies and pleasures, loving-kindness is the most powerful response to cynicism and despair; through it we rediscover the reason for being alive.

Kindness is the most faithful of all qualities. Many years ago a friend's mother said, 'When you're young you look for a partner who's attractive and fun. But when you get older what you really want is someone who's going to be kind.' Her words stuck in my mind, as did those of a man who told me about his last conversation with his dying father. At the time he was still unattached, so he asked him what qualities he should look for in the girl he hoped to marry. He expected his father, who was an orthodox rabbi, to make some pronouncement about the importance of religious observance, but instead he told him simply, 'Be sure she's truly kind'.

Genuine kindness is rooted in love; it's an intuitive response to the feelings and needs of others, the spontaneous concern that the child shouldn't be cold, the visitor lost, the sick person left alone. But kindness has its discipline too, demanding wisdom and selflessness, the ability to step back from our own wants and desires. Even in the middle of tension and conflict, when we're prone to react in anger, it calls on us to consider the sensitivities of the other person and remember what may be their pain, their fear, their weakness and the causes of their defensiveness. It requires us to endeavour, even under the greatest pressure, never to respond without compassion and respect.

Kindness is ultimately a spiritual quality, an expression of partnership with all that lives. That's why we should be kind to animals too. The Psalms speak of God's mercies extending to all God's works;[5] Buddhists include all sentient beings in their prayers. For the animals are our partners on earth; they too are susceptible to suffering, they don't deserve our cruelty. I appreciate people who respect animals and are gentle in their presence. It's surely part of what the prophet Micah meant by 'walking humbly with God'.[6] How can that be compatible with the desire to hurt another living being?

But truly kind people don't act out of pious or self-conscious motives. They're kind because they're kind, because kindness is love in its everyday form and because its opposite, cruelty, is simply unthinkable to them.

Over two thousand years ago, Simeon the Just taught that kindness is one of the three pillars upon which the world stands.[7] If we really practised the laws of loving-kindness, how much more securely established the world would be.

From a Family of Rabbis

Was du ererbt von deinen Vätern hast,
Erwirb es, um es zu besitzen.

What you have inherited from your fathers
Acquire, so as to make it your own.

Goethe [8]

On my grandfather's grave are the words *migeza rabbanim*; they translate, inelegantly, as 'of rabbinic stock'.

According to family legend my grandfather was still a small boy when he climbed onto the dining room table and delivered his first sermon; his younger brother, the sole auditor, was evidently unimpressed and disappeared off to the nearby forest for a ramble. He later became a doctor and a keen naturalist.

My grandfather's behaviour was scarcely surprising. His own father was a rabbi in Erfurt; as a young man he had walked from Hungary to Vienna in search of the opportunity to immerse himself in both rabbinical and European literature. The story goes that he attached a rope to his leg and hung the other end out of the window so that the man who extinguished the gas street lamps at five o'clock every morning would tug on it and rouse him to his studies.

At eighteen my grandfather travelled to Berlin and enrolled at the *Hochschule für die Wissenschaft des Judentums*, the progressive academy for rabbinical studies, as well as at the Humboldt University of Berlin. By state decree every German rabbi, whether liberal or orthodox, was required to possess a doctorate. He recorded in his memoirs how when he returned from the *viva* on his thesis, which he completed in Heidelberg, his landlady congratulated him and presented him with a bunch of flowers. 'But how did you know I was going to pass?' he asked her in surprise, to which she replied, 'When someone works as hard as you have, he is sure to do well.' In 1909 he graduated to the news that he could choose between a pulpit in Berlin or a position in Frankfurt, the two most prestigious Jewish communities in the country. He opted for the latter and officiated there, except for the four years of the First World War, when he served as army chaplain on the western front at Verdun, until the Nazis forced him and his family into exile in 1939.

My grandfather met my grandmother at a party on the festival of Purim. She was beautiful and he invited her to dance. It soon transpired, however, that he hadn't the least idea of even the most basic steps (an inability which I've ably inherited), so they sat down to talk. At the end of the conversation, he invited her to his Bible class. She was astonished; this was scarcely the most romantic invitation she'd ever received and anyway, weren't all rabbis old, with grey beards? But she went and, at the completion of his lecture on the famous saying in The Chapters Of The Fathers, 'Make yourself a teacher and acquire yourself a friend', she raised her hand and asked, 'What if the two should prove to be the same person?' 'That,' he replied, 'is such a good question that I think we should meet afterwards to talk about it.' Before they became engaged they sat in the empty auditorium of the main Frankfurt Synagogue and discussed, in true German philosophical fashion, whether their love was 'Objektif oder subjektif'. Only when this question had been resolved to their satisfaction did they allow themselves their first kiss.

Of course, I knew as a child that my grandfather was a rabbi. But, in spite of the occasional game of 'synagogue' in which I considered myself to have been relegated to the lowest of positions well beneath my brother in the hierarchy as 'mere' *shammes*, or orderly, while he was *chazan*, or cantor, I failed to appreciate what that really meant until a year or two before his death. Only then did I begin to ask him serious questions: 'How could Jacob be a hero if he cheated his brother and deceived his father?'; 'What was it like to study Talmud?' But his presence had made its impact on me and in the weeks after he died I spent a trial month at rabbinical college.

I never, however, inherited my grandfather's inner certainty about his future career and, in the difficult years after I completed my degree, I was filled with doubts and conflicting plans. I spent time in Israel, then returned to England and trained and worked as a teacher, all the time taking on an increasing range of roles in the synagogue. Still not quite sure, but encouraged by members of the congregation, I began to study for the rabbinate. Then at some point in my second year at college the doubts disappeared. The learning, the work itself and all their many challenges engulfed me; I was committed. Life had decided for me and the question now belonged to the past. The real issue became, and remains, how to strive not to fall too far short of the many responsibilities entailed by the position.

Only later did I learnt about the rabbinic tradition on my father's side of the family. When my cousin cleared the flat in Ramban Street in Jerusalem where the family had lived since 1940, she discovered large numbers of papers and photographs going back at least three generations, many of them seemingly untouched since our grandparents arrived in Palestine as refugees from Nazi Germany. There were effusive letters of appreciation to my great-grandfather, who had been head of the rabbinical court in Berlin, congratulating him on his seventieth birthday. One was written on parchment in beautiful classical Hebrew; another was signed by the renowned scholar and leader of the German Jewish establishment, Rabbi Dr. Leo Baeck. My great-grandfather died in 1937 while on holiday and was buried, according to his express wish, not in Germany but in the cemetery of the nearest Jewish community, which proved to be Holleschau, the home of one of his previous pulpits. The bundle of papers included several photographs of the long procession of mourners following the coffin through deep snow. His wife Regina perished in the Holocaust. I found, in an old white bag of unsorted papers from the years 1938 and 1939, the letter informing her that the quota imposed by the British authorities on immigration into Palestine had been filled and that it would therefore regrettably not for the present time be possible for her to join her son, daughters and grandchildren in that country. It was presumably this document, dated 9th November, 1938, hence written on the day preceding *Kristallnacht*, which sealed her destiny. Brief details of her fate were later inscribed by the family on her granddaughter Eva's tombstone. Eva died young, possibly of complications following diphtheria, and was buried in the Jewish cemetery on the Mount of Olives, overlooking the Old City of Jerusalem which her grandmother never lived to see.

My great grandfather, Rabbi Dr. Yaakov Freimann, himself came from a renowned family of rabbis. I recently studied details of an important legal decision by his grandfather, Rabbi Yaakov Emden, known, as are so many Jewish scholars, after his most important work as the *Aruch LaNer*. I regret that until now I've spent so little time researching such matters.

The two sides of my family came from very different branches of the Jewish tradition, and I find myself ideologically somewhere in the middle ground between them. My mother's father was a traditionally minded, but nevertheless progressive rabbi, although he only ever travelled by car on the Sabbath after the family had been exiled to London and the distance to his new congregation, composed of refugees like himself, proved simply too great to walk. The rabbis in my father's family were strictly orthodox scholars of Talmud and Jewish law in the classical manner.

Yet both were engulfed by the same fate; both sides of the family were exiled and scattered across the globe, between Israel, Europe and America. On both sides the immediate family escaped while members of the wider circle of relatives perished. On both sides, too, there have been slower, more insidious and persistent kinds of loss, breaches in the continuity of family culture, a host of absences around the table on Sabbaths and festivals, an ongoing struggle to re-establish the learning and confidence of the past, and, in our small part of the family, few marriages and fewer children.

These gaps and wounds leave a deep and demanding sense of responsibility.

The Ladder

Jacob left from Beer Sheva and set out towards Haran.
And he lighted upon a place and there he spent the night . . .

Genesis 28:10 –11

For the first time in his life, Jacob is utterly alone. The night is pitch dark and full of dangers; he has neither home nor shelter. He has left his family behind, his father and mother dismayed, his brother enraged. There can be no question of returning; there's no way back to how things used to be. Before him lie many days of journey and an unfamiliar land. There's no escape from the unknown. Here in his dispossession he has only *hamakom*, 'the place' upon which he has lighted, the middle of nowhere with its stones. He gathers them into a pile, lays down his head and in his aloneness has his great dream:

> Behold there was a ladder placed towards the earth and its top reached to the heavens; and behold angels of God were ascending and descending on it. And behold, the Lord stood upon it and said . . . 'Behold I am with you . . . ' [9]

Four times in the course of the dream the Torah employs the word 'Hineh, Behold!' Four times we are drawn towards a different and deeper perception of the world.

'Behold there was a ladder . . . ' There's an etching by William Blake which I used to think was inspired by this dream. A man is positioning an enormous ladder in order to climb up to the sky. The feet of the ladder are placed on the earth and the top ascends among the stars.[10] But on reflection the picture and the Biblical narrative prove to be quite different. Blake's work suggests a combination of curiosity and greed, a drive to explore mixed with a desire to possess. Imperial man reaches out from planet earth. The caption beneath the illustration reads 'I want! I want!' But in Jacob's vision the ladder, like the dream itself, descends from heaven; its feet are only set 'towards the earth', it seems they don't even touch the ground. The potential connection indicated here is primarily spiritual: is there anything which links the heavens and the earth?

It's fascinating to listen to children's perceptions of God and to hear adults recall how and when they first encountered the idea of such a being. Theological problems are quick to emerge. Small children often ask 'Where is God?', a question which doesn't disappear as we get older. When four-year-old Mossy was given the conventional reply that God was everywhere, he said, predictably, 'What, here in my tummy too?' Libbi experienced related difficulties at the early age of two and a half. We always insisted that the children say the appropriate blessing when they were given new clothes. She refused. Her argument was simple and cogent: 'Mummy bought me the trousers, not God'. But pressure was brought to bear and she relented. The result was that when I took her visiting and an elderly lady asked her who had given her the smart item in question, she answered: 'God and mummy'. Nor was this the end of the matter. She later inquired in all innocence, 'What does God do when God isn't buying trousers?' – a question to which many of us would still like to have a good answer. As regards the rabbinic legend that the unborn baby is taught the entire Torah in its mother's womb but forgets it all when it enters this world of blindness, the evidence argues at best only for the thoroughness of the forgetting.[11] God, for most children, is a word which enters their vocabulary as a threat, 'God will be angry'; as a promise, 'God will be pleased'; as a way of palliating the fear of death, 'The dog's with God in heaven now'; or as an agent to whom the everyday laws of sense and reason fail to apply, so that adults feel justified in making such apparently meaningless assertions as 'God's in everybody's heart' and 'God knows everything'. Yet many children do, at moments, have a deeply spiritual response to the world.

At what point, if at all, does the idea of God become part of our actual experience? How is genuine spiritual knowledge obtained? I don't believe in absolute proofs of God's existence, in the possibility of producing evidence of the kind that would satisfy the rigorous demands of the empirical method of scientific investigation. A few years ago I was on holiday near Loch Ness and the legendary monster was everywhere in evidence. There were Loch Ness monster mugs, T-shirts, pens, pencils and cuddly toys of every size to beguile the gullible and extract money from their pockets. 'So much stuff and no one's even seen the creature,' I complained. 'So what do you do for a living?' came the reply.

Yet at certain points life prompts the intuition that there is indeed something which ascends beyond the material reality of this world. Slowly, experiences begin to accrue which nourish this sensibility. These may be moments of ecstatic joy when it seems as if the whole world sings in our small being and our consciousness hears the speech which rises from the living earth, its plants, trees, birds and animals, as it rotates on its trajectory of days and nights, seasons and years about its star, across the universe. Or maybe in the stillness underneath the sores and complaints of sorrow we apprehend the voice of a great silence saying to us, 'Be still, because I am'.

'Behold there is a ladder . . . '

And on that ladder are angels, ascending and descending. In Hebrew an angel is a *malach*, a messenger, one who is sent on God's behalf. I've seen many angels over the years, and I trust I'll meet many more, though none of them has the six wings to which Isaiah testifies in his vision. My angels are human beings. They ascend God's ladder and inspire me to try to climb up after them through the quality of the lives they lead. In my view, the conduct of such people constitutes the most compelling testimony that the spiritual life is not a fantasy, but real, and that it remains the most important pathway towards what is selfless, courageous and good. Whether their achievements reach the public domain and they become figures of international and intergenerational stature, or whether, which is far more likely, scarcely anyone knows of their existence beyond their family and friends, they bear witness through what they make of life that this being to which we give the inadequate title God, this all encompassing vitality and presence, is the most profound and absolute reality and that it is this which in our lives we have to serve.

I've met many people who, through faith in life, in love or in God, climb high on the ladder between heaven and earth. I think of the woman who, despite being terribly ill, danced at her son's Bar Mitzvah just a month before she died. With fiery red hair, a gift for joy and laughter, kind, vivacious eyes and an intuitive wisdom, she lived, as her family told me, at two speeds: fast and very fast. She loved life, every minute and every day. She was a wonderful friend, had a tremendous sense of fun, but never could understand quite how it was that she brought others so much laughter. Her children described her as a big kid, game for anything, 'the amazing Scottish mummy' whom their companions adored. When she became ill with cancer, she never resented the disease. On the contrary, she spoke about how the experience was changing her, of what she was learning from it. She always believed that others had it worse. The one thing she could not bear was the thought that she might ever have to wake up in the morning without hope. Mercifully, she never did. She was concerned for others and engaged with life until the night before she slipped into unconsciousness, dying the next morning in her sleep.

I think of all the people whose testaments are recorded in the book *Dying We Live*.[12]

I remember exactly where that volume sat on the lowest shelf above the sideboard in my grandparent's dining room. When my grandfather died I asked, before I even knew anything of its contents, to keep it in his memory. It proved to be an anthology of final letters written in prison by Germans who had resisted the Nazis and were now awaiting execution. Most of them were believing Christians. I often think about the faith which, sixty years later, still communicates itself quietly and profoundly from the isolated cells of those courageous men and women.

Through faith in life, in love and in God, such people gain ascendancy over the selfishness, querulousness and material preoccupations which we so often allow to govern our lives. In so doing they transform the ordinary into the inspiring and, by sharing their gift for living, bring heaven down to earth.

'And behold, the Lord was standing on [the ladder]' . . .

How could Jacob look at God, even in a dream, when Judaism teaches that no one can see God and live? Maybe a dream is different, or perhaps

Jacob didn't actually see; he felt God's presence and knew. Rabbinic legend compares perceiving the divine to examining the colours of light which emerge from a crystal ball. The configuration of rays and shades appears different to every person and changes all the time. Each of us has only a momentary, partial, indirect and subjective glimpse of an infinite number of possibilities which expand and diminish, transform from tone to tone and transmute from shade to shade every moment. For God is limitless and cannot be described. Therefore we cannot define God in words or pictures, or even imagine a single other person's experience of the being whom Jacob perceives to be standing at the top of that ladder in his dream.

But perhaps, as the great Hasidic teacher Rebbe Yehudah Aryeh Lev of Ger notes, we can know the experience by the effects. Jacob awakes and is afraid. Startled, he exclaims, 'How awesome this place is!' It's a moment of inner realization; the heart responds with awe to the awareness of the presence of God. The mark of a genuine spiritual experience, the proof of its authenticity, is that it engenders a profound respect for all that is. How awesome is this place, this world, this life, this companionship in creation. Struck and humbled, the heart determines never to inflict any form of hurt on anything. All it desires is only to serve and to cherish – the grass, the trees, the animals, other people. For all of us are part of the articulation of the same divine creative energy, which we are commanded to hold inviolable in every form. In the moment of realisation, in the experience of awe, this commandment is no imposition, but our one overriding desire.[13]

Then God speaks to Jacob and says: 'Behold I am with you and shall protect you wherever you go'. This is the final 'behold' in the dream and appears to introduce a lie.

Is it really possible to believe in a God who literally protects us wherever we wander and brings us safely home? It would be wonderful to do so but I, for myself, cannot.

Does God really prevent accidents and disasters and preserve the innocent? It would be lovely to live in such a world, but we don't. To claim that we do is deceitful. We're forbidden to imitate the moralising of Job's comforters whose heartless faith required them to blame the

91

victim in order to keep their theology neat and tidy with its convenient and predictable God. 'If you're suffering, you must be guilty', is the catechism of the cruel. In the Book of Job even God testifies that such a premise is a lie. Terrible things happen all the time to those who don't deserve them and this serves neither as proof nor disproof of the reality of God's existence.

Yet on a different level God's words to Jacob are profoundly true. For God's assurance, 'Behold I am with you,' is not a promise of constant protection but of inalienable companionship. History testifies to its power. 'Behold I am with you' is the secret of the inner strength which faces tyranny down. It's the source of the spiritual resilience of the persecuted. It's the underground stream which feeds the inner well of those who suffer without losing faith. It's the message which somewhere, in some throat, no matter how many are slit or burnt, survives the slaughter.

But the voice which says 'I am with you' is not easily heard. This isn't because that voice is silent, but rather because our heart must be open enough and our spirit humble enough to hear it. And when the voice does come, it often only stays to speak for a single, bare moment. It soon becomes alienated by our heedlessness and our many preoccupations, however justified and however noble.

'Behold a ladder placed upon the earth . . .' Jacob, alone in the middle of nowhere, couldn't have had a more favourable dream at a more propitious hour. But dreams come and go; they don't constitute life's challenge. That challenge is to live by them.

God's Being

'I am the Lord your God' isn't a commandment. The deepest experiences don't need to spell out their own implications. We know.

I remember moments when I've been most in love with life, when I've felt bound in a spirit of thankfulness with the leaves, the trees, the hillside and the night, when I've laid myself down so that my heart would sing next to where the grass sings, and have got up and walked on in joy. Such prostrations are acts of fealty, when I make my vows to life: 'I promise not to hurt you; I promise to carry the love of you with me. So may you, too, be with me when I need you.' I admit that I've forgotten since, sometimes for years at a time; I know I've behaved faithlessly. But I've never for a single second considered the commandment to be abrogated by which I'm bound to love and honour life.

There are other kinds of realisation, different moments of commandment. I remember the picture of the young girl and the bird. It was during a prolonged and vicious drought in Africa and the girl was struggling to reach the camp where a relief team was supplying food and water. She had only a little further to go but her strength had come to an end and she sank to the dried out earth. The bird, a vulture, sat scarcely a few yards away and watched. It knew: the girl would never reach the food and water. Surely we, like the photographer, are commanded: 'If you do not carry such children with you . . . '

'I am the Lord your God' is not written in the imperative form. It instructs us to do absolutely nothing. Yet once the truth behind these words has been experienced, once we have in any way felt the presence of God in our lives, we are utterly commanded. There can be no thought or action which is not, explicitly or implicitly, a response to the deepest reality we know. We can call it by many names, God, Allah, transcendent being, the consciousness which comprehends all life. But however we name it, it is present, whether or not we realise it, in every interaction and in all consciousness at all times.

Moments of awareness, and for most of us awareness is rare and momentary only, belong among the great treasures of our experience. We cherish them like the presentiments of a great love. They are the stars by which we navigate our existential darkness. All such moments are revelatory and form part of a continuum with the great revelation at Sinai. For, as Rebbe Yehudah Aryeh Lev of Ger, known after his work as the *Sefat Emet*, the Language of Truth, explains, in those seconds when God spoke, 'All creation was focussed upwards toward the root of its vitality . . . When God said "I am the Lord your God" all created beings understood the words to be addressed specifically to them . . . Then everything was perfected as is most fit.'[14] Any moment in which any consciousness apprehends the universal being is part of the same revelation.

Faith is a way of experiencing life. It is often misrepresented. It is not simply a dogma, a set of mental convictions that certain propositions are true. It is not a master plan for how to play chess with life's contradictions or an escape route from life's anguish. Faith is in the living, including the doubt, the anxiety, the pain and the long periods of ignorance and forgetting in between short moments of knowledge and realisation. Thus faith is never an entitlement to complacency.

Neither can faith ever justify zealotry. To disregard life, to insult, wound and kill in the name of God is to betray the very God in whose name the deed is perpetrated. How can the living God, whose presence is manifest in all consciousness, be served by killing? How can God be present potentially among my people, in my land, in my consciousness, and not potentially in your people, your country and your heart also? For there is no Jewish God, no Muslim God, no Christian God, no 'your God' and no 'my God' but only God.

On the contrary, faith is always a moral challenge, a constant struggle to be faithful to life. As the *Sefat Emet* goes on to explain, in the moment when God speaks and creation hears, 'No one is capable of committing wrong. For nature itself prevents anyone from transgressing the intention of the Creator.'[14] In the moment of knowledge, when we understand that we and all existence belong to God, we are filled with such reverence for life that our only desire is to honour and cherish it. All selfishness, all desire to do wrong and to hurt, is abrogated.

The problem is that the moment falls away and we forget. We live in a world of concealment and hold weakly to the memories of rare and exceptional experiences of beauty which are soon contradicted and eroded. It is in this muddled and jaded reality that our faithfulness is constantly put to the test. It is tried in the rush hour, at the supermarket, in the way we talk to our family, and in our responses to difference, indifference and hatred.

Everything we do matters. A thoughtless deed always drives something precious away. The incident may be relatively trivial. The other day I had a misunderstanding with a man on the pavement. I thought he was waiting for me, so I slowly backed my car out of the drive. He thought I was waiting for him and walked on. The next moment he was right next to my car window shaking his fist. Although I had no intention of behaving rudely, I had become part of an unpleasant interaction and felt ugly, as if on some level of being I had inflicted damage. Such incidents happen to us every day and leave a wake of violence or grace. That is not even to speak about the great divisions and hatreds which afflict humanity.

On the other hand, a moment of beauty brings the hidden wonder of life into conscious recognition. Outside, a jay sits on a pine branch. A small bird hops into a nest. The tree is filled with life. Ultimately the same being whose vitality traverses all worlds holds us together as fragments among all the countless manifestations of the same consciousness. Here is God's presence, in the birds, in the tree and in between us.

That presence is latent, too, in the care we feel for another person. I watch a child hug her grandmother outside the school and run off into the playground. Tenderness, compassion and understanding invoke a deeper sense of being; we are drawn together by what transcends us all and which, through our loving, we all serve.

Every moment of life presents the challenge of faithfulness or betrayal.

But there are, mercifully, unanticipated experiences of beauty and grace. However brief and transient to us, the eternal vitality flows through them like a hillside stream. Silenced and awakened, our spirit recognises that being which encompasses and enfolds it. God is speaking to us, the everlasting 'I am'.

95

Hinneni

Master of the universe	*I will sing a song to you.*
Where will I find you?	*And where will I find you not?*
Where I go, there you are.	*Where I stay, there are you.*
Only you, you alone,	*You again, and only you.*

Rabbi Levi Yitzhak of Berditchev [15]

At the heart of life a voice is singing. We heard it when we walked that dusk along the canal, when the tiny grey-brown cygnets climbed out of the water onto their mother's back and she hid them under her feathers and carried them beneath her wings. The voice answers nothing and says everything, without uttering a single word.

A voice is singing. Perhaps one shouldn't say 'voice' because there are no lips and there is no sound. The world is filled with the paradox of its silence: 'Day utters speech to day and night communicates knowledge to night', reads the Psalm, before continuing, 'There is no speech; there are no words; their voice isn't heard at all.'[16] For there is nothing which offers an explanation.

Part of the problem is that we want so much of God that we forget God in thinking of what we want. We don't hear because what we're listening for is something else. Perhaps it's the Bible's fault for leading us to expect revelation in similar proportions as in ancient times, or at least a word from heaven the way God used to bestow it on the prophets. But what if God has long since done with that kind of disclosure? What if it never actually happened quite like that? What if it never occurred that way even then, but the creators of narratives recorded it thus, – with all that speaking, acting, stretching forth of mighty hands, deliverance and wrath, because they understood that God had indeed been present in some decisive form, had been the essence and the inspiration of their history, and all other kinds of language had failed them in trying to describe the silent absence of God's utter manifestation?

We crave answers: 'Answer us on the day we call,' begins the evening service. 'Answer us, father of orphans; answer us, judge of widows,' conclude the penitential prayers. The words are at once an impassioned demand for a response and an articulation of the baffled anguish of the moment: 'God, in the midst of all this sorrow and confusion, help us!' But God appears recalcitrant and no voice speaks from the sky. Or maybe God isn't that kind of God. For God descends in no obvious way either to explain the past or to indicate the future.

Struggling to live with what we can't understand, we often impose fictions on the silence, making it noisy with our justifications. How many people think, despite themselves, when someone dies before their time: 'The way he lived his life, always running'; or, less cruelly, 'God wants her in heaven'; or, more simply, 'There must be reasons for everything in God's book'. Maybe such constructs do ease the pain of suffering. After all, what comfort is there in the thought that fate is largely random, that what happened may have occurred for little, if any, reason at all? But that doesn't suffice to make those statements true. They are born of our anguish, of our incapacity not to know, of the need to turn life into a coherent story. The process of composing them about our own sufferings and struggles, with if's and but's and maybe's, may lie at the heart of our search for meaning. But proposed as truths which explain the destiny of others, they are frequently harsh and sometimes punitive, even if not consciously intended in that way. Thus they aptly reflect life's own imponderable cruelties, to accommodate which we require them. We need the stories to silence the silence of what we do not know.

Yet at the heart of life a voice is speaking. We heard it together in the hospital room when my friend said with his characteristic frankness and courage, 'It's *Ne'ilah* now; this is the end'.

But the voice says nothing about either the why or the wherefore and we badly need explanations. Abraham wants an explanation. 'Should the judge of all the earth not do justice!' he demands.[17] He even argues God down to the concession that the city of Sodom should be saved for the sake of just ten righteous people within it. But what the text fails to address is why God should allow even a single innocent person to burn to death. The next morning Abraham looks out at the smoke rising from the city in flames. One wonders what might be his thoughts.

Moses wants to know the answer. At the moment of his greatest achievement, when he saves Israel from God's wrath after they make the golden calf, chastising the people for their sin and God for God's destructive intentions, he demands of heaven: 'Make known to me your ways'.[17] According to rabbinical tradition, what he actually asks is the age-old question about why the wicked so frequently prosper while the righteous have to suffer. But even the Talmud can produce no credible answer.[18]

Job wants to know why. His pain is terrible enough, but what goads him into fury are the lies his so-called friends keep telling him about God. It isn't true, he insists, that everything conforms to a single pattern in which suffering means punishment and the punishment invariably fits the crime. No, he conceals not a single secret sin which could justify his misery. God does eventually vindicate Job and admonishes his friends for speaking falsely about the deity. But God fails to provide Job with any logical explanation for all his gratuitous pain; God offers him no alternative interpretations. There is only the inscrutable wonder of creation. 'Only'; but it is enough, that voice singing at the heart of creation.

So, if Abraham, Moses and Job receive none, why should we obtain answers? Yet it's almost impossible to escape the compulsion to seek them. How can one say, in the face of misery and injustice, that there is a God, yet maintain that that God is not implicated, is not the why and the wherefore? What use then is God, if 'believing in God' justifies nothing and fails to explain anything? Wouldn't it be simpler to concede and agree with the atheist?

But a voice is speaking at the heart of creation. It is not there for use or function. It is, because it is. It is here in the tumultuous bird song of dawn; here it is in the sudden quietness at dusk. Stilling the restless, agitated mind, still in the stillness of the conscience, taut in the heart's attentiveness, reverberating in the soul that permeates and dissolves us, is this voice.

'*Hinneni*; here am I.'

Who said that? Was it that voice again? No; it was me, experiencing myself addressed. But the voice itself is more like silence, endless being overheard in the process of its own articulation. It pervades all, all is interpenetrated with it; it transcends all, and all is transient within it; it is at once the entirety of love and the totality of destiny. When we hear it, all it says is 'I am what I am'. Or rather it says nothing, for names are merely human words and the voice is not merely human.

After all, it isn't actually true that all we want of God is explanations. We want God.

A young man is very ill. Others are asking, 'Why should this be?' For some time he, too, is haunted by that question, creating many painful answers. But at a crucial point, at a moment of healing, it loses its central relevance, though never entirely absent from his thoughts. For he is listening to something else, if only for a few moments, if only now and not then, and then again for just a moment. The singing of the silence is embracing him.

'*Hinneni*', he says, 'Here am I. This is me. I have nothing; will you have me just as I am?' It says, 'But I am already with you; we have each other always.' It says, 'Look! The world is mine from the root to the leaf, from birth to death, from the earth to the sky.' It says nothing at all.

Who was it who said '*Hinneni*'?

God, say something more! There are so many essential matters we need to hear you address!

On a pond in the dark, two ducks are swimming close to one another. It seems at first as if they are silent, but between them is a constant, quiet chattering, an almost inaudible intimacy. It calms the spirit; it reassures the heart. Asking 'What is that voice really saying?', demanding 'Tell me more!': these are not the proper questions.

'*Hinneni*, I am what I am': Is there anything else that needs to be said? What it means is clear without demanding that every clause be set down. Each moment is subject to life's commandments: to respect, to honour, to love, and never through injustice or unkindness to be faithless.

In articulate silence; listen!

Soul

The soul is a faculty of being, the most reclusive of our sensitivities, an almost secret receptivity to the presence which it knows and for which it longs, though all the world deny that it exists. The soul often therefore seems to sleep beneath the other senses. But at the speech of its invisible companion it wakes, at the vibrant silence of that being which at once inheres in all things and transcends them all. There is no sound more immense than the great rushing, and the vast stillness, of this silence.

The soul is the register of living faith. Its condition is almost constant yearning, its happiness is to feel itself addressed, its joy is the exhilaration of love, its fulfilment the communion of awe. All is, and nothing is except this all, its instantiation in countless forms, in every consciousness, each seemingly distinct, the starling, the rabbit, you and me, while it courses through every one of us and unites us all.

The soul requires the constant sustenance of vital relationships. The issue is not with whom; such connections are possible with everything, animals, people, silence, the wind and the sea. The question is to what depth. Deprived of nourishment, the soul first yearns, then mourns and finally withdraws, contracting itself into a recess of the consciousness where it sleeps, concealed as if it had ceased to exist. But the soul never dies within us. It lies, like a dehydrated seed in parched earth, like the rose of Jericho in the desert, inert, without stirring, even for many years. Yet when the rain falls it unfolds in a moment; it comes alive in an instant and matters more than all that seemed to matter more than it.

The soul is in love with the world; it rejects no form of life. It is moved by the longing to draw near, to come close to God and to whatever speaks to it of God, though it may never call God by that or any other name. It is for this reason that the soul so often feels lost in the world. Like a refugee child, bewildered by an incomprehensible culture and disempowered at every juncture by the rupture of exile, it seeks the companionship of anyone who can talk to it in the familiar language of home. Such company may be provided by the comfort of a safe, substantial tree whose leaves and branches speak to one another, especially at night, by the breath of a sleeping animal, or by poetry and music, maps through which hearts and minds born a thousand years apart can still discover the paths of spiritual fellowship. The soul longs to hear the sound of familiar voices. Its love is unconditional and unassailable; what it loves is ultimately nameless, eluding all nomenclature including even that we use for God.

The soul is nourished by listening. The more the soul listens the more it refines its capacity to hear. Correspondingly, the more it hears, the more it becomes capable of listening. This is the meaning of the simple but compelling explanation of the opening words of the second paragraph of the *Shema* meditation by Rebbe Yehudah Aryeh-Lev of Ger, the *Sefat Emet*: The emphatic repetition of the verb in the clause *im shamo'a tishme'u*, known grammatically as the infinitive absolute, should not, he argues, be translated as 'if you truly listen and obey', but rather as 'if you truly listen, you will surely hear'.[19]

However, the soul's receptivity is not developed in a similar manner to that of the bodily senses. It is enhanced or diminished not by physical but by moral training. It is marred and clouded by wrongdoing. Cruelty, carelessness and self-centredness alienate the soul and dull its presence within us; compassion, just behaviour, self-restraint and gentleness restore and purify our sensitivity to it. There can therefore be no such thing as spiritual growth accompanied by moral corruption. The soul's awareness constantly expands or contracts within us according to our conduct.

The languages of the soul are prayer and meditation. Their most important form is silence, as in the story of the old man who used to sit at the back of the church. Day after day he returned until at last, curious and impressed, the pastor asked him what he was doing there hour after hour. Was he perhaps speaking with God? 'No,' he replied. Perhaps, then, God was speaking to him? This proved equally incorrect. What then, asked the pastor, was he doing there all this time? 'We just listen to each other, God and I,' answered the old man.

Sometimes the soul's silence is satiation, the undistracted joy of simply being, wanting for nothing, as if it were saying, 'I am here, content', though at such moments there isn't really any 'I'; or 'I am here by the river', but the sound of the water is no longer merely something other.

The soul doesn't often offer prayers of supplication, except for those requesting spiritual companionship itself. But the heart has a right to pray as well, as has the body, for everything we and others crave and need. When the soul does ask, its request is essentially a summons to partnership itself, a call to the branches, to the wind which moves them, to the vitality which moves the wind, that it should come to cauterise all pain, bringing healing and effecting peace.

But, most of all, what the soul seeks in prayer is the source which nourishes it, the resonance beyond all words and melodies which animates their pulse and rhythm, the almost inaudible vibrancy of transcendent being, immanent in all that exists.

The soul is the garner of the stillness which cannot be contaminated. Amidst the turmoil of mental anguish and restless self-torture it says to the racing mind, 'Stand still and be quiet'. In the misery and bewilderment of grief, when even to put one foot in front of the other is a struggle and dizziness threatens to engulf a person on the pavement, the soul has the capacity to hold together the bleeding flesh of the heart's wounds. It says to the heart: 'Be still and know. I am with you and within you, attentive and intact. I am your strength, deeper that everything which has been broken. No, don't say anything. Just let me be, and when your spinning thoughts grow still, then you will understand.' It's difficult for most of us to summon the self-possession to listen to the soul for more than a few brief moments. But even in that small interstice something speaks to us saying, 'I am life. Life is not impossible. Life contains unfathomable sadness, yet its beauty still persists'.

Listening to the soul requires courage. This may initially involve the determination not to be drawn into distractions, the currents of envy, anger and competitiveness which carry us swiftly into forgetfulness. If we live as if the soul doesn't exist, the soul humbly obliges; eventually we no longer even experience the malaise prompted by the inner awareness that there once was something which we used to feel. But if we do continue to listen, sooner or later the soul summons us to a deeper discipline. In the clarity of its stillness it challenges our responses: 'You need not have done that,' it tells us in the silence following our outburst. 'Nothing compelled you to react in that way. That was not at one with life.'

The soul has moral knowledge; it can never assent to evil. It cannot sin against its very nature and, in those moments when it is predominant in our consciousness, nor can we. How can we harm the infinite, the beautiful? An overwhelming longing for integrity nullifies all other desires; we are at one.

But the soul is reticent unless aroused. It rarely demands our attention, it sinks beneath the threshold of our sensitivity. 'Soul,' we then say, 'What's that?' and can provide no evidential proof, no tangible answer. There's enough in life to worry about without engaging in such delusions.

But the soul bides its time. It never dies. One day it will remind us of itself and confound the silence of its seeming absence with the silence of its presence.

Three Mysteries

Three mysteries hold me in thrall: the mystery of beauty, the mystery of endurance and the mystery of unity, the ultimate oneness of all. These mysteries have the power to turn our days into service and our years into pilgrimage. They redeem our life.

It's late February and in the protection of the hedgerows the snowdrops are flowering in clusters. The cold rain clings to the coarse grass around them; the leaves of the snowdrops are almost invisible, they match them so closely in colour. But the flowers are wonderful, thirty, forty in a patch the size of a hand; they bring brightness to the roadside verges and to the banks scattered with dead leaves. They illumine the late winter; one sees them and rejoices.

Across the valley the wooded hills are radiant with the sunlight which pours in brief abundance through a breach in the clouds. The forest is a quilt of many colours. The tips of the young birch branches glow orange and red, calmed by the grey beeches and the oaks to which half of last year's leaves still cling amidst the knotty twigs. The trees are rich with gathering sap; they're preparing to create the spring.

The ewes have been brought down from the hills to give birth in the shelter of the barns. In the farmyard a dozen pens are already full of mothers and their lambs. A sheep is trying to give birth. The other animals watch carefully; their turn to be delivered will follow soon. But this lamb will not emerge, its shoulders refuse to pass through the canal. The farmer draws the half-born animal gently forwards and at last it slips free of its mother onto the hay. It's a big lamb and its front legs are spindly and weak. It wriggles and pushes against the ground but it can't stand up; it looks as though it isn't going to make it. Maybe one of the shoulders was dislocated during its difficult birth.

Across the barn, ewes call for their lambs and they cry out in turn in little, high-pitched voices. At last the newest born stands up, then falls, stands again and succeeds in staying upright on its long, lanky legs.

At night an owl shouts, unanswered, across the open land. The cry penetrates it like an ultraviolet searchlight; it knows the fields, hedges, stands of trees and all the outhouses. But there is no reply, only an awakening, an alertness in those who hear. This is how it is to be alive.

*　　*　　*

It's late at night and I walk down the solitary lanes for miles. In the entire range of hills there is no light except from two or three far separated farms, and from the stars.

The presence of a tree looms before me like instantiated darkness. It reminds me of a conversation. Viktor Frankl is talking to a young girl shortly before her death in Birkenau. The girl is sick and knows she's dying but is cheerful in spite of everything. 'I am grateful that fate has hit me so hard,' she says, 'In my former life I was spoiled and did not take spiritual accomplishments seriously.' Still, when she points to a tree as her only friend and explains that she often talks to it, Frankl wonders if she's delirious or hallucinating:

> Anxiously I asked her if the tree replied. 'Yes.' What did it say to her? She answered, 'It said to me, "I am here – I am here – I am life, eternal life".'[20]

In Baladiyat prison in Baghdad, in Iraq under Saddam Hussein, a group of tortured women who are regularly burnt and beaten to the point of death call themselves comrades in tears. The guards rush in with truncheons and drive them against the wall; the women are sure they're about to die. But one of them begins to sing. She sings to the tune of a centuries-old Iraqi lullaby, altering the words to fit the moment:

> "I lost my mother,
> When I was only a child,
> But I remember how she held me,
> Loving me in her arms.
> Now I beg you,
> Walk softly on this soil.
> Perhaps they buried her in this place,
> So walk softly on this soil."[21]

105

The Jews of Salonika sang as they were taken away to die. I've heard survivors testify that there were people of faith who walked upright in the death camps, not as a show of defiance, but because they knew that the values by which they had lived were insuperable and could not be erased by death. They would not die, they were not susceptible to being killed; their spirits had touched a domain beyond the reach of annihilation.

Tyranny loathes genuine faith, whether in God, life, justice or freedom. For such faith is incapable of being destroyed. Though tens of thousands lie dead, a voice will always remain to tell of the treacherous deed and to proclaim freedom. Freedom escapes the confines of every jail: the gas chambers could not exterminate it by fire, the Siberian gulag could not paralyse it by cold, concrete cells cannot contain it within their impenetrable confines. 'You gave me my shoe-size in earth with bars around it,' wrote Osip Mandelstam out of exile in Voronezh:

Where did it get you? Nowhere.
You left me my lips and they shape words, even in silence. [22]

Mandelstam died in a transit camp three years later. But his words remain.

There is no end to the suffering, the killing and the struggle to survive. One has to honour not only the great deeds of defiance, but also all the daily acts of endurance exacted from so many by ordinary, everyday life – the effort of a weak and very old man to stand, the will-power of the sick to lift food to their lips, the determination of the terrified woman who says to herself in the hospital in the middle of the night, 'No, I'm not going to die'. One has to admire the courage with which innumerable people have faced their inescapable fate and given up their lives undefeated.

For, in spite of everything, the soul can retain its light and illumine even these dark paths.

*   *   *

I often wonder what is the one which unites the all.

This oneness cannot be named because names are inevitably merely human and suffer from human limitations: they evoke the finite, suggest specific associations or are considered to be the property of one or another particular group. But the ultimate oneness is not finite and no one can own it. On the contrary, all things belong to the one. It fills all forms, traverses all forms, sings in all forms and transcends all forms.

I am puzzled both by what it means to apprehend this oneness and how easy it is to fail to perceive it. The Hasidic master Rebbe Yehudah Aryeh Lev of Ger taught that the Hebrew noun for song, *shirah*, is related to the word *shurah*, indicating direction. Song emerges when the soul is directed towards the one, when nothing impedes the awareness that it belongs to this ultimate unity, the oneness of God. For everything has its own song, the specific melody which pertains uniquely to its nature. This, he says, is the meaning of the ancient tractate *Perek Shirah*, the Chapter of Song, which lists the particular praises which each animal, bird, tree and blade of grass proffers to God every day.[23] Thus, for example, the elephant proclaims, 'How great are your works, O Lord,'[24] while the barley whispers, 'A poor man's prayer when he grows weary and pours out his words before God.'[25] If the author of the Chapter of Song had known about snowdrops, they too would surely have had their place in this composition.

As for us, if our consciousness were not continually distracted, but if, rather, we were filled with true awareness, our lives would be filled with such songs. And it is precisely these melodies which the most cunning and powerful tyrant cannot prize away from the soul. That is why, after they had crossed the divided sea in safety, the Children of Israel sang together 'My strength and my song is God'.[26] God is our strength in so far as God is our song, and our ability to sing God's song is the true measure of our strength.

The world secretly nourishes our capacity for song: 'Day utters speech to day and night communicates knowledge to night.'[27] We, overhearing this almost inaudible communion, experience the silent replenishment of our soul until it, too, begins to sing. Its music, which may remain unheard even by the grosser parts of our own personality, does not belong to us. It expresses our participation in a greater harmony, an assent, a dance in abandonment to that which transcends the self which appears to be the singer.

Ultimately we are not, in the one.

Another World

*Sometimes it seemed to me that what saved me were the animals
I encountered along the way, not the human beings. The hours I
spent with puppies, cats, and sheep were the best of the war years.
I would blend in with them until I was part of them, until
forgetfulness came, until I fell asleep alongside them. I would sleep
as deeply and as tranquilly as I had in my parents' bed.*

Aharon Appelfeld.[28]

It's midnight and the narrow road is empty across the moors and into
the woods. A pony emerges from the gorse and steps slowly onto the
street. Soon another follows, walking a few paces behind its fellow.
Their presence makes me happy. The steady fall of their hooves is
reassuring; the darkness feels companionable now. For a few minutes
we are travellers together, then they turn away into the forest. This world
belongs to them.

The sky is clear and there are hundreds and hundreds of stars. The
great woodland trees, oak and beech, frame them in the intersections of
their branches and their twigs are like fingers stretching out to catch
them. Birch bark glistens in the black light; the tarmac gleams in the
cold. I could walk on forever.

I turn a corner and see a patch of even deeper darkness in the grass.
A foal is lying down asleep. I notice another beside it, its legs curled
beneath its stomach, while two more ponies stand above them
watching, keeping guard. I sit down very quietly, wanting only to
listen, hoping not to be excluded from this night time tenderness. The
animals look at me, completely still; then one of them gets slowly to its
feet and they all move away. I can't be trusted; I'm the outsider here.

By day the ponies are a charming part of the landscape; the tourists
say: 'Look at that foal over there. It's got the sweetest face!' Even then
they are mostly shy, turning away should anyone approach too closely,
trotting off across the moor. But at night the forest is theirs. They know

where the longest uncropped grass remains, where the leaves are most tender and where the trees and hedgerows intertwine to provide the densest cover from the thin, persistent rain. They know these things by instinct, with a faculty for immediate and intuitive knowledge which, for all our book-learning, we humans of the cities have forsaken and whose loss leaves us alien on this earth.

Yet something has woken up inside me now; I still have an instinctive relationship with the world, it is not entirely forfeit. The forest is mysterious not only because I am so much a stranger but also because I still belong. To feel at home on earth, unreservedly, graciously, would not be entirely impossible. Yet even with all these stars by which to map my path, I could not make my way by night between the forest's thickets.

Our connection with the animals shows both a physical and a spiritual kinship. We share with them being born and dying, blood, muscle, nerves and sensations. According to the philosopher Maimonides, we even share a part of our emotions, 'For the love and tenderness of a mother for a child is not consequent upon reason, but upon the activity of the imaginative faculty, which is found in most animals just as it is found in man.'[29] Our spiritual bond is discovered in the experience that we and the animals are different forms of manifestation of a single reality, that we are encompassed together in the one consciousness which both gives life and withdraws it.

The ponies turn and trot away. I go back to the road saddened, hampered by a burden which feels like faithlessness and makes me foreign to my fellow creatures. Is it simply the instinct for survival, or is it the long history of betrayal by my species which makes these animals watch for my slightest move, then run from me in fear? There's a painful diminishment for humans in the forfeit of their trust. When Noah released the animals from the ark, God showed him the sign of the rainbow and promised a more peaceful partnership between them. But God also said that from then on the fear and dread of man would rest upon all the beasts of the earth.[30] I've often puzzled over this change in our relationship. Was it our fault? Was it because of the great destruction which human beings wrought, of which the animals were the hapless victims? Or was it always thus; while to what the Bible really testifies, in its fantasy of an Eden before and after, is our longing to be at one with all the world – and our feeling of loss?

Nevertheless, I return home filled with a song of gratitude for the clarity of the night, for the frost across the moor and for the presence of the ponies. Moments of companionship are privileged, a few dozen paces taken together on the road through the forest and a score of breaths shared by its verge in the frozen night.

CHAPTER FIVE

Conscience

Those Who Care for Others

One who says: 'What's mine is mine and what's yours is yours' is an average person. But there are those who say that this is the way of Sodom.

Mishnah: Avot 5:13

I never grew up feeling that my life belonged to me. It certainly never occurred to me that it might be mine to do exactly as I liked. This must have been something I had simply absorbed through being a child of refugees. I often used to ask my parents to tell me stories about their childhood when they came up to say good night. I loved to listen. But even before I was consciously aware of the nature of the events which had overtaken my mother and father and their families, I understood that something very different lay beneath the safe environment of school and games and that it could break through the unsettled surface of our world at any time. I soon knew that my father had fled overnight from a childhood as comfortable as mine to a Palestine where, in the late nineteen thirties, there was hardly anything to eat. Isca would tell me how, when times were very bad under the Nazis, she would put her head down on her pillow and hope that she would wake up safe the following morning. I also knew that she had found herself in a strange land at the age of sixteen, training to look after babies in what sounded like a cold and dismal Yorkshire institution where mice ran up and down the curtains during the long night hours on duty. Anything could happen. My grandmother, reflecting on her experience of flight and total upheaval followed by the reestablishment of her life in a new country, would observe, '*Es ist eine verrückte Welt* – it's a crazy world'. It was clear to me that it certainly was.

I often felt guilty or frightened. Readings in assembly at school about drought and hunger, or predictions of how the world would shortly suffer dire shortages of water, terrified me. At the same time I felt increasingly that I lived in a fragile and threatened enclave beyond which violence and disaster were a frequent reality. That made me anxious; I often worried that this safe world would collapse. I still do and, in a way, parts of it have indeed fallen apart.

At school I was transferred in year twelve to Mr Barber's French class. This lovely man also ran the school's voluntary service department. He took me with him to meet lonely old people living in bed-sits in Kilburn. On our first visit a very ancient lady whose wrists were as thin as sticks had an epileptic fit. Mr Barber showed me how to use a spoon to prevent her from biting off her tongue, then issued strict instructions to watch over her while he rushed to call an ambulance. For years and years I visited one of the old ladies to whom he introduced me, long after she had left her room and moved to a home. I was one of just a handful of mourners at her funeral. Then I lived in Jerusalem with a wonderful, and very frail, old couple whose influence on my Jewish life was inestimable. On one occasion the elderly man adamantly refused to take a bath unless it was I who helped him. How foolish I was to agree. He was far too weak to climb back out of the tub. I still remember how heavy and slippery his body seemed as I strove to find a safe but comfortable grip and assist him. I also volunteered to work with children, both in London and in Jerusalem; I still think often about the neglect and abandonment to which many of them were subjected. Later, when I was teaching at a primary school in Brent, the deputy head-mistress went to visit a little boy in hospital who had TB. 'You're the first person to come and see him for a whole fortnight', the nurse told her.

But it was much later before I really began to understand what so many more adventurous and devoted people were doing to care for others. I remember watching a programme with my father about Médecin Sans Frontières: 'Look at how these people are helping others,' he said, 'What about you? What are you doing with your life?' I still recall my feeling of shame.

For many years it's been clear to me that two common assumptions need to be inverted. Firstly, we who live amidst so much privilege must always remember that the world doesn't owe us a living; rather, we're in debt to the world for being alive and must constantly strive to give back to life something of what it has given to us. The earth itself commands our respect and people require our compassion and understanding. To live a purely reactive life is insufficient. We must work to increase the amount of care, understanding and tolerance in the world. The greatest Jewish, and universal, values are justice and compassion. There isn't a day which doesn't present us with the challenge of practising them more fully. Secondly, we mustn't think of God as some sort of dispenser in the sky to whom we turn from time to time with a shopping list and prescriptions. We must rather consider what we can do for God so that this earth entrusted to our care comes closer to resembling the kind of world of which the true prophets and visionaries of every faith have always dreamt.

I've met all kinds of people whose work I admire. Every day we should think with gratitude of the nurses and carers who sit up all night with sick and dying people, helping them turn over in bed, assisting them on the slow, difficult journey to the toilet, calming their restless fears, checking on their pain relief, watching with them through the darkness until brief sleep finally brings them a few hours of respite. Every day we should acknowledge those who look after groups of people so often invisible to the rest of us, refugees, outcasts, the homeless, people whose families are in camps and prisons in countries devoured by tyranny and war, people who have no means of ascertaining even whether those they love are alive or dead. Every day we should say a blessing for those who struggle to replace prejudice with knowledge and hatred with understanding, who, where it is so easy to generate bigotry and contempt, strive to engender tolerance, friendship and vision. Every day we should pray for those who risk their lives to bring justice to the persecuted, while evil regimes greedily turn a half-blind eye to their murder. Every day we should ask ourselves how we can do likewise.

In the description of his arrest following *Kristallnacht*, my grandfather recalled what might be regarded as a small detail. As he and his fellow Jews were sent to the trains which would take them from the hall in Frankfurt where they had been tormented and humiliated to Dachau concentration camp, they passed a man who quietly handed each of them a bottle of milk. When I first heard about this incident, I imagined this as an instinctive and spontaneous act of kindness. But that cannot have been so; the man must have made careful preparations. He'd have had to buy the milk, establish from which exit the detainees would leave the building, transport it to the correct place without attracting attention and then stand there handing out bottle after bottle for a long and dangerous period of time. Almost sixty years later, I'm inspired by this man's courage and the bravery of those who do likewise.

Moral Imagination

My friend turned quietly to his wife and suggested in a whisper, so that no one else would notice, that she move the heavy jug of water lest it be in the way of the elderly man sitting next to her who was now too weak to lift it. It was such a tiny gesture and I only caught it out of the corner of my eye, but it made me realise what a special man he was. There are some people who have an exceptional capacity for intuiting what the world feels like to others. I always admire them. Perhaps that's the real secret of love, love the way the Torah means it when it teaches, 'You shall love your neighbour as your self,'[1] love the way the Torah stipulates when it repeatedly insists that 'You shall love the stranger, for you were strangers in the Land of Egypt.'[2]

We don't know. Nobody actually knows what the world is like for others. One should be wary of those who say, 'I know exactly how you're feeling'; it's a kind of tyranny to assume that others experience the world precisely as we do. Maybe what bothers us doesn't trouble them; maybe they suffer deeply for things we scarcely notice. We don't know.

But we are obliged to care, and to care we have to take note. I'm always afraid that I'll fail to do so. If there's anything of which I've become more aware as I've got older, it's how much I fail to realise. None of us can see into the heart of the person sitting next to us. When, in our isolating society, we do come across a person in pain, it can be hard to know how to respond. I saw a young man sitting on a bench in the park crying. I turned off the path and asked him, in the inept idiom, 'Are you all right?' He obviously wasn't all right at all, but, responding according to the same conventions, he replied 'I'm OK.' What's one supposed to say next? He wasn't a small child for whom it might have been appropriate to assume responsibility. He didn't appear to be in any physical distress; he hadn't fallen or broken any bones. One can't interfere; one has to respect a person's privacy. So I went uneasily back to the path. But then I remembered that I had a bag of buns in my hand so I took one and placed it on a paper next to the crying man: 'That's for you,' I said, and added, not wishing to impose, 'But if you don't want it, I'm sure the birds will enjoy it.'

We're obliged to behave in ways which make us aware. When the rich man told the rabbi that, out of humility, he was going to live from now on off black bread and water, the latter was furious. 'You must eat goose and white bread every day!' the rabbi retorted. When asked to explain himself, he said: 'If he eats only stale bread he'll think the poor can live off stones, but if he has goose perhaps he'll realise that at a very minimum the poor must have bread.' At least in that society the rich and the poor bought and sold in the same market place and met in the same house of prayer. We live in a world where the opportunities for ignorance are much greater. Television and letters from charities, however graphic and however important, are no substitute for what we see with our own eyes and ponder in our heart. There's a constant danger that we will not love our neighbours as ourselves, but merely those of our neighbours who are just like ourselves, because they're the only ones we ever really notice.

We have many ways of preventing ourselves from feeling. Isca told me how once when she was in hospital a person in the same ward died suddenly in the middle of the night. When the flurry was over and the body had been wheeled away, the sister on duty told the other patients to go right back to sleep. 'To my amazement,' said my mother, 'most of them did.' The world is full of suffering to which we never wake up and, when we finally do so, we're always liable to fall back asleep.

But there are moments when we learn to perceive with different eyes.

Such was the impact on me of my first visit to a home in a Palestinian refugee camp. We had driven no more than three or four kilometres outside Jerusalem; only a few minutes earlier we'd been travelling along roads with which I'd been familiar since my early twenties. But here it appeared as if there were no municipal services at all. Rubbish lay in high piles by the verges. Tracks and alleyways divided at all angles; without guidance I would never have found my way back out. When we reached the home of the family whom we'd been brought to meet, it seemed at first as if familiarity had been restored. We were offered coffee

116

and we all endeavoured to overcome the barriers of language and make what polite conversation we could. But as soon as we stepped outside onto the flat roof and looked across to the suburbs of Jerusalem it was impossible not to be cognizant of a divide incomparably greater than the few hundred metres which separated the two worlds. There, cars proceeded along wide avenues and people walked along pavements planted with pleasant trees. How deep the wadi was in between! The children were bewildered. 'Whose fault is it?' asked my son.

I realised that I'd visited Israel not less than thirty times without once entering a Palestinian house, though I have now done so several times since. How I wish that those who call for the destruction of Israel would spend time in an Israeli home, in history as it has been experienced by the Jewish people, in the heart of an Israeli who simply wants to live, work, love and raise children in peace.

I used to attach great importance to the words of Cain when God asked him where his brother was now: 'I don't know! Am I my brother's keeper?' he retorted.[3] I used to believe that if only we were unable to say 'I don't know', we would never be so brazen as to fail to care. But now I realise that even peoples who've lived together for years, such as Christians and Muslims in Bosnia or Kosova, can be taught in a matter of weeks to betray a lifetime of peaceful and cheerful relationships and turn a pitiless eye on theft, deportation and, ultimately, murder.

That's why I admire those who have moral imagination, to whom the suffering of others is not invisible, for whom it isn't happening to people too insignificant or too alien to count, or occurring in a place simply too far distant to be worth bothering about.

Without moral imagination, the other will always remain outside the limited circle of our compassion. Without moral imagination, we condemn ourselves to living amidst indifference to misery and sorrow, so long as the afflicted person is merely someone else.

Solidarity

There are questions we insist on asking of God, but what about the questions God insists on asking of us?

We want to know why. There are always issues: droughts, floods, earthquakes, famines. The world is never at peace and the heart can never be at ease. We want to know why God let it happen. Two hundred thousand people perished in the Asian Tsunami, the terrible waves following a great earthquake beneath the Indian Ocean. As many as twenty million people more were left homeless, hungry, grief-stricken and shocked. It's said to be the worst natural disaster in recent history.

Down at the garage the man behind the counter pointed at the picture on the front page of the newspaper. It showed a British soldier at a base in Iraq humiliating a prisoner. 'That's terrible,' he said, 'the Tsunami is a natural disaster; but that? That didn't have to happen.' Then he added: 'I'm from Sri Lanka.' I asked him if everyone in his family was all right. 'My close family are OK, but many relatives have been killed.' I said, 'I'm sorry.' He gave a shrug and commented again on the difference between the Tsunami and the picture in the papers. 'One can't ask "Why?" about the Tsunami,' he said.

But we do. I've heard the question not only from people who saw the devastation on television at a distance of many thousands of miles, but also from men and women who clung to each other and grasped at branches as the water rose around them. They watched other people drown; they saw the bodies of the children. 'The children,' someone told me, 'rushed back to the beach after the first, much smaller wave, to look at all the fishes the sea had washed up. Then the second wave came flooding in and drowned them.' Asking 'Why?' is really a gesture of incomprehension; there's no actual anticipation of an answer.

Noah must have asked the same question after he came out of the ark. The Torah notes that he lived for a further three hundred years after the flood, three centuries in which he said, as before, not a single word to God. How fatuous the promise of the rainbow must have seemed to him after the experience of opening the door of the ark, when, according to the Zohar, he wept because out there before him in the endless mud there was not one single being left alive. Condemned to exist with this unbearable and inexpressible knowledge, he planted a vineyard, harvested the grapes and became the first person in the Bible to get drunk.

Noah did, of course, have a theological answer at his disposal. The Bible is quite explicit about that: All those people who died were wicked; they deserved their fate. So, presumably, did all the animals, except the few who came in two by two (strange that they should be the only ones we ever think about). Or does that miserable and unconscionable explanation belong rather to the moral problem posed by the story than to its solution? What kind of God behaves like this? What dreadful things do we have to say to make God's ways look just?

That's exactly what Job asserted. Robbers and a catastrophic storm shattered his world; all his children were killed. He challenged God from the rubbish heap and with increasing frustration begged the Master of the Universe to be less recondite, less reclusive, and step forward to provide the answer Job so surely deserved. Why, God should at least have the decency to talk to him! No, his companion's claims were false that he, Job, had to be the evildoer. It wasn't true; suffering was not invariably the consequence of sin. God had to have some better explanation. But when God does finally respond to his impassioned pleading, God fails in that magnificent declamation to match Job's interrogation in any ethically coherent way at all. Yet Job is satisfied; he feels he has found God at a new depth. He has acquired a faith which is content to live without answers.

Milton believed he could, 'Assert eternal providence, and justify the ways of God to men'.[4] But one can't tidy up the morality of the universe. One can't explain why the child who cried 'Look, daddy, look,' and rushed to examine the silvery, flickering fish, should have to die in the terrible waves.

We can't not ask. But the answer will be silence.

Is there anything, nevertheless, in that silence for us to hear? To

Elijah, hidden in a cave on the mountain of the Lord, it carried a different kind of question, the question God was asking of him:

And, behold, the Lord passed by, and a great and strong wind tore the mountains, and broke in pieces the rocks before the Lord; but the Lord was not in the wind; and after the wind an earthquake; but the Lord was not in the earthquake; And after the earthquake a fire; but the Lord was not in the fire; and after the fire a still small voice. And it was so, when Elijah heard it, that he wrapped his face in his mantle, and went out, and stood in the entrance of the cave. And, behold, there came a voice to him, and said, 'What are you doing here, Elijah?'[5]

'What are you doing here?' is not a question about causation but response. It's the sound of the fine silence which follows fate's blow. It's the long, steady stillness of life's interrogation. The vibration which ultimately fills it is the passage of our own breath, as if its rise and fall were asking the same question Elijah experiences as emanating from the very mouth of God: 'What is my existence for?'

Elijah answers; Elijah repeats exactly the same arguments as he had cast at God before his revelation. He talks about his mission; he's the only prophet left, he's exceedingly zealous for his God, the Children of Israel won't listen to him. It's hard to escape the feeling that he's missed the point. The classic Biblical answer to such a question from God consists of just one word. Abraham gives it; Moses knows it. It is the word '*Hineni*, Here am I'. What do you want of me, God?

This is the moment at which life becomes service. Service is a response to the realisation that the voice which addresses us, the question in the silence, is an appeal to our heart's commitment. That, and our love, are all we have with which to answer for our lives. Nothing else constitutes a satisfactory reply to the quiet, unrelenting question: 'What are you doing here?'

At the Memorial in Minsk

It was obvious that we would want to say the Memorial Prayer and the *Kaddish*, so why had I foolishly forgotten my *Siddur* on the coach? I ran back up to fetch it, leaving everybody waiting.

It was then that I noticed the figures. The Yama Memorial in Minsk marks the place where thousands of Jews were herded from the ghetto and slaughtered on October 21st, 1943. Yama means pit; presumably it was previously a small valley, though it seems strange to think of it as a place that might once have possessed any natural beauty. The site is neither far away nor hidden; it is well within the city limits and all around it large buildings lour. A series of steep concrete steps leads down to the obelisk at the centre of the pit. But a recent and powerful addition has been made to that old memorial with its inscriptions in Russian and Yiddish. Now the visitor is accompanied in his descent by a harrowing procession of figures, men, women and children, old and young, carved in bronze in their final, terrifying moments. Some look steadfastly ahead; some reach out to their wife or child in a gesture of helpless consolation; others stare to the side, unable to confront in the eyes of those they love most in all the world their inability to do anything whatsoever to protect them. They are all naked and they all proceed irrevocably downwards to their deaths.

As I rushed back up the path beside them to retrieve my prayer book, these people caught me by the eye and held me, hailing me without words: 'You there, who heedlessly runs past us, hastening back up to life along the path that was denied us, who are you? Halt, if you are human!' I stopped. To this day, years later, something is still stationary inside me, interrogated by those faces: 'Tell us by what prerogative you live, while we go down to death. Consider if you walk worthily upon the earth, you who inherit this world where we were dispossessed and slaughtered.'

I stood stock still next to the figure of a woman whose seeming gaze now held me transfixed.

'What do you want from me?' I asked, half-afraid, yet half-complicit in this interrogation of my life. 'What have I done?' I felt that she could see my home and the food on my table, could see my heart and the very wars of good and bad inside me which formed the light and shadow on my face.

She was frozen in the dread of her final moments of life. But suddenly I remembered how at Auschwitz-Birkenau, as I wandered between the ruins of the crematoria and looked up at the fields behind them full of ashes, I felt the grip of voices calling as if they were still possessed by the desperate desire to recount their lives before they died, saying, 'Don't remember us like this. Consider how we lived! Don't deny us our existence for a second time by thinking of us only in our dying!'

So, too, I imagined how this woman next to me turned to one side and withdrew, stepping backwards from this terror and humiliation. In a moment she surveyed the long, descending path of degradation that had led her to this place. She moved still further back and saw herself, a child at her father's table: there was her mother holding her hands in front of her eyes as they blessed the candles at the first twilight of the New Year. A melody without words floated through the window pursued by the sounds of a brisk Talmudic argument. Those were the years of un-assailable safety in the shadow of her parent's love. Then swiftly, it was she herself, leading her own children to the house of study. And there, at the bottom of the field was the apple tree, her final sight of the village that was home from the road which led to the ghetto and this pit.

What will she ask? Whatever she says to me, I will apprehend it as a judgment of everything I am. Very quietly, and with penetrating gentleness, she puts her questions:

> 'Are you faithful?'
> 'Faithful to what? How do you mean?'
> 'Just faithful; surely you understand the word "faithful"?'

She watches sharply, as if the issue of whether the term 'faithful' is or is not meaningful to me were itself an implicit examination of my life. Maybe in that moment of failure to understand I have already given her my answer?

But I do comprehend, though maybe it is her gaze which makes everything so clear. I recognise that this simple word penetrates all my interactions since I was a child. Yes; you mean faithful to life, faithful to the trees, faithful to the birds, the grass, the clarity of the stars by night. You mean faithful to the human heart, to love, to trust, to yearning, tenderness, vulnerability and joy. You ask me whether I am faithful. What you mean is: Do I essentially and intuitively honour life? Or am I hurtful? Do I take without acknowledgement; do I drain without recognition the well of people's giving? Do I set my teeth mercilessly into the flesh of life? Do animals cower when I come near? Do I alienate the heart?

You ask me God's questions. You make me listen to the sound of my own footsteps on the face of the earth.

'And do you love?'

I am silent. I haven't answered your first question yet.

'And is this Jewish life, for which I die, an instrument of music and a way of loving to you? Or are you, its guardian, ignorant of its melodies? Tell me, for were anything to redeem my suffering it would be this, do you love God's world and love this soul of being in which are garnered so many of its songs?'

'Yes,' I heard myself say, 'I love it'. But then, afraid that maybe I was lying, I immediately added, 'But I am often unworthy and impure.'

'Then you will seek for purity?' she asked; it was a stern demand rather than a question. With that she turned away and I saw before me only the frozen figure facing death.

Since then the consciousness of those unspoken questions compels the promise I make most readily in my best and purest moments, to love and honour life and to endeavour never, at any cost, to betray that love.

A Dialogue

Because you say, 'I have not sinned.'

Jeremiah 2:35

'You don't know me, but we share the same world.'

Since the moment at the Yama Memorial in Minsk when I was seized and challenged by that implacable interrogation, other voices have emerged from the uneven static of my conscience and summoned me for reckoning. Their insistent presence refuses to leave me alone:

'We share the same world but you don't know me.'

Who are you?

'You don't know me, nor do I know you. But sometimes I imagine you, eating the fruits of my labour.'

What is your life?

'Work. The soil and labour. Being poor, but not the poorest. Existing. But you will say that your life is also work. Tell me, do you drink coffee?'

Yes.

'Do you have chocolate?'

Yes.

'And bananas, pineapple, fruit?'

Yes.

'So you know the lives of those who grow them, who toil in the heat in the plantations and pick and pack?'

No.

'Yet you drink our coffee. So the world has connected us, you and me! Tell me also, do your children have shoes?'

Yes, they wear shoes.

'I set my hope that one day my children too will have shoes and clean clothes. I labour so that they will go to school for long enough that they won't have to go out to work until they have an education. How old are your children?'

Ten and twelve and fourteen.

'Do they work?'

I look ahead and give no answer.

'One day my children too will not go out to labour either. They will study until they are grown up.'

'But tell me, how often are your children hungry? How often do they go to bed thirsty? How often are they afraid that in the morning there'll still be no food and water?'

*   *   *

I remember the Tibetan teacher who came from Dharamsala to observe the way we ran our youth camps in England. He was moved and impressed, but he also had his criticism. I can still hear what he said: 'I've watched the children in your country and they're good children. But they waste their food, which my people never do. They play with it; they fuss over what to eat and they leave their meals unfinished. These are things which we never see among my people. They also leave their books, even holy books, on the floor. They don't treat them with respect. Our children would never do this.'

A visceral feeling of ugliness often takes possession of me when I shop in the supermarket. I sense that I've become complicit in a great rape of which the entire earth is a victim. We buy greedily and blindly. We concern ourselves with the wrong questions. We want to know what's cheapest and why the price has gone up yet again. We complain that our favourite brand is unavailable that day, or that the shelves are arranged in an inconvenient manner, or that the products have been moved from where we always used to find them. But if, whenever we touched an item, a miniature film began to play on the tin or packet and we could see how those who produced it laboured, how they and their families lived, and at what cost to the environment the food was grown and transported, we would turn away in self-disgust and buy only a small fraction of the items we eagerly purchase now. Instead of going round complaining about how expensive everything is, we would say, 'I'm buying this product because it's more just; I'm choosing this item because the farmers have been properly paid'. If 'organic' and 'Fairtrade' brands are decried as lifestyle choices for the middle classes, then it's in support of them that farming subsidies, so long blamed for fostering environmentally degrading practices, now have to be spent. I recently read how little it costs to produce a packet of tea because the women who pick the leaves are given such paltry wages that they can hardly survive. There's injustice in our cupboards, in our fridges, in the pots on our stoves and in the mugs in our hands.

Of course we can excuse ourselves by saying, 'Everybody does it; that's just how we live around here'. But social acceptability is not equivalent to moral justification. We can all be wrong and, in this case, we definitely are.

Moral Conscience

– Why do you risk your life in dangerous
places taking these pictures of suffering children?
– So that people should see and change how they behave.

The world is so beautiful, and so unfair.

There can be no reason to justify why one person should rise in the morning and go outside to walk in a green garden full of songbirds, while elsewhere a child wakes up hungry and thirsty to another day of hopeless slavery. It is as inconceivable that we should be ignorant of this fact as it is impossible that we should be indifferent to it and still consider ourselves fully human.

Our humanity is contingent on our commitment to be morally engaged. Within the sphere of my immediate personal life whether or not I have a clear conscience depends on my own conduct; at any given time I may, or may not, deserve to feel innocence or remorse. But as regards the wider world I have no right to experience a conscience at peace. If I never feel anguish, if the misery and grievance arising from so much suffering and injustice never touch me, I cannot call myself a human being. For to be human is to be permeable to the pain of others. Though in Jewish law we are entitled, even commanded, to live our own lives to the full and to rejoice in them when we can, we are not allowed to block out the faculty of moral knowledge. We can't spit out the apple. Since Adam and Eve picked the fruit and ate it we are defined as a species who know good and evil and can tell right from wrong. It is only Cain who, challenged by God, insists that he 'does not know'. But his dead brother lies before him, contradicting his protestations. Most of us are not Cain, we did not kill him; but the voices of the blood of our brothers and sisters cry out to us from all over the earth, as does their poverty, sickness, hunger and thirst. If we claim that we do not know, we mark ourselves as the moral progeny of Cain.[6]

The Torah commands us, saying, 'You shall not stand idly by the blood of your neighbour'.[7] But what are we supposed to do? Again and again we feel powerless before the depth of suffering and the extent of violence across the globe. Perhaps it's all simply beyond us; surely not every one in the world is our neighbour. Yet that cannot be allowed to mean that there are no bonds of kinship at all between their humanity and ours, as if it could be right to watch a starving child struggle to find water, or hear of an asylum seeker forcibly returned to the very country where she was tortured and raped, and feel no reaction whatsoever. We must, at the very least, protest. Long ago the *Mishnah*, the code of law and ethics compiled in the Galilee at the close of the second century by Judah the Prince, condemned those who failed to give evidence in capital cases on the grounds that they didn't want to get involved and that it was all too much bother. It's not legitimate to say to ourselves, 'Why should I get entangled in all this trouble?' We should therefore remember that 'Whoever saves a single life is considered as if he or she had saved the entire world'.[8] This *Mishnah* was concerned with trials theoretically carrying the death penalty, a punishment in practice abolished by the rabbis. Today we hear from all directions of suffering which is absolutely and immediately an issue of life and death. Do we say, 'So what? Just leave me in peace! My cup of tea is more important to me than your dying'? Or are we commanded to speak out and become involved, to remember that every life is an entire world, and at the very least send food, blankets and medicine?

The failure to testify diminishes the humanity of three groups of people: the victims, to whom it is a face averted from the sight of their pain and dying; the perpetrators, who read it as only once removed from the nod of complicity; and the indifferent, who hasten the atrophy of their own conscience.

In the years of the Yezhov terror under Stalin the great Russian poet Anna Akhmatova spent seventeen months queuing regularly outside the prison in Leningrad. One day someone recognised her and called her by name:

Standing behind me was a woman, with lips blue from the cold, who had, of course, never heard me called by name before. Now she

started out of the torpor common to us all and asked me in a whisper
(everyone whispered there):

'Can you describe this?'

And I said: 'I can.'

Then something like a smile passed fleetingly over what had once
been her face . . . [9]

It was only when I had read this short passage several times that I
took proper note of the crucial words 'what had once been her face'. The
very thought that there might be someone who would testify, who had
the capacity to set down such suffering in writing, was sufficient to
restore the features of this woman whose face and identity had been
almost entirely obliterated in the anonymity of collective misery.

To be silent, as if their victims were not even worth the protest, makes
us partners to hunger and sickness, violence, persecution and death.
We are effectively saying: 'Who cares whether these suffering people
were once human beings? Affliction has robbed them of their names and
faces and reduced them to masses and numbers. They don't belong
among those to whom empathy is due; they merit no feeling.'

It is true that we feel overwhelmed. There are so many tragedies all
over the world that we quickly become bewildered and inured. Before
they entered the news as the sites of some atrocity or disaster we often
hadn't even known that the peoples and regions in question even
existed. It's as if they had risen suddenly from nowhere to make a claim
on our conscience. We cannot possibly respond to the needs of them
all. We haven't sufficient time, heart or money.

Yet Rabbi Tarfon's famous teaching from the second century remains
as relevant as ever: 'It is not your duty to finish the work, but neither are
you free to desist from it'.[10] The fact that we cannot be engaged the
whole time doesn't render us free to disengage all of the time. Over the
course of our life we have to choose our issues and become involved. For
one day we will have to give an account before the restored gazes of
those whose suffering we have ignored. They will not simply say, 'You
did not help me', because they will realise that it is impossible for each
one of us to have assisted every single one of them, just as they could not

all have helped us in our times of pain and terror. Rather, they will say, 'Why did you not help any of my brothers and sisters who were hungry? Why did you not help any of my brothers and sisters who were sick? Why did you not help any of my brothers and sisters who had their limbs blown off by land mines?' We will be filled with unbearable shame if we can give no answer at all.

Presumably there'll be no actual conversation between us all in the presence of God. But from time to time such dialogues do take place in our conscience and the indictment is no less real. If we are inured to its conclusions, if the thought of the suffering of others does not trouble us, it can only mean that the moral imagination has withered away inside us.

Worst of all, indifference is an invitation to the perpetrators. It assures them of society's, of the world's, non-intervention; it grants them moral immunity. There is therefore no such person as the 'innocent bystander'. Indeed, the bystander may well be the next person on the list, as in Pastor Martin Niemoeller's famous indictment that by the time the Nazis had come for the Jews, the communists and the trade unionists and he had done nothing to protect them, there was no one left to stand up for him when his own turn arrived.[11] But in the meantime such bystanders have allowed themselves to become, at least in part, fellow perpetrators, if only by virtue of allowing the abuse to proceed without dissent. One who sees and is silent, not from fear but from indifference, becomes an accomplice.

We have only to look at ourselves. If no one tells us that something is wrong, we persist in our behaviour. From the child who isn't scolded for stealing her friend's sweets, or for never helping with the family chores, or for bullying his playmates, to the adult who considers it acceptable to beat up strangers, exploit the poor and watch the dismemberment of civilians simply because they live in the wrong country at the wrong time, if there is no one who stands up and declares 'This is wrong!' then we allow ourselves to become morally enfeebled and behave with ever greater disdain for the difference between right and wrong.

Yet somewhere inside us we surely do know. Or if we are no longer instinctively aware because our conscience has for so long failed to protest, then at least we know that we once knew. But if we fail even to know that, then the perpetrator we are hunting for must be not only outside of, but within us as well.

That is why the most basic declaration of the Jewish faith, '*Shema Yisrael* – Hear, O Israel, the Lord our God, the Lord is one!' – is also an appeal to bear witness. For the letter *ayyin* at the end of '*Shema* – Hear!' and the letter *dalet* at the end of '*Echad* – one' are written in the Torah in enlarged letters, spelling the word '*Ed*', which means 'witness'. To testify to the unity of God is to bear witness to God's image in every human life; to hurt or destroy other lives, or to be indifferent to their pain, is to violate God's presence in them and to hold God's oneness in contempt.

Perhaps this is why Primo Levi called his bare and forceful poem by the same name, *Shema*:

> Consider whether this is a man,
> Who labors in the mud
> Who knows no peace
> Who fights for a crust of bread
> Who dies at a yes or a no . . .
>
> Consider that this has been:
> I commend these words to you.
> Engrave them on your hearts
> When you are in your house, when you walk on your way,
> When you go to bed, when you rise . . . [12]

Shame

Wer nie sein Brot mit Tränen ass,
Wer nie die kummervollen Nächte
Auf seinem Bette weinend sass,
Der kennt euch nicht, ihr himmlische Mächte!

Who never ate his bread in tears,
Who never through the wretched night
Sat weeping on his bed, such a person
Knows you not, you heavenly powers.

Goethe [13]

By what right does a person walk the world at peace and at ease?

'It's forbidden to fill one's mouth with laughter in this world,' taught the third century sage Rabbi Yochanan in the name of the ascetic Rabbi Shimeon bar Yochai.[14] Only at the time of the redemption will we experience the full abandonment of joy. But for now, there is simply too much suffering on the earth to warrant such unbridled happiness. The world is beautiful and failure to appreciate it would be a sin against the generosity of life itself. But how, in this present reality of poverty, pain, sickness and struggle, can we be so oblivious as to laugh with all of our laughter?

It's Rabbi Yochanan, too, who taught that God told the angels not to join in. The Children of Israel had just crossed the Red Sea on dry land while the pursuing Egyptian soldiers were drowned in the returning waves. So the people of Israel sung of their great liberation in jubilation and relief. But when the angels wanted to sing too, God, according to Rabbi Yochanan, rebuked them, saying, 'My children are drowning in the sea and yet you are planning to sing!'[15] These so-called 'children' were the vanguard of the best-armed cavalry in the ancient world, soldiers intent on killing everyone in sight. Yet even they are described as God's children.

In this world there are always children drowning in the sea, starving, thirsty, lonely, unloved, abandoned from the moment they are born. But their suffering is generally beyond the range of our mental horizon; we do not see or hear them and, while they perish, we are often to be found singing about entirely different matters. Rabbi Yochanan cautions us: until everyone can participate equally there must be a limit to our song and laughter.

It was Rabbi Yochanan, also, who would take the bone of his tenth child with him when he went to comfort mourners. 'This is the bone of my tenth son', he would say, showing them the tiny fragment in a gesture which it seems hard to imagine could have provided any real consolation.[16] But perhaps it was not intended to do so. Maybe, rather, what he was trying to say was that he too had suffered and knew what it was like to feel pain. He was offering not comfort, but companionship.

How can we live as if there were no misery and injustice in the world? There is a time to sing and a time to dance. But there is also a time to wake up in the dark and know the shame of our conscience. This may not necessarily be prompted by guilt for any specific act. It's not the same as remorse for the thoughtless way we sometimes treat the people we really love. It's the shame of living in a world where there is constant violence and endless and unfathomable suffering. It's the shame of knowing that we are witnesses to hurt and degradation. It's a shadow of the feeling which Primo Levi perceived in the faces of the first Russian soldiers to reach Auschwitz Birkenau:

> They did not greet us, nor did they smile; they seemed oppressed not only by compassion but by a confused restraint, which sealed their lips and bound their eyes to the funereal scene. It was that shame we knew so well, the shame that drowned us after the selections, and every time we had to watch, or submit to, some outrage: the shame the Germans did not know, that the just man experiences at another man's crime; the feeling of guilt that such a crime should exist, that it should have been introduced irrevocably into the world of things that exist, and that his will for good should have proved too weak or null, and should not have availed in defence.[17]

We could say: 'Why should I bother about the fortunes of others? I struggle hard enough to ensure that my own family is all right. I deserve the fruits of my labour. After all, I've earned them by honest hard work so why shouldn't I enjoy them in peace?' But it's precisely to this attitude that the Mishnah refers when it teaches that the person who makes the seemingly unobjectionable claim that 'What's mine is mine and what's yours is yours' is following the way of Sodom[18]. What appears to be a healthy and law-abiding respect for property in fact conceals a callous sneer, as if to say, 'I've earned my portion; you deserve your lot'. Who can explain by what right he or she is born to prosperity while someone else is a slave by the age of four? We can neither answer that question nor, if we have any integrity, sweep it away. It's precisely when we do succeed in deleting it from our consciousness that we should worry most about our moral health. When our conscience never registers anguish over such matters we have entered the path of moral decline and, in forgetting the humanity of others, have lost the essence of our own.

There are two sides to this existential shame; shame for what we do and shame for what we fail to do.

The twentieth century Jewish theologian and philosopher Abraham Joshua Heschel asks: 'Who is worthy to be present at the constant unfolding of time? Amidst the meditation of the mountains, the humility of flowers . . . we are hating, hunting, hurting . . . Suddenly we feel ashamed of our clashes and complaints in the face of the tacit glory in nature.'[19] We wish we could prevent or avoid not only the effects, but the very coming into being, of such hatred.

The first time I realised that there were people nearby who wanted me dead and who, had they not been afraid of the consequences, might have killed me, was when I was walking through the streets of the old city of Jerusalem thirty years ago and a stone whizzed past from a sling. I understood then that my life was protected by two realities, fear and force. But I don't want to live by force and fear. Their very existence pains me, and inwardly I'm ashamed, even when they function on my behalf, even when there's a measure of necessity or justice in their deployment, because they mean for certain that there are others whose hearts are filled with anger and humiliation. The world of my hopes and ideals is therefore broken. That is why all and any violence on earth is a call to each and every one of us to examine our souls. It invariably afflicts the innocent in the end. What would we say if it was our child's leg which was blown off by a mine while he was playing in the grass? But that's precisely what happens to little children every single day. We are all at fault.

Not only do we fail to prevent suffering, we cannot even estimate the damage we ourselves inflict. When we die, our bodies will at least rot down. But the consequences of our actions remain. The poor who stayed poor because of the side effects of our way of life don't get a second chance at life. The animals whose habitats we polluted won't come back. We could say: 'What difference can one person make?' We could say: 'Everyone else around us lives like that!' But to argue that we're only doing the same as all the rest is a weak excuse, no better than that of the soldier who fired his gun because someone in authority told him it was all right. Everyone knows what consequences follow from that kind of morality.

Then there is the shame for what we fail to do. We need only think of children who've got nothing to eat. If one hungry child in every million were to look at us and say, 'How could you not have fed me?' we would have no adequate answer to give them. The relief of poverty, said Nelson Mandela, is not an act of charity but of justice.[20] This is precisely the Jewish view, which describes helping those in need as *tsedakah*, righteousness. No other choice is moral; we have to accept a share of responsibility for the vast injustice in which we participate every day.

No, we cannot entirely fill our mouth with laughter in this world. It's forbidden to us to seal our conscience. Our aim must be the opposite, to extend the horizons of our moral imagination and deepen our compassion. This means that sometimes we have to feel ashamed; were history marked by true moments of collective shame, we would long ago have transformed the world.

Nevertheless, Rabbi Yochanan's attitude seems unduly severe. Are we really not allowed to laugh and to be happy? Aren't happiness and laughter an essential, and often a courageous, part of our response to suffering? Life would be unbearable without them. To refuse to smile and laugh with life must surely also be wrong. It's a characteristic of many of the greatest people that they almost always communicate a sense of equanimity and are frequently full of laughter. But that has nothing to do with the complacency to which Rabbi Yochanan is justly opposed. Such true laughter is an expression of the confidence of those who are at peace with themselves because their life is devoted to others.

Being Judged

You know the secrets of eternity . . .
You examine the kidneys and the heart

Prayer for the Day of Atonement

An ancient Aramaic rendition reads this as the issue that led to their fatal quarrel: 'There is no judge and there is no judgment', declared Cain. 'But there is!' maintained Abel, and paid for his insistence with his life.[21]

I believe that we are judged. I believe that every act is registered and known, that all have consequences, that none are neutral, that there is not a moment of existence which does not have its moral implications. The very quality of our consciousness transfers itself almost imperceptibly to everything around us, affects it every moment and is recorded there.

'You shall fear your God,' says the Torah after instructing us not to curse the deaf or place a stumbling block before the blind. Because, explains the mediaeval commentator Rashi, we can always deny what we did and the only witnesses can either not see or not hear, the Torah reminds us that there is one who knows our thoughts and who is invariably present.[22]

That was Macbeth's great mistake when he boasted to his wife that there was none to call their power to account. She, presumably, already knew better, rising nightly in her sleep to that futile washing of hands. He had reckoned neither with conscience, nor with other people, nor with destiny. But there is never no one who can call us to account. They may of course refrain. Fear may cause them to demur. Even in domestic life we all know people to whom one can say nothing; one sits there in cowed, resentful silence. Meanwhile, across the globe tyrants with the power to imprison and murder at whim order arrests, reprisals, tortures and executions. But, unlike individual people, truth grows new tongues. Eventually, as the Psalmist says, 'Truth springs from the earth,' and no amount of slaughter can entirely kill it off.[23] Perhaps it's because of this very awareness that it can never exterminate everyone who saw, heard, or somehow came to know of its ill deeds, that evil is followed by paranoia like its shadow.

Surely we are known.

There's a compelling ambiguity in a key line of the famous meditation for the Jewish New Year which describes how God opens the Book of Memories. *Umei'eilav yikarei*, says the prayer: Are those two Hebrew words to be translated as 'He reads from it', meaning that someone reads out the contents of the volume in God's presence? Or is the Hebrew better rendered as 'It reads of itself', indicating that the book in some manner orchestrates its own articulation? Or is there indeed any difference between the two interpretations? Maybe God's speech to us consists precisely in our ability to listen to the book reading itself. Significant parts of that challenging volume may consist of pages, even whole chapters, we never allowed ourselves to hear, or never even previously intuited at all. For the leaves of the 'book' are the flight of a frightened bird, the atmosphere in the room where we sit and harbour our thoughts, the unspoken feelings of the heart which we ourselves may not recognise, nor wish to, but which others perceive and know, our words, our deeds.

Where does our responsibility end? Will it be my fault if my grandchildren are brought up too strictly, or with too little restriction, because I shouted too much at my children? Will some of their love of nature be my creation too? The ink of me gets paler, its colour dissolves in the future, but it is transformed, it transmigrates into lives and interactions of which the causality is a million different behaviours regressing to the very origins of matter. For that which for a while became me was only the temporary confluence of atoms among the innumerable permutations of what has been and what might be. Yet now, in this very hour, I am making a difference. In ways I do and do not choose, consciously and unconsciously, I am having an effect. That must have been what God meant in instructing Abraham to 'be a blessing'.[24] Is the way I live my life, am I, a blessing or a curse?

There are two interrelated moral questions. The first concerns the record itself. Is there a moral legacy? Are our actions inscribed in 'the book of life', if there is such a book? The second is about our ability to hear that book being read, and change. There is all the difference in the world between being known, and knowing that we are known. The former may be no more than the truth but the latter is also an opportunity.

How many voices speak! They address me from within, intuitions from the conscience, feelings of unease which presage realisation, 'My God, what have I done?' I push the thought away, 'It's nothing'. I tell and retell the story to myself, 'I didn't do anything wrong'. A friend assures me, 'Don't worry. You were fine!' But only I know the tone of what I said, the intent behind what I did. Deep within myself I recognise the futility of these efforts to fortify what, in some place fatal to them, I've always known are only fabrications.

The voices speak in memories and intimations; the phone call I never made and the anxiety afterwards about having failed to do so; the person who for no apparent reason never called me back; the lapse of a friendship. The associations fade, then return. Finally I ask myself, 'What did I do?' and begin to piece together the hints of realisation.

The voices speak directly. A good friend, suggests Rabbi Yehoshua ben Hananiah, who lived in the first century of our era and was renowned for his humility, is one who can reprove us lovingly, in such a way as enables us to accept what he or she has to say. It's an art, the Talmud admits frankly, in which virtually no one is skilled.[25] How quickly we react with anger to words we don't like, often the more so if we suspect that they contain a truth we've been seeking to repress. How long it usually takes before we are able to be open with ourselves and say, 'Yes, that's right; it really was like that,' before we realise that we are in fact capable of surviving the humiliation of the admission. How hard it is to learn! Sometimes a phrase echoes for years, blown angrily about the mind until it finally settles in a corner capable of receiving it honestly. We have to face the fact that we find it hard to face the facts about ourselves. But who we are is articulate in everything we've ever done, and failed to do, in the friends we keep, and in those we don't, and in the quality of the consciousness which sweeps like the tide over the sea-floor of our mind.

As important as the question, 'What have I done?' is the question, 'What can I learn?' In the end, I'm more frightened of proving unable to learn from my past conduct than of the shame of having to recognise some of the less pleasant contours of who I am. I don't want to be a person who leaves behind a trail of damage while humming away to myself that what I'm doing is really fine. I don't want to inflict hurt. I want to be a person who is grateful, gracious, appreciative of this delicate privilege of life.

That's why I've always felt that when, from time to time, I do manage to reach the simple place of truth, I'm not alone. God is there, God with the face of justice and God with the face of love. I, in being truthful, have ceased to evade the God of truth, who was present all the time. I now encounter also the God of love, who wills and inspires me to do better.

CHAPTER SIX

The Privilege of Life

Gratitude

The hidden things belong to the Lord our God.

Deuteronomy 29: 28

The night before I'd gone walking at midnight with my wife. 'Take the disused railway line,' they told us, 'You can carry on for miles'. I'm sure they hadn't imagined that anyone would set out at so absurd an hour on a freezing winter's night. But the walk was wonderful. Below us lay the the rivers and valleys of Exmoor; scarcely visible in the darkness, they would preserve their mystery until morning. But the sky was alive and luminous, a canopy rich with stars as I'd only ever seen it once before in my whole life, when I lay on my back in the desert thirty years ago and stared up at the heavens.

So many stars were visible in the cloudless sky that night. It stretched above us, vibrant, cosmopolitan, rich with unknown stellar life, yet silent, embracing and vast. I thought of Abraham, commanded to look up and count all those stars, if only he could. Such, he was promised, would be the number of his descendants. To me, it would be enough to know that I had children who appreciated them, that one day they might stop on a night like this, with a cold wind and a clear sky, far from the inhibiting smoke and light of cities, and look up with wonder and say, 'The stars! How many stars there are in the sky tonight!'

I want our children to know God in their hearts; I want them to experience wonder, I want them to feel the breath, on the earth, amongst the stars and in the immense spaces beyond them, of the eternal presence which fills the whole of this unending, vital universe. I want them to apprehend the greatest of all life's gifts; I want them to be able to stand at those most special and most private moments of their lives in happiness and awe and say, as much to themselves as to the world at large, and to the horses in the field and to the trees in the hedgerows, 'Thank you for this being, this privilege, this moment in eternity we share'.

The following night our youngest daughter came with us on our midnight wander, she and Mitzpah the dog. Like her brother and sister, she'd inherited the family craziness, long may it thrive in them all, and thought nothing of setting off at such an hour in the pitch black dark following the white tip of the dog's disappearing tail. We took the same old railway cutting and Kadya walked between us, holding our hands and chatting merrily away. 'We've had so many holidays,' she said, and we talked about the different walks, the walks on which we'd got lost, the walks which had been too long, too steep, too boggy, or too short, and those which had been our favourites. 'The fifteen mile walk last summer was the best,' she said, 'I like the way we had to ford those rivers above the loch.' But there were many other rambles she remembered as well, always an adventure and always leaving each of us soaking, muddy and contented.

It was then that we realised how much she too loved these times together, loved the dogs, our family companions, loved the moors, the woodlands, the rivers and the bogs. Ferns, heather and blueberrries, streams and rock pools, wild deer and ponies, these are the witnesses to the love which has made us its conductor, to spring across the generations.

Later that morning I took the steep path down the hillside on my own. A fast stream flowed through the woodlands along the valley floor and past a gabled farm house, hidden from the road above by the steeply rising contours of the land. Among the tree roots by the river bank, high above the level of the water, were sweeps of glistening snowdrops. There they were, the pale green stems against the brown earth and the fallen twigs, the white flowers all together, hundreds and hundreds of them. What wonder and what grace, the beauty and humility of February.

With Whom God is Comfortable

Kol sheruach haberiyot nochah hemenu,
ruach hamakom nochah hemenu.

With whoever God's creatures are comfortable,
God is comfortable too.

Rabbi Chanina ben Dosa:
The Chapters of the Fathers 3:10

Rabbi Chanina ben Dosa's saying is notoriously difficult to translate. What does *ruach haberiyot* really mean? Pious, ascetic, devoted, he lived a poor man's life. Surely he cared about the animals too; according to legend even his donkey refused to eat untithed grain. Perhaps, therefore, that key phrase is best rendered not just as 'people' but as 'creatures', to include all living beings. God, then, is comfortable with a person with whom not only other people, but even the very animals, at least the domestic species, feel at ease. It's hard to imagine that God would wish to be near anyone who had a cruel and intimidating spirit.

Love of animals is not, at first thought, a spiritual issue. It's often regarded as a sentimental quality, a quirky 'English' trait which doesn't quite compensate for a lack of social grace, or, worse, a basic inability to get on with people. But in truth there can be something much deeper about the fellowship between humans and certain animals, a trust, an acceptance of the shared destiny of life and death, a spiritual companionship.

From the first, Jewish sources make a distinction between wild and domesticated animals. As for the wild animals, whole tracts of the world are intended to be theirs: 'The high mountains are a refuge for the wild goats; and the rocks for the badgers . . . You spread darkness and it is night; then all the beasts of the forest creep forth.'[1] The hunter has no business to intrude into their domains unless out of desperation, writes Rabbi Ezekiel Landau of Prague. The abode of wild animals is dangerous; the Torah does not permit a person to undergo risks for no good reason and, anyway, Nimrod and Esau, the great hunters of the Bible, are scarcely uplifting role models.[2] But should hunger drive animals to adventure into cultivated lands, then the produce of the sabbatical year belongs to them too.[3] Only if wild animals enter human habitation and pose a threat to human safety may we kill them. Their existence is a source of wonder, testifying to the immensity of life: 'Do you know the time when the wild goats of the rocks bring forth, or can you mark when the hinds calve?' God asks Job. Job is somehow satisfied with this response, which, though it answers not a single one of his theological questions, nevertheless reconciles him to existence in a world which is neither just nor fair, but full of the unfathomable mystery of life.[4]

I've heard it argued that Job accepted nothing; he was simply cowed by God's power. I don't agree, especially since listening several times to dying people say that what has brought them reconciliation is the knowledge that it's to this vast world of living beings that we yield our body and entrust our soul.

I therefore fear these unnatural hot summers, the parched grasses and dried up rivers. They are the damning evidence of an unquantifiable sin, a destruction which is already withering up our spirit and may extend to shrivel and burn our bodies as well. 'Do not destroy my world,' says God, 'because there is no one after you who can come and put it right.'[5] It's not just a question of material destruction; it's as if, with the decline of so many species and their habitats, something of the wonder of God's presence is forever lost.

Domestic animals are permitted by the Torah for our service and even, under strict controls, for our consumption. Still, according to the Bible this has applied only since the time of Noah, who emerged from the ark to discover a different world familiar with ubiquitous death. In the Garden of Eden, and once again in the future when we return there in the Messianic Age, the taking of animal life will be forbidden.

But even today, in this utilitarian and exploitative era, our relationship to domestic animals should be one of partnership. 'The just person feels for the life of his cattle,' teaches Proverbs,[6] while the rabbis ruled, according to some opinions with the full authority of the Torah, that we mustn't inflict pain on any animals.[7] Indeed, they, too, must be allowed to rest on the Sabbath.[8] They must be fed before their owner eats and shouldn't be taunted with the sight or smell of food they are prevented from enjoying. Human beings have to go to the aid of a fallen animal, even if they hate its owner. After all, that's scarcely the ox or donkey's fault. The parental feelings of animals must be respected, because, as Maimonides explains, 'In these cases animals feel very great pain, there being no difference regarding this pain between man and the other animals'.[9] It therefore seems to me only right to be a vegetarian.

Even for those who do eat meat, rabbinical rulings define not only what species are permitted and how they must be slaughtered to minimise their pain, but also how they are to be treated in life. Force feeding geese is forbidden, as is keeping calves or other livestock in crates where they can't exercise or on an unnatural diet laced with chemicals to prevent the very diseases which those same conditions provoke. Hence even the person who eats milk, cheese and eggs has to be sure that the animals from whom he or she benefits are leading a pain-free life.

We live in partnership with nature; the purpose of its existence is not purely for our exploitation. Every morning we pray, 'Blessed be God who has mercy upon the earth; Blessed be God who has mercy upon the creatures', indicating that the world and the animals are precious before God in their own right and not simply as an adjunct to human life. According to the ancient tractate *Perek Shirah*, The Chapter of Song, all of nature serves God through its particular melody. The land itself says, 'The earth is the Lord's and the fullness thereof'. The deer says, 'I shall sing of your might, and of your kindness in the morning; for you have been a fortress to me, a refuge in the day of my trouble.' The elephant says, 'How great are your works, O Lord.'[10] Maybe that's why there's such comfort in feeling the breath of a horse, in watching the way it chews its hay or moves its ears, or in hearing the sound of its hooves, why there's such exhilaration in seeing the flight of a dipping bird, the slow beating wings of an owl at night. Animals often bring a humbling simplicity to life and death. At times it feels as if there's something they comprehend, which we, amidst the sophistication of our knowledge, have managed to forget, or never in the first place understood.

That's my excuse when on certain mornings when I can't concentrate on my prayers, I spread my prayer shawl over the dog's head and listen to God through his breathing.

Mossy's Wood Turning

The sound of the turning lathe drones through the thin wall which separates my half of the garage from my son's.

I'm no longer sure when Mossy's interest in wood turning began, but he'd been talking about it and taking lessons for a long time before the exciting morning when the lorry stopped with the enormous parcel which it took two of us to unload. 'We want to be sure that it's a passion, not just a fad,' we said. The lathe was his big *Bar Mitzvah* present from Isca and my father. Everyone else joined in to buy him the accompanying tools.

It was their gift in other senses too. My father was always a maker. When he was a boy he created his own *Chanukkiah* out of brass. He used to tell us the story of how he had just soldered a section together when his father came in and, picking up the hot pieces, dropped them instantly, burning himself painfully. 'Was it too heavy?' someone interjected, rather cruelly. Since then, asking 'Was it heavy?' has been a tasteless family joke whenever anyone picks up something too hot.

Perhaps the family love of wood owes its origins to the timber mill which my grandfather owned in Rawitsch. Apparently the premises still exist; a photograph from the sixties or seventies testifies how, long after the war and the destruction of the Jews, a large sign with the name Wittenberg was still attached to the building. As I recall it, the photo also shows railway tracks running right next to the mill and I find it impossible not to experience in that innocent picture the presentiment of something sinister.

From my earliest childhood I associated my father with timber and tools. He worked together with the joiner to build the attic room of the house in Glasgow where I was born. I remember the electric saw and the sight of the bare wooden stairs leading upwards. My father taught me how to strip a surface clean and paint it. He explained the proper use of each particular tool. He made me watch carefully several times before trying them out for myself. 'Never leave a tool lying on its working surface,' he would say, 'and never use a tool for a purpose for which it wasn't designed.' Together we built shelves, put up wall paper, cleaned the rust off the garden gates with wire brushes and repainted them in black metallic paint, and removed the offending muck from blocked drains. It seemed to me as if there was nothing, from a malfunctioning toy to a chair with a broken back, which he couldn't mend. For years after my father wasn't able to manage those activities anymore, Mossy would still say: 'Why don't you take it to Grandpa? He'll fix it!'

The sound of the lathe stops, then recommences. We came across a craft shop in South Wales where the owner gave lessons in wood turning and for two hours I watched Mossy being taught the basic pre-requirements: how to stand, how to hold a tool, how to move the body with it, from the shoulder, as the chisel travelled steadily along the spinning wood. 'Are you sure you're really committed to this?' we asked him. 'Have more lessons first; then we'll think about buying you a lathe.' His room filled up with catalogues, he sent e-mails to manufacturers, inquired about prices and specifications and deluged Robert, a family friend with twenty years' experience in the craft, with his questions. In the end, he determined precisely what he needed and the best places, and prices, to obtain it.

The lathe arrived and was promptly installed. Or rather, Mossy immediately began the process of its installation, because it took weeks to fix up shelves and round up tools. Robert and he spent many hours in the garage together tightening bolts, testing parts and arranging equipment. From time to time they would emerge thick as thieves talking of jaws, angles and grinder speeds. Even now the catalogues are still in evidence and Mossy's next birthday looms.

I'm proud to watch him standing over his lathe, engrossed, proud to listen to him talk about challenges I can't fully understand, let alone help him resolve: how to sharpen rounded blades, tighten inaccessible bolts, fit the jaws to an obstreperous piece of wood. I can even forgive him the (now less frequent) disappearance of my own tools. He's developed the capacity to concentrate for hours and the skill to create beautiful things. Above his bed is a chart showing bowls made from dozens of different kinds of wood. The other night we compared our favourites: purple heart, ebony, olive, oak, woods with rich grains, not too pale, not too bland.

I know that he will receive a spiritual education from these materials. A true craft trains the hands in actions which become more skilled and more intuitive with the practice and patience of years. It absorbs and disciplines the mind in observing consequences, determining how to apply appropriate tools, thinking, puzzling, learning, researching, devising new ways to solve intractable problems. Not least, it develops the awareness of what is harmonious, proportionate, complete, and thus refines an aesthetic sensibility which, in its instinctive recognition of beauty, may be the closest of all our faculties to spiritual apprehension.

This art of turning a fine bowl from a rough piece of log involves not only a mechanical but an artistic laying bare; it requires the development of a knowledge of and feeling for what's already present in the substance of the timber, the grain, the contrasting rings around a knot, the texture of a burr. The more skilled the maker, the less there seems to be of creation and the more of revelation.

I trust my son's teachers, not only the experts in the craft who've so kindly and skilfully instructed him, but the trees of the forests and gardens, and the secrets concealed in their woods by the years.

The Void

When does the awareness of death first come to consciousness? When does the fear of death first begin to pick apart the web of life we carefully weave around our children? When does the mind first conceive of its own annihilation and the dread of the void first settle on the heart?

'It's that feeling again,' says the boy. He's spoken to me about it many times.

People often say that they're not afraid of being dead, it's the process of dying which terrifies them, the suffering, the dependency, the indignity, the loss of faculties, the thought of being trapped, unable to move or even speak, inside a useless body pumped by a relentless machine.

This child, however, is afraid of death itself, of the vastness of the universe, of the endlessness of time, of nothingness, of ceasing to be.

We try to weave ties of grace and beauty between our children and the world. We hold their hands and stretch out their fingers to feel the cat's fur. We encourage them to go running through the rain and stick out their tongues to taste the falling drops. We hurry them outside in boots and scarfs to throw snowballs. We take them on trips to the coast and cry out, 'It's the sea!', our own child-self filled with the old, irrepressible excitement. We want life to be gentle and generous to our children, to all children; we want it to be a marvellous and compelling adventure. We want them to go out in joy and come home with wonder in their souls. That's why the death of a child feels like the betrayal of life's very purpose and the killing of a child is the ultimate desecration.

Yet even as we make love and conceive we set in motion the slow organic transformations which inevitably lead to death. When the sperm meets the egg, time emerges out of eternity and the sand begins to flee through the glass. Afterwards, then what? I will die, you will die, the child will die; we simply shall not be. This is a basic fact we cannot hide from our children. Somehow, too soon, the intimation settles on the heart.

The boy says he's frightened.

'What's the matter?'

'It's that feeling again.'

'Describe it to me; maybe that will help.'

'I can't. It's like the world is so vast and I'm going to be just nothing.'

We try to talk about it. I say to him that many people feel ready when death comes. Those who die suddenly don't know in advance and have no time to be afraid. Those who are aware often find reconciliation; many people are able to yield gracefully to death and some even manage to embrace the rhythm of living and dying.

But he says he's still afraid. No amount of explanation can take the reality away.

He wants me to discuss it with him again. It's not as if I can't identify with him; I have my own fears too. When I don't feel frightened of death, I can't tell if I'm just fooling myself. After all, the consciousness is incapable of contemplating it's own not being; it cannot by definition comprehend what it would mean for that very 'I' which thinks and feels to cease to exist. Therefore imagination and its terrors remain. I'll tumble from the edge of the precipice into the unending void. No one will hold me or reassure me as I fall. There, beyond the reach of all who ever loved me, I'll disintegrate and dissolve. I'll have no voice with which to cry out and, anyway, no one will be there to hear me. I'll enter the nothingness of infinity and eternity, for annihilation, nothingness, is the true import of those magnificent sounding words. In that nothingness all I ever have been and everything I've ever loved will neither exist nor be remembered. Annihilation will devour the dog whom I cradle for comfort; it will silence all the sounds which signify safety.

If infinity and eternity are the ultimate reality and time is only an interstice, a temporary delusion, then all things are already nothing in potential. Maybe even now we're all as good as dead.

The boy says he's frightened.

'What's the matter?'

'It's that feeling again.'

I try to tell him, 'Love life while you have it. It's the only way to live.' I tell him to say blessings over life with wonder and respect. He mustn't miss the snowdrops by the verge of the mountain road. He should go out and sit by the daffodils when the smell of spring is rising from the grass. He must get up in the middle of the night and watch the autumn clouds fly past the moon. He should fall in love and bear his heart's pain and fall in love again. He should stay up the extra hour and bother to write the letter to that old man who befriended him, telling him how much his words have meant and how deeply he treasures their conversation.

I tell him to live by the words of Dylan Thomas:

> Time held me green and dying
> But I sang in my chains like the sea.[11]

You can't stop time, but you can sing within it.

Yet the fear still remains.

Then I remembered the teaching of the sixteenth century mystic, Moses Cordovero. Maybe there's another way to face the vastness of the universe:

> Then you wonder, astonished: Who am I? I am a mustard seed in the middle of the sphere of the moon, which is itself a mustard seed within the middle of the next sphere. So it is with that sphere and all it contains in relation to the next sphere. So it is with all the spheres – one inside the other – and all of them are a mustard seed within the further expanses. All of these are a mustard seed within further expanses.
>
> Your awe is invigorated, the love in your soul expands.[12]

How can Moses Cordovero not be frightened by these immeasurable comparisons and unimaginable distances? How can it be possible that he not only doesn't feel afraid, but even experiences an increase of awe and love in his soul?

Or can it be that death, like life, entails not nullification but participation? Though a mere mustard seed within spheres inside even vaster spheres, perhaps the human consciousness yet remains a participant, an infinitesimally small fraction, but still nevertheless a fraction, of that being which comprehends totality? So what, then, if we ultimately lose ourselves in the whole? In the interim, the soul receives its vitality from God and the heart absorbs its love. Afterwards, that which is, that which encompasses and transcends us a million million fold, will transform us into itself. In death we will belong to the source of life. Hence 'our awe is invigorated, the love in our souls expands'. For the vastness which embraces us is not in fact a void. It loves us, yes, it even loves us, and that love, in its source and essence, and not merely in its transient and peripheral forms as we experience them on earth, is what ultimately awaits us.

What do we know?

Meanwhile the child still says he's afraid.

Libbi

Our second child, Libbi, was born at the Royal Free Hospital in London at a quarter-past three on an October morning. Her entry into this strange world must have terrified her because she soon began to cry. But I remember the first quiet moments of her life in her mother's arms and how, after weighing her and checking that she was breathing freely, the nurse passed the delicate package of baby and towel to me. I held her carefully and, looking down for the first time at the new person in my arms, noticed at once her big, lucid eyes.

Delighted with our young son, I desperately wanted our second child to be a girl. I'd always known that she'd have to be named Libbi, Libbi Shulamit, after my late mother; Libbi to preserve the initial of my mother's first name 'Lore', and Shulamit because that had been her second, Hebrew, name, chosen by my grandfather for its association with his beloved Song of Songs. I also had friends in Israel whose daughter was called Libbi, and I very much liked both the family, the child and the name.

Libbi is Hebrew for 'my heart', though the name is also apparently connected to the Russian *Lyuba*, meaning love. The word Libbi appears many times in the Bible and the Hebrew liturgy. Nicky and I have developed a special sensitivity to such occurrences. One of my favourite references is found in the chorus of the Sabbath song written by the mediaeval Spanish Jewish poet Abraham Ibn Ezra: '*Libbi uvesari yerannenu* – My heart and my flesh shall sing to the living God'. But most frequent have been the times when, despairing of persuading her to go to bed, we've recalled the verse from *The Song of Songs*, 'I sleep but my heart, *libbi*, is awake'.[13] Sometimes we would simply give up and leave her, a busy but sensible three year old, to potter around, knowing that as soon as our backs were turned she would reliably make her own way upstairs and settle herself down between the covers. One morning we found her sleeping with a large segment of over-ripe brie trickling down over the edge of her pillow. She'd evidently considered that the malodorous cheese would make a pleasant midnight feast and carried her booty off with her to bed.

'Say the *Shema* with me Daddy,' she says as I look into her room between eleven o'clock and midnight and invariably find her light still on and her nose stuck in a book. Like our other children, she always loves to read. Just recently she advised me on how to dry the pages of a book of country walks over which I'd spilled a cup of water. 'How do you know how to do it?' I asked her. 'From all those times I've dropped my book in the bath,' she replied with cheerful confidence. Picking my way across the untidy floor, I sit or stand by the bed and Libbi and I say the night time prayers together. It's a rite which both of us love.

When my father was very ill and we all knew that he was dying, we took the children to say their last goodbyes. They were well aware of the situation. It had been important to us all to include them; we'd hidden nothing from them except certain medical details with which there had been no point in burdening them. They'd visited regularly before; only by now my father was scarcely conscious and responded rarely, other than to appeal to Isca or sometimes to us to help him, or to call out for his sisters, all three now dead.

Libbi, who was eleven and a half at the time, went into the downstairs room where we'd set up the special hospital bed loaned by the Red Cross and simply stood there, her hands on the rail, silently looking at my father with her big, clear eyes. She made no noise, she was absolutely still. Her presence seemed to draw the quietness together and deepen the silence in the room. We'd thought the children would just look in for a few moments and say their farewells or at most maybe sit with my father for ten or fifteen minutes. After an hour we said to Libbi, 'You can come home now.' But she refused. 'I'm staying here all night,' she insisted, and so indeed she would have done had sleep not overcome her. We brought a chair and persuaded her to sit down. She said nothing but simply sat and continued her vigil with the same steady composure. 'If she wants to stay here, let her,' said Isca kindly, equally moved by her quiet concentration. We ceased appealing to her to come home. Her grandfather's death belonged to her experience too; we had no cause or right to intervene.

Later, when I returned with a few necessities, I found Libbi overwhelmed by tiredness, swaying in her chair, startled awake only by the movement of her own body a second before her balance would have been irrecoverably lost. Then at last I said to her, 'Come now, Libbi', and she consented to go home.

She didn't speak about her thoughts that night, either later back in her own room, or when my father died, or when we buried him. It was many weeks afterwards before some pretext led me to ask her about her feelings. She grew still; she simply looked at me with her big, unfathomable eyes and, quite capable on other occasions of providing a running commentary on the smallest details of her experience down to the way one opens the wrapping round a loaf of bread or fixes the lead to the ring on the dog's collar, said nothing.

The Silence and the Song

Once Rebbe Lipmann of Radomsk, son-in-law of Rebbe Shlomo of Radomsk, went to visit the great sage, Rebbe Menachem Mendel of Kotsk. 'Tell me words of Torah from your father-in-law,' requested the Rebbe of Kotsk. He replied: 'It's written of Aaron that he was silent [when his sons died] and this indicates a very high degree of spiritual attainment. But King David, peace be upon him, attained an even higher level when he said, "So that [we] may sing of you in glory and not be silent".'[14]

The Torah records that on the eighth day, the day of the dedication of the Tabernacle, two sounds were heard, the ringing cry of joy and the silence of Aaron mourning for his two older sons who died at that very hour.[15] So it has been ever since; the life of every individual and the history of all humanity are characterized by those same two responses, the silence and the song.

The eighth day represents the seven days of creation, which, in the Biblical context, symbolise the natural cycle, plus one extra day, the day on which God delivers the divine work into human hands so that we may cherish it and bring it to fruition. It was on this eighth day that the people witnessed the revelation of the glory of God through the fire which descended from heaven onto the altar. That was the day on which they saw and sung.

We, who live almost two thousand years after the Temple was destroyed, have seen no such miracles. But we still from time to time find ourselves in the presence of that radiance and beauty which are the manifestations of the sacred fire which burns secretly in the heart of life everywhere. At such moments of deeper perception, we too sing in exaltation.

The Bible commentator Rashi explains that the people felt great joy on that day, not simply because of the proximity of God's glory, but specifically because that glory was revealed, 'in the work of their own hands,' in the Tabernacle and on the altar constructed by their, human, endeavour.[16] All human creativity and all ethical conduct may be described as making a home and altar for the sacred. 'How do you decide whether a certain course of action is right?' asked the Hasidic teacher Rebbe Moshe Eliakim Beriah of Kozhnitz, before answering, 'By carefully considering whether or not the result will lead to the revelation of God's glory.'[17] Though it may seem far from the mundane and confused reality in which we see ourselves as living, there is not an hour of existence or a field of endeavour in which such revelation isn't possible.

As his skill as a wood turner has developed, Mossy and I have looked together at bowls of all kinds and sizes, some made of exotic timbers like olive and purple heart, others from branches of ash and oak gathered by craftsmen from the local forest floor. Almost all the work we've seen is competent. But the bowls which are truly beautiful have a quality which sets them apart; it's as if the essence of the wood has been revealed, the flow of the grain, the texture of a burr, the edges where the timber meets the bark, its very scars and faults. In these bowls, as in great sculpture, one senses that what the artist has achieved with such skill and intuition is the liberation of what was always intended to be.

Something similar can be attained through the art of human interaction. A nurse recently told me how much she'd enjoyed giving a bath to a patient. This woman knew that she was soon going to die. She had little mobility left and taking a bath was only possible through the use of sophisticated aids and with the help of a specially trained nurse. But my friend said that once the lady was in the water she found great physical and mental relief and the pleasure she experienced liberated a flow of delicate and touching conversation. It had been a privilege to share that special hour; they had felt a sense of joy, even fun, together.

The deepest love seeks not to encircle but to liberate. Good parents want their child to become the best person he or she is capable of being. I've often listened to husbands and wives who've found themselves becoming carers, struggling with the limitations of their partner, walking slowly by their side, looking with acute concern for the next safe place for him or her to place a foot. Such attentiveness shows not only great patience but great love, the love which, if we are fortunate, accompanies us from the first, which both holds us and lets us go, both challenges us and comforts us and helps us to become the truest human being that we can. Such love prepares the wick and the oil so that the light of our spirit can burn.

'All the people saw and sang':[18] There are many reasons for singing, for the sheer joy of being alive, for passion, for the rain, for sorrow, for the rush of a stream across the stones. The deepest music is inspired when God's fire descends upon the altar and the wonder of the sacred is revealed.

But there is also the silence.

'Aaron was silent': He had just seen two of his sons die, consumed in the very flames which had so inspired everyone else. Moses had tried to comfort him, but Aaron had said nothing. He simply remained silent.

There are many kinds of silence. There is the stillness of close companionship, the quiet of reflective thought, the speechlessness of rapture. Aaron's is the silence of grief, the silence which it is impossible to live and not know.

Alfred Feldman describes how he and his father survive the Nazis by hiding in Vichy France and, later, in the Italian Alps. On their journey home to Belgium after the war they gradually learn the terrible truth from which their isolation has kept them ignorant. Back in Antwerp their property is restored to them, but their loved ones will never return: Alfred's mother and sisters are dead. They open the trunk and see the dresses neatly arranged just as they'd packed them years before. Father and son say not a word to each other. But the next morning when Alfred wakes up, the clothes are gone, folded away into the silence.[19]

History is full of such silences. So is every individual life. 'The dead do not praise you, nor those who go down into the silence,' says the Psalm.[20] I often wonder what those words really mean. The first clause is perfectly clear; the dead don't speak of God's glory, or of anything else, because they're dead. But what does the second half of the sentence add, unless it's simply an example of Biblical parallelism, the repetition of the same idea in alternative words. But it strikes me that perhaps 'those who go down into the silence' refers not to the dead, but to us, we the living, who mourn. All of us have chambers of silence in our heart, rooms full of memories and sorrows. To visit them is to descend into realms too sad for speech, it is indeed to 'go down into the silence'. There, grief overcomes us and we recognise that life inevitably entails losing, letting go, and staring through the impenetrable barriers of time at the love from which we have been severed.

'Aaron was silent,' and we in turn shall be silent too.

So what do we do? How are we supposed to respond? What did the Rabbi of Radomsk mean when he declared that David's reaction was greater than Aaron's because he sang, defying the silence?

Most of us are afraid of the great emptiness beyond. When we die, will it be like falling off the edge of the earth into a bottomless abyss? Will annihilation engulf not only us but eventually the whole of this living planet? Will everything that ever was be turned back into nothing, until not a single memory or sound or echo of a sound of anything we ever loved remains?

Perhaps.

So what do we do?

We can manage no more than this: to rejoice in the privilege of being alive so long as we are able, to love as truly as we can, to be kind and generous, to conduct ourselves with humility, strive for justice, act compassionately, appreciate beauty, listen in wonder, and dedicate ourselves to the service of life. That's as much as we in our mortality can achieve. We must pray, too, that what good we do will survive us to grow in further hearts and be fostered in other lives than our own.

It's with this faith that we seek the courage to confront emptiness, pain, misery and grief. It's through this faith that we continue to sing, embracing the very silence in our song. For that silence never goes away; therefore our only recourse is to address it, include it, encompass it in singing.

That's what we have to do in life and there's nothing else worth trying.

'Let Us Make Man'

'And God said: "Let us make man," –
God says to every person:
"Let us make a true human being, you and I together." '

Rebbe Avraham Mordechai of Ger [21]

If we had the use of God's gifts to create the ideal person, a man or woman with all the qualities and sensitivities with which a true human being should be blessed, what faculties and characteristics would we want him or her to have?

My person would have an open and listening heart, for the heart is the core of the human being. 'Then let them anatomise Regan, see what breeds about her heart. Is there any cause in nature that makes these hard hearts?' demands the vexed and distraught King Lear.[22] I would give my person a soft but stalwart heart. To tyranny and cruelty it would be as tough as beaten steel; to helplessness and anguish as penetrable as silence to the fall of a bract of leaves. 'I will remove their heart of stone and give them a heart of flesh,' declared Ezekiel, summarising in a single prophetic sentence the cause of the difference between good and evil.[23] The heart should rarely be heavy, only when there is deep cause for anguish. It should be amenable to joy; happiness should flow into it while it sleeps and it should awake in the morning singing. The heart should be pure, like a clear mountain stream, as the Psalmist prayed, 'Create me a pure heart, God, and renew a ready spirit within me.'[24]

The soul should seek wonder, beauty and grace. As the moisture underground seeps invisibly into the well, filling it with cold, sweet water, so the presence of God restores the soul, so that the tired and frustrated consciousness can drink and be refreshed. For only the soul can wash the mind and heal the anxious, overburdened heart.

The mind should be curious and eager. It should investigate, discover, process, analyse, compare and comprehend. The mind should be rigorous regarding truth; it should be honest and free of fear. It should be ready to forgo what it thought it knew when compelling evidence questions its assumptions. It should challenge prejudice. It should not be cowed by falsehood and refuse to perpetuate lies. Yet the mind should also be ready to accept not knowing, attentive to the recurring questions, the mysteries which, through all our explorations, remain the object of our wonder. For the mind is partner with the heart in the search for wisdom and understanding.

The mouth should be full of laughter, the expression of happiness in times of joy and the resource of defiance in the face of pain and fear. My ideal person would have the gift of quiet speech, because 'a gentle answer turns aside anger' and there's already far too much aggression and self-assertion in the world.[25] Two short phrases are especially important: 'Thank you,' the capacity for appreciation, and 'I'm sorry,' the humility to acknowledge being wrong. But a listening ear is more important than many thousands of words.

The hands should be creative and gentle. When I was a child the cantor from my grandfather's synagogue in Berlin came to visit us not long after our cat had given birth to three black kittens. He was a tall, well-built man with giant, powerful hands, and Isca was at first reluctant to let him hold the tiny creatures. But he picked them up with the greatest of care and they sat purring in the cradle of his palms. Hands should also be creative, skilled at holding tools, adept at the precise movements which direct a chisel across the grain of a piece of wood, strong to keep the saw singing through the timber. But they should be gentle, too, for stroking the hair of a young child or supporting the arm of an old man. Hands should convey faithfulness, as when their protector Janusz Korczak held the hands of the smallest children and refused to be separated from them while they were forced to leave the orphanage in the Warsaw ghetto and board the train to Treblinka.

These are some of the qualities of a true human being.

I would also want such a person to have two further gifts, the greatest assets anyone can wish for in this world: a loving and supportive family and the companionship of loyal friends. In times of tragedy our most important resources are a strong family and devoted friends. In times of contentment they are the source of our happiness and our partners in joy.

My ideal person would live in good health and in a world at peace.

But, unfortunately, life isn't like that. All around us are not only beauty, love, generosity and grace, but unhappiness, loneliness, injustice, hatred, cruelty, caprice, violence, misery, sickness and war. We ourselves aren't like that either. Human nature is not only loving, humble and kind, but greedy, jealous, angry, arrogant, selfish, vengeful and blind.

It's in this painful and uncertain world, with our complex and conflicted tendencies of character, that we are nonetheless required to develop the heart, the mind, the soul and all the other faculties which make us into a true human being.

By the Stream

He makes me lie down in green pastures
and leads me beside tranquil waters.

Psalm 23:2

It was the day before the first day of spring, but already the fine green of the small leaves was filtering the sunlight and the forest floor smelled of new growth.

It was only a tiny stream. I wouldn't even have noticed it, looking down the hillside to the lane. But then I saw the wooden bridge and caught the faintest sound of running water. I made my way eagerly towards it.

Safi the dog climbed down into the water at once. He was old and placed his paws carefully, cautious of jumping. Still, he enjoyed the stream, drinking first, then paddling in the small current. It seemed to soothe the ache in his legs, it made him feel young again. The children followed, throwing their coats over the railings of the bridge and quickly taking off their shoes and socks. This was the moment they'd been waiting for, the release from grey skies, homework and reports. Happiness overcame us all.

I lay down on the grass and looked idly around. Kadya, our youngest child, was curled on her stomach over a hummock of moss, playing with a twig. Her thoughts wandered between the end of her oak stick and the patch of fallen leaves she was using it to explore. Her consciousness was content with itself, absorbed, but prepossessed by nothing; she was basking happily, caught between the green earth and the sun, which soothed her from above and from below. 'Mummy,' she said, 'this moss could be my bed.' Tranquillity had found its home in her.

The other children were exploring the area around the stream and trying to play 'Pooh Sticks' from the bridge, though there wasn't really enough of a current to carry the twigs in the race underneath it. Nicky was lying near me on the grass examining a flower. 'Have you seen the

163

wild strawberry plants?' she asked me, then observed, 'There's a little geum flowering over there.'

I'd lost the capacity not to be tense; for a long time now my state had been constant apprehension. But something was healing the agitation inside me, sunlight was restoring my soul. There was no need to worry about anything; all I had to do was to accept this joy. It was a sabbath to calm a whole season, to cure an entire year. It was a holy day of sunlight and trees; the water was running through my head, the little stream was cleaning my soul. There was neither servitude nor oppression in my mind, only freedom and the sound of the river. 'Heal me and I shall be healed': the small current swirled across the gravel and fell lightly over the edge of my thoughts down to a pool beneath.[26]

It was too early for the oaks to be in leaf, but even in these magisterial trees the summons to the new season had begun. Vitality was gathering in the buds; spring was inevitable. No one was going to prevent life now; fear, at this moment, was inconceivable.

I don't know for how long we stayed in that place. Maybe it was three quarters of an hour, I doubt if we were there for much longer. But it was time experienced in a world beyond time, a world like the best of childhood, filled with trust.

I've visited that world at other points in my life, not often, but the occasions seem to connect with each other, on the beach at Mull, in a meadow in the Alps where I sat with Michal, my Israeli cousin, when I was five, looking at a gentian in the grass. It's from this world that I would like to leave when I depart, because it holds no apprehension, no anguish and no envy. I hope it will stay present inside me.

There is only the radiance of life within, infusing and traversing the heart. There is only the abundance of life without, drawing the roots of the trees downwards and nourishing the young leaves in the buds.

CHAPTER SEVEN

Struggles

Loneliness

She said: 'I thought this would bring us closer, but we simply aren't speaking the same language.'

In the little patch of woodland even the leafless trees looked cold. It was March and the rich smell of spring should have been rising from the earth. Instead, a few meagre snowflakes were blown about the trunks by an icy wind. The grey branches pointed upwards to an equally grey sky. A solitary squirrel scattered last year's leaves, not a single bird was singing. A forlorn and wintry beauty had withdrawn to the hearts of the trees and hidden itself behind the bark.

My friend turned to me: 'I want to talk to him about it, but as soon as I begin he changes the subject. My sister, who's usually more open, won't say very much either. She tells all her friends, "We just have to carry on. We'll make it through this." She says exactly the same to me. As soon as I try to encourage her by creating an opportunity to take the conversation further, she repeats the same thing like a mantra. It's as if she can't bear to let anyone in.'

I often hear such words. People are very different in the ways they respond to fear and sorrow. Sometimes there's nothing to be done about it; sensitivity never was distributed equally, not even in the same family. Sometimes misery has rubbed so persistently against the heart that a thick callus keeps everyone outside and no one knows what's actually happening within. Sometimes one person feels the need to talk when in pain, while their partner remains tight-lipped.

Still, I wonder why it happens so often in suffering that at the very moment when we most want to reach the heart of another we are kept so stubbornly on the threshold. Maybe our very attentiveness threatens to dismantle the barrier which keeps misery at bay. I was once speaking to a woman who immediately began to cry, 'I can't bear to be among people who're kind,' she said. 'As soon as I hear the first words the tears come and I can't listen to anything any more.'

What are we to do, then, with the loneliness of pain? We listen, we hold hands, but even the most adept love cannot enter the space where the consciousness abides on its own. Who can touch the inside of someone else's heart? Who can sweeten the mind of another in the moment of its despair?

In a house at the edge of the woodland lives a person who is sick. I think she's at home now, but she's often at the hospital for treatment. What's in her thoughts as she sits waiting while the liquid in the bag slowly passes down the tube and through the needle into her veins? How does she integrate her illness, absorb her chemotherapy? What are her feelings when she wakes up in the night? Does she rouse her husband, who's only half asleep anyway; do they talk about their fears? Or does she turn to the window and, realising that her questions extend beyond the reach of human knowledge, interrogate the spaces between the stars: 'My God, my God, why have You forsaken me? Far from my salvation are the words of my cry.'[1] Is she alone with nothing and no one? Is God a meaningful word for her? Or does the blue-black darkness bring comfort as the great vitality which wakes the birds enters her too; does her soul finds solace amidst the singing voices of the dawn?

I'm often asked what we should say to people who are suffering. There are no perfect phrases. Tentative words can be withdrawn should they prove unhelpful, so long as they are spoken with humility. It's not the semantic meaning of what's said but the feeling and intention which matter most. Though even our loving cannot in and of itself bring healing; we can only illumine a similar love in another, or, more often, be illumined by it. Then sorrow can rest on that love, like a robin for a moment on a still, gentle hand.

The frozen branches extend upwards to the grey sky and the snow falls in small, broken flakes. The squirrel runs away. How lonely the trees appear, how isolated the houses.

Bitterness

Give me an ounce of civet, good apothecary,
To sweeten my imagination

Shakespeare: *King Lear*, Act 4, Scene 6

The lady came into the room and sat down. She recounted what had happened then put her head in her hands and said: 'I don't want to become bitter and twisted like so many people around me. I'm a good person; at least I think I am. I'm basically kind at heart. But now I'm afraid I'm going to lose all that. Thoughts of hatred and revenge keep surfacing inside me. So tell me what I have to do so that I don't become a sack full of misery and rage.' Then she began to cry.

It's said that a man once came to see the hasidic master Rebbe Menachem Mendel of Kotsk and told him how wretched his life had become. Once a reasonably cheerful person, he had sunk into depression and now all he wanted to do was to die. The rebbe referred him to a statement in the Talmud about the bitter herbs which the Torah commands us to eat on Passover night: 'If you swallow down the bitter herbs [without chewing them] you haven't fulfilled your obligation,' says the Talmud.[2] The whole point of eating bitter herbs, explained the rebbe, is to experience the taste. In the same way, the bitterness in our life can't simply be avoided. First we have to chew it; only then can we begin to digest it.[3]

Time and again I encounter people who accept pain and suffering with good grace. Young or old, straightforward or sophisticated, it's impossible to know in advance who they'll prove to be. 'This is my philosophy,' said one lady when, after her third major operation, her prospects looked grim. 'I'm not very religious, so I hope I won't offend you, but this is what I believe. There's life and there's death; all the time the sea and the earth are full of creatures being born and dying. When something's dead it dissolves and then it becomes part of life again. I hope I shall live, but if not, my death will simply be part of the tide.'

Which of us really knows what kind of person we'll prove to be when life confronts us with the ultimate test? None of us can tell in advance what will happen in the hidden vessels of our flesh where sweetness and bitterness fight for possession of our consciousness. Which of the liquids stored away in our heart and spleen will ultimately impart its taste to our being? Almost invariably, when I'm moved by a person's courage, or patience, or love of life, or humour in the face of pain, or when I witness bitterness and resentment, I watch myself worrying in a corner of my mind about how I would deal with those circumstances which could one day be my own. A simple prayer has formulated itself in my mind and I catch myself saying it often: 'May the sweet juices within me prove stronger than the bitter waters'. I, too, don't want to be bitter and twisted, neither in old age, should I reach it, nor while I'm dying, nor if I should have to go on existing after life has brought sufferings which feel worse than death. For dying is often a release.

Just as there are different degrees of physical pain, so there are many kinds of mental suffering. Death, especially if it's timely, may not always be the worst. People generally gather round the dying; amidst the suffering and sadness an environment of love is often created. The best memories are brought to the fore and shared. Sometimes the dying hear life itself calling out to them with a completeness hidden from them in the midst of their journey. It addresses them at once from within the soul and from far beyond it, saying, 'You are with me and part of me now. You are absorbed into my seasons and my tides'. Maybe the very chemistry of dying releases some compound which fosters reconciliation. Perhaps that's what led one of my teachers to say, 'I've never seen anyone die bitter'. I'm not so sure; I have seen people die tormented by anger, guilt and despair. But mercifully, that doesn't occur very often. For most of us there will at least be some moments filled with a new kind of peace and a deeper integration.

What voices, though, speak to the person whose husband has gone off with another woman after deceiving her for years? Maybe a small handful of faithful friends rally round her disaster. There can be no sense of peace, only the shock and pain of betrayal, the anger, the self doubt, the feeling of failure, the worry about the future, and the long war between the instinct for revenge and the vexed, reiterated questions of how to let go and whether or not it's possible to forgive.

Ten years after her husband left her for another man, a woman said to me: 'Even now there are moments when it still comes surging in upon me. Most of the time it's fine. Life's moved on. But it never goes away completely. I feel that I've actually managed to let go; I think I've even forgiven. But suddenly something little happens which triggers it all off. Then huge waves of anger come flooding back over me and in those fierce moments all I want is revenge.'

The notion that it's possible simply to forget is a fiction; however thoroughly we repress an event, some drab or painful detail is liable to surface in the consciousness after ten, twenty, or even fifty years. Absolute forgiveness is equally unreal. Until we die, the inner struggle is never irrevocably over. Love, courage and sheer persistence are permanently pitted against the invasion of hopelessness and hatred.

What must a person do? Some years ago there was a competition on the radio for the best short story. Short in this case meant very short indeed; submissions could be up to one minute in length. A sentence from the winning entry stuck in my mind: 'Undulate your spleen'. I'm not sure exactly what the writer intended, but it struck me that this was an art it would be good to understand.

The Ritual of the Waters

Let me not be bitter,
Lest I cloud with my bitterness
The pure blue of the sky,
My companion of old.

Rachel [4]

Is the bitterness in the cup, or do the waters only become bitter inside us? Everyone has to drink from the cup of sorrow. But will the liquid poison the heart and embitter the mind, or will it encounter an inner sweetness strong enough to turn sadness into wisdom and suffering into compassion? I've seen people accept tribulations and grief with extraordinary love and patience. Everybody gathers around them. They say they can't understand where such an outpouring of support has come from. But the truth is that it originates in their own attitude, as a result of which everyone else feels uplifted and inspired. Other people become embittered, or angry and preoccupied with recrimination. Their hurt makes them indiscriminate in their targets; they alienate their former friends whose patience and understanding begin to fail. They become isolated and then feel doubly victimised: 'No one wants to speak to me anymore. Nobody has any time. My neighbours avoid me like the plague.'

Perhaps we really are afraid of contagion. Maybe we see in the people we avoid an omen of what we ourselves might one day become. Maybe bitterness has already crept into our own soul? Bitterness is truly to be feared; so we edge nervously around the borders of its forbidden territory. Yet we too may well have to pass through its strange and disturbing terrain.

The Torah addresses the subject of bitterness through the ritual of the so-called deviant woman, the *sotah*, whose husband suspects her of adultery. The Book of Leviticus outlines a procedure which seems unjust and cruel, indeed abusive, to us. The rabbis abolished it some

170

two thousand years ago, if it was ever practised at all. Yet its details fascinate me. The woman is tried by being forced to swallow what the Torah calls the *mei hamarim hame'arerim*, the bitter and accursing waters. She is literally made to drink the cup of bitterness, and in one manner or another, we too are bound to drink after her.

This is how the Torah describes the process. If a man became jealous of his wife, he could take her to the temple and present her to the priest together with an offering of plain barley flour. He was entitled to do so whether or not his suspicions were well founded, though according to the Talmud they could not be entirely without warrant. The priest would then fetch water from a special supply within the sacred precincts and mix it with dust from the ground. He would tell the woman that, if she wasn't guilty, the drinking of the waters would prove her innocence and she would subsequently become pregnant. But, if she was guilty, they would make her belly swell and her thighs collapse, turning her into an object of public contempt. The woman was then forced to swear her assent to these conditions, answering 'Amen, amen'. Before she finally drank, the priest would write out the full text of the oath, including God's name, and dissolve the writing in the waters.[5]

Mercifully, the rabbis banned the entire procedure two millennia ago.

But no one can deny the fact that people do drink bitter waters, all the time. Careful reflection reveals many points of contact between the strange, obsolete ritual described in the Torah and the struggles we all undergo with injustice, misery and gall.

In the first place, there is precisely that question of justice. Men, as the maid Emilia, outraged on the part of her falsely suspected mistress Desdemona, says in Othello, are 'not ever jealous for the cause, But jealous for they are jealous'.[6] Jealousy is not rational. So why should a misguided husband have the right to treat his wife in this shocking and humiliating manner? The Torah makes no mention of any sanctions against him should his suspicions prove groundless. Even if the woman is at fault, who's to say that the husband wasn't at least partially responsible? The Talmud does concede by implication, prior to declaring the whole practice null and void, that women would never think to do such things if their husbands weren't at least partly to

171

blame.[7] Yet it was always the women who had to drink the bitter waters.

But that is exactly the issue. All too often there's nothing fair whatsoever about the contents of the cup of destiny which life presents to innocent, good-hearted people, demanding that they should swallow. They don't even have the choice of 'drink or die'; if death were a legitimate option, there are plenty of times when, in the face of utter grief or prolonged physical pain, a person might well prefer to perish rather than carry on existing. It's the causeless nature of it all, the injustice of the situation, which makes the necessity of drinking so cruel, the water so bitter and the whole affair so utterly outrageous.

Then there is the complex nature of guilt itself. Guilt can be inferred; people often come to feel that just because a certain event happened to them, that very fact is proof they must be guilty. How else can their destiny be understood than as a punishment? Equally, guilt may be displaced from a different area of a person's life which now comes to be seen as the true cause of the tragedy: 'My child was run over because I'm not very nice to my husband'. Or the mind begins to impute to itself motives which were entirely absent at the time, so that the innocent woman ends up wondering, like so many tortured prisoners on the brink of a false confession, whether she wasn't in fact somehow guilty after all, had given a sign, made some unintended gesture, or harboured a fantasy which had somehow become reified in ways which, hunted and afraid, she can no longer distinguish from reality, from the actual physical deed. Thus the victim of destiny, or of other people, ends up the victim of his or her own psyche as well. 'You let the poor become guilty, then you abandon them to their misery,' wrote Goethe, thinking surely not of a specific and juridical, but of a constant, haunting existential guilt.[8]

The trials of the innocent woman who had to drink the wretched water almost certainly didn't end after she had swallowed it. Granted, she'd gone through with the whole nasty ritual and was now in the clear (except for the fact that she was still living with the husband who'd forced her to do all this.) But who knows how she might have felt afterwards? Maybe she became possessed of the feeling that she was being forced to drink again and again, as if the liquid had fostered a culture inside her and was reproducing itself in her digestive tracts, burning the lining of her stomach, flowing through her heart and poisoning her thoughts. For, as we all know to our cost, once we begin to harbour guilt and bitterness they well up over even the smallest concerns and the most steadfast consciousness has to struggle to control them.

A unique and striking feature of the *sotah* ritual is that God's name is erased in the waters before the woman drinks. But, as every Jewish child learns, the Torah teaches that God's holy name may not be destroyed; writings which contain it must be preserved or buried but may never be thrown away. Yet here, in this unique instance, God's name is obliterated. The Talmud attributes this to God's great love of peace. For the sake of restoring harmony between husband and wife the divine name itself may be effaced.

But perhaps there's a sadder explanation. There are liquids so bitter that there's nothing they can't corrode. By the time we've finished drinking them, even God has been eaten out of our hearts. We have simply no faith left. 'I don't believe any more,' says the man who's lost his young and beautiful wife. 'If there is a God, then he's a vicious and capricious deity. Or else there's no God at all.' Worse than the loss of faith in heaven may be the loss of faith in life, in the value of getting up in the morning, in the capacity of the heart to receive love, in the hope that the soul will ever again feel calm or receive the blessings of tranquillity. No, we are marked down for bitterness forever; it is present in the very substance of our thoughts, rotting away the consciousness from within.

It's foolish to imagine ourselves immune. Who knows until after the event whether our imagined beliefs, in God, in life, in hope, in love, in humanity, in trust itself, amount to anything more substantial than the mercy of never having had the kinds of experience which could have erased them entirely from our hearts?

The ritual of the *sotah*, long abolished, was centred precisely around the question of faithfulness: Had the woman been unfaithful to her husband, or had she not? It's strange how, in a very different manner, the way we drink our own cup is a prolonged and searching test of our fidelity. With whom and what will we manage to keep faith? What values will we succeed in upholding in spite of anger, bitterness and grief? What kind of person will we become? An undiscovered self awaits us all on the other side of pain.

People sometimes tell me that what they're most afraid of is becoming a misery, a kill-joy, a bitter spirit whose company no-one can stand. One woman recently said to me, 'Maybe it's already too late'. She paused for me to contradict her which, of course, I did. But I fear such contradictions will never reassure her. I'm frightened of the same thing myself. I struggle to control my consciousness if even for an hour it starts to poison itself. Hardest of all is to witness all good memories, all consolation, all hope and vigour draining away into nowhere through some internal hole, while the vial of bitterness leaks its poison into the blood. Perhaps that's why the Torah refers to the bitter liquids not as 'accursed', in the past tense, but as 'cursing' in the present continuous, because they continue to perpetuate their maledictions.

Yet maybe the struggle with bitterness will give birth to something entirely different. Perhaps we shall find the courage and serenity which is so marvellous to observe in other people, my heroes, those who love life and are full of grace and gratitude in spite of everything. That is why we have to garner love inside us while we can, and trust that it will turn us, too, into gracious, patient, forgiving and generous people.

What's the Point of Dying?

On the New Year it shall be written
and on the Day of Atonement it shall be sealed:
how many shall pass away and how many shall be created,
who shall live and who shall die . . .
But repentance, prayer and charity
remove the evil of the decree.

The High Holiday Liturgy

A friend sat down in my kitchen and burst into tears: 'How can I pray to be written in the book of life when I've been told I may not live to see another year?'

That same day a woman explained to me why she'd stayed at home on the New Year: 'I couldn't face adding insult to injury by declaring that good deeds can change God's decree when I lost my son last winter.'

Then Kadya, aged just nine at the time, prompted by the tone of some conversation she'd overheard about the house, asked simply, 'Daddy, what's the point of dying?'

The idea that there is a book in heaven originates in the Torah; the Talmudic rabbis developed from it the powerful image of God inscribing in separate volumes, open only between the New Year and the Day of Atonement, the names of those who shall live and those who must die.[9] But nowhere does this picture attain the impact it achieves in the unforgettable lines of the unknown poet whose work was placed at the very centre of the liturgy of the Days of Awe:

> On the New Year it shall be written
> and on the Day of Atonement it shall be sealed:
> How many shall pass away and how many shall be created,
> who shall live and who shall die.

I most certainly do believe in the existence of the books of life and death. Only they're all about us, not volumes in the sky. That frightening Talmudic image serves primarily as a forceful metaphor to make us ponder the entangled strands of life and death and review the uses to which we put the years of our fragile and limited sojourn.

I did a short exercise; I wrote my own books of life and death. I took a sheet of paper and set down what was most important to me in the book of life: Immensity, the sky above the sea in the dark; immersion in Torah; phoning a close friend late at night and talking through the day; family affection; moments of intense love; the movement of animals; work; writing; planting a garden; concentration; the creative imagination on fire.

There is suffering in the book of life too. People tell me, 'I'm lonely'; 'I'm broken'; 'I'm finished'. Their friends say, 'If only we could take your pain from you'. Too often they can't. I hear the cry of the old, demented woman in the hospital, 'Don't leave me alone. I can't take it a moment longer. I'm going to jump; I really will.'

Always, too, there is the awareness of time, time threatening, time fleeing, time haunting us with visions of the irrevocable past. Already when the dog was young I began to worry about the number of his years, knowing a dog's life is shorter than ours: He's ten and slowing down. He's fourteen and limps behind us on arthritic paws. When will his day of judgment come and must we be the judges? I count my own years differently after that day has passed: forty-seven, forty-eight, forty-nine . . .

I took a page and wrote down everything which spoke to me about death. Vasily Grossman accompanied the Red Army from the retreat to Moscow until the advance on Berlin. He described two dead soldiers lying together at Stalingrad, a Romanian clinging to a child's picture of a sailing boat and a Russian with a letter from his daughter, 'Come and visit. I wish I could see you. I am writing this and tears are pouring. That was your daughter Nina writing.'[10]

I see a young woman holding her unconscious husband's hand while their seven-year-old child sits watching. Most people are more afraid of dying than of death. We don't want to become a burden; we don't want to lose the ability to speak or become trapped in a body which doesn't function anymore. There are hospital rooms where the only sounds are the steady, disconsolate bleep of the monitors and the irregular rasp of indrawn breath.

I wonder about my own death. Moses Ibn Ezra, eleventh century bon-viveur, penitent and poet, visited his parents' graves:

> I greeted them, but no one heard or answered;
> Had my father and mother forgotten me then?
> Wordlessly they called me to themselves
> And showed me my own place by their sides.[11]

The books of life and death are open about us all the time.

'So what's the point of dying?' asked Kadya. I was in the middle of saying that it wasn't a question of 'point', that dying was a fact and we had no choice in the matter. But something made me realise that she knew this already. She was voicing the question we all have to face: What difference does dying make to the way we live? The answer is as long as life itself and as short as a single sentence: Death gives life its urgency.

This is what it means to be written in the book of life: If there's something good, kind, exhilarating and worthwhile which we can do, then we should go right ahead and do it now. All Jewish teaching is posited on the principle that we 'stand this day before the Lord your God'.[12] This day, this very present day, is all we have. Tomorrow is another world which may, or may not, include us. The time, therefore, is always now. When I was younger I didn't understand this; I had plentiful reasons for putting things off. Today I have a different attitude. I'm mindful of the line Shakespeare gave to Richard II as he languished in prison: 'I wasted time; now doth time waste me'.[13]

We must write others in the book of life too. This is no mere metaphor; people die all the time of hunger, disease and neglect because we fail to bring them food, medicine and companionship.

We must write ourselves in the book of other people's lives. What we call our own is basically their gift; we're beholden to others for everything which composes our lives. Even our capacity for love doesn't come from nowhere; we owe it to the love which we have received.

What, then, can we give back and how, in the time available to us, can we do it to the utmost? Love owes its urgency to the fact that we will die; there is indeed such a thing as 'too late'. Whoever has experienced the reality of those inexorable words will surely want to spare others the same suffering.

That's the theoretical answer to Kadya's question. The real response must be made through the quality of our lives.

What about the woman who stayed at home, unable to stomach the thought that more earnest prayers and better deeds might have persuaded God to spare her child? In the face of all the tragedy to which so much of humanity is witness, I regard such a theology in its unqualified form as obscene. I cannot believe that our destiny is clearly and necessarily determined solely by the quality of our character. There are of course connections; reckless living won't lengthen our days. But in general, I don't believe God works with simple equations; experience contradicts this all the time. The fact that a person dies young of cancer, is run over in the street or is blown up by a suicide bomber is not a direct divine judgment.

But that is not to say, in the words which the ancient Aramaic translation puts into Cain's mouth just before he murders his brother, that there is no judge and no judgment.[14] The moral and spiritual quality of our life produces innumerable effects and counter-effects, some palpable, others invisible, which return all the time to bless us or afflict us. In this way our life is indeed judged every day and every moment according to its intrinsic qualities. It is in this sense that our deeds do indeed write us in the book of life: They inscribe us in other people's hearts, they change the quality of our own existence and theirs, they bring the difference between misery and hope, love and loneliness, sometimes even life and death. However, our outer fate, the number of our days and those of our children, may have little connection with this process.

We sat at the kitchen table and my friend spoke to me about her illness. Life, she acknowledged bravely, can't be measured by quantity alone. In the face of imminent death one has to see each day as an entire universe and every hour as an opportunity. A beautiful morning, a walk in a park, a few minutes at peace, these experiences have intrinsic value and cannot be regarded as of greater or lesser value because of how much time may lie on either side of them.

We talked about how much bigger the book of life is than the extent of our own existence. Who knows what other hearts have nourished our own? Had someone put blue dye into our great grandmother's deeds and we could watch how the colour spread over many generations in the love and affection she inspired, we would find that it emerged in shades and hues in hundreds and thousands of lives in ways and places she could not possibly have imagined. We exist, even in this corporeal world, far beyond the self and belong far more deeply to life than life belongs to us.

We can therefore do no better, in the interim which is ours, than live as deeply, generously and lovingly as possible.

Three Dimensions of Forgiveness

'Forgiveness means giving up all hope of a better past'

The Forgiveness Project [15]

The very contradictions between the trite, familiar sayings, from 'Forgiven and forgotten', to 'I'll never forgive him, never!', point to the unfathomable complexities of the question: What is forgiveness?

From the Mishnah onwards, the first code of Jewish law edited at the close of the second century, Judaism has distinguished between forgiveness between persons, and forgiveness between a person and God: 'For sins between a person and God, the Day of Atonement atones; for sins between a person and his or her fellow human beings, the Day of Atonement cannot atone until he or she makes peace with his or her fellow human beings'.[16] There is, in addition, the profound challenge of how to forgive life itself when terrible events occur.

It's difficult enough to understand the meaning of forgiveness between one person and another. The popular saying already referred to, 'Forgiven and forgotten', points to part of the dilemma. Does forgiving mean erasure of the offence from the mental record? Have I only forgiven if it is as though the attack, the painful words, the hurtful action, never ever happened? Do I have to regard myself as unforgiving, must I feel guilty, if a shadow of my former anger should cross the sky of our now supposedly unclouded relationship?

It's impossible that forgiveness should require of us such an act of mental amnesia. Everyday experience testifies to the fact that we cannot simply remove past events from our memory. Furthermore, there's no such thing in life as the status quo ante; we can never go back to how things were before. Forgiveness cannot therefore mean that we have to behave as if the event never occurred, or at least never affected us. Happen it did, and it is as irrevocably a part of our relationship with the persons concerned, and of each participant's life, as yesterday forms the way we experience today.

However, this does not mean that forgiveness is therefore a fiction, a mere pretence at forgetting, while deep down the hurt still endures. It's instructive to consider the meaning of the classical Hebrew word for forgiveness between people, *mechilah*. In its general rabbinical usage *mechilah* signifies remission of a debt, letting go of the claim to something which might justifiably be ours. Thus, in striving to forgive we do not forget what happened but rather let go of our 'claim', which in this instance may be the anger, the desire for retribution and the hurt, or at least part of them, which the original events engendered. This is never simple.

But it's certainly possible, and it may be helped by a number of factors. It's far easier to forgive if we truly value the other person. If we generally respect and like them, we will be ready to weigh this particular upset in the scales of the relationship as a whole. Furthermore, we may encounter a degree of remorse which awakens in us so strong an empathy or love that there's simply nothing left to think about.

But more often forgiveness requires the discipline of seeking to understand what happened from the point of view of the other person; such understanding is a core part of the process. If we really care, we will try to find a way of asking, 'Why did you do it? What made you hurt me so much?' Judaism teaches that we have a responsibility to offer such an opportunity, wherever we can, when other people behave in a way which seems to us hurtful or wrong. It may emerge from the subsequent conversations that we ourselves were largely to blame; we were blind to the pain caused by our own conduct. Or we may realise on reflection that the other person was under a lot of pressure and this may help us to reevaluate his or her behaviour. Even if we can't have such a discussion directly with the person concerned, it may still be worthwhile to hold it in our own mind.

Understanding doesn't take the past away but it can transform it retroactively. Events are now seen as part of a rather different story and, as a result, we may no longer feel the same intensity of hurt. This transformation may take hours, months or years, but through it we come to see the past in a new light, and, in so doing, reclaim the future for a potentially renewed relationship. Of course, the other person may be stubborn, insistent and unyielding, in which case we may ultimately decide to end our connection with them. But we will still be left to heal our own pain and frustration.

Understanding and letting go of hurt and indignation are always a struggle. But if we do not attempt them, we often end up twisting the knife in our own wounds and becoming the victim not only of what others do to us, but of our own attitude as well.

Forgiveness of life itself is at least as difficult. Here we face an inner examination which may prove to be one of the most challenging ways in which experience ever tests us. It may be life itself which is 'to blame' because it has hurt us, bringing upon us a sudden or creeping disability, killing the person we love most in all the world, depriving us of a joy, such as having children, which everyone else seems to take for granted. We suffer, and we very likely suffer again, for after the tragedy comes the pain of what it exacts from us, the cup of inner bitterness which we are left to drink. For who suffers most when a person cannot accommodate himself to the tragedy by which he has been overtaken? Here we are faced with an inner battle often beyond our conscious control, an extended struggle between those qualities within us and those experiences we have garnered which nourish our sense of gratitude and enable us to appreciate what we have gained from life, on the one hand, and those parts of ourselves which feel malnourished, cheated or even abused by life on the other. Until we ourselves are fighting, none of us can know for certain who we really are. We cannot be sure what juices have been brewing in our heart and whether sweetness or bile will prove the stronger. Again and again I think with admiration of those who face suffering with cheerfulness and courage, who remember and value the blessings life has brought them. Again and again I wonder what sort of person I will prove to be. For all of us will be tested, though not equally.

Perhaps the struggle is similar when it is not life itself which has brought the suffering, but some other person, some definite agent, who is nevertheless to all intents and purposes inaccessible. Perhaps he is dead and we struggle alone with the unresolved guilt entailed by the relationship, talking to the gravestone, to the voice inside our mind which continues to disturb us, or to the very air. Or perhaps we cannot speak to her because the breakdown in our relationship has placed her outside the reach of significant communication. Maybe he or she is an ex-partner and although we can exchange basic information, it's impossible to talk about anything of substance any more. So it's left to each party to cauterise on his or her own the flow of pain from wounds borne in solitary despondency and self-doubt. Or perhaps a person we love is the victim of a tragedy, a terrible accident, war, a suicide bomber, murder. With whom can we conduct a dialogue? In our grief and outrage we strive to construct what reasons we can to ameliorate our misery. Perhaps at least we will be able to say, 'If I can make something good come out of this, it will not have been entirely in vain.'

Bound up with these struggles is the question of forgiveness between ourselves and God. Judaism teaches that forgiveness from God follows on from our efforts to forgive and seek forgiveness from one another. We cannot turn to God while steadfastly ignoring the justified claims of our neighbours. Judaism also teaches that God is forgiving if we truly regret the offence, resolve never to repeat it and to do our utmost to make reparation. The Bible reserves the word *selichah* for God's forgiveness alone, thus symbolising the unique and unfathomable nature of the divine mercy.

Ultimately the nature of God's forgiveness is a mystery. The very concept is problematic, with its anthropomorphic attribution of such human feelings as anger and mercy to the deity. Nevertheless, it may be helpful to think of God's forgiveness by analogy with how we see the world while we are depressed and after our heaviness has lifted. When we feel dejected, listless and without spirit we have no eyes for the beauty of the world; our gaze is bound to the painful vacuity inside. But as we manage to clamber away from the destructive magnetism of that mood we look up and see the trees and the sky once more. We hear the birds and say to ourselves, 'Listen! Look!' The ordinary glories of life take us by surprise. They were there of course before, they were present all the time. It is we who were somewhere else. So it may be with God's spirit. It is here all the while. But so long as we are possessed by anger, hurt and the feeling that life owes us, we cannot feel it. We forfeit access to our own heart; if someone were to speak to us during such periods about the spirit, we would feel as if we knew what they were talking about in memory only, if at all. But in stillness, or stirred, perhaps even shocked, into a different level of contemplation, we are drawn back down to the deep pool of water which is our own soul and we discover that it is there within us as before, reflecting an unpolluted heaven. So God's forgiveness is present all the time, part of God's very being, pure, generous, filling all things which do not obstruct its radiance with their own obscurity. Our own soul has been there all this while also, silent and unnoticed.

All our life we are liable to lose our sense of God's closeness. But sometimes, in moments of true blessing, we rediscover our God and feel the joy of integrity restored. On such occasions we are 'forgiven', welcomed, despite our errors and our coarseness, back into the unbounded purity of the one.

Anger

Remove anger from your heart.

Ecclesiastes 11:10

I'm never sure about the value of anger; I'm don't believe that it's 'all right to be angry'. Yet I recognise that for almost all of us getting angry is sometimes inevitable. For myself, I invariably regret it within moments when I lose my temper; I always feel bad afterwards. I feel as if I've defiled myself and wish I had the wisdom to be more patient and rid my soul of this affliction.

Anger isn't the same as indignation. Indignation is formed of the combined fires of justice and compassion. I admire people whose conscience burns on behalf of the oppressed, whose sense of outrage gives them the courage to challenge tyranny. Slavery, trafficking in women and children, contempt for refugees and strangers, blindness to the fate of the poor, cruelty to any sentient being, hatred for others simply because they are other, disdain for the community of humanity and nature, these are matters concerning which we should be far more indignant than most of us actually are.

Such anger is not the opposite of patience but of indifference. In Judaism it's a sin not to care. 'You must not stand idly by the blood of your neighbour', teaches the Torah, commanding us to engage with the destiny of our fellow human beings, whoever they are and whenever they're in trouble.[17] Most of us are too content with our ignorance, too much at peace with our complacency. I used to be afraid of those who challenged my conscience; I used to wish they'd leave me alone and not activate my sense of guilt. Now I'm grateful to them for waking me back up.

In our world there's too much anger and too little indignation.

Personal anger is usually, if not always, destructive. There are plenty of people who don't agree; anger, they argue, may be a bad master but it's a good servant. I remain unconvinced about the division: when am I in control of my anger and when is my anger mastering me? If I'm in

185

command, is it really anger? Wouldn't it be better to remain calm? If I'm not in control, anger rules and I and those around me may be damaged.

Perhaps a short outburst of anger doesn't really matter. One 'gets it off one's chest'; one 'says one's piece' and 'clears the air'. At least it's open and honest. If there's a cause for anger, it's usually better shared than harboured until it turns into a grudge. It's wiser to express our feelings calmly, but if that's beyond our patience, the kind of anger which bangs the door but soon returns shamefacedly is to be preferred above the civil rage which shuts it quietly it in icy contempt, never to open it again. For anger and pride often prove an invincible combination, as William Blake's poem *The Poison Tree* testifies:

> I was angry with my friend:
> I told my wrath, my wrath did end.
> I was angry with my foe:
> I told it not, my wrath did grow . . .
>
> . . . In the morning glad I see
> My foe outstretch'd beneath the tree.[18]

Something almost always lies broken after a serious bout of anger. It isn't the smashed cup or the splinters of glass which are so terrible; one can always sweep up the pieces. But how does one put together shattered trust? How does one remove fear from the heart of the child who witnessed the outburst? 'I'm sorry', the adult says, 'I'm so terribly sorry. I love you and I never meant to do that.' But memories are not so easily unmade and fear is not so swiftly removed.

Sometimes, of course, the tears which follow an argument restore a bond which reemerges stronger and clearer than before, powerful as the rage which preceded it. The partners weep and embrace, saying how much they love each other after all. They put it all down to a bad day, or to too much pressure, or to a major irritation at work: 'I'm so sorry, darling, I know I shouldn't have taken it out on you.' But what if it all repeats itself a second time and then a third? Eventually the heart retreats; inside, one readies one's defences and goes semi-permanently on guard. No one is prepared to expose their inner world to regular assault. Love and friendship are founded on trust; trust and fear are incompatible.

Anger has an impact on the wider environment as well. It's as if the soul has bad breath. My dog sometimes walks out of the room when people are angry. Nature itself retreats. If even a careless act of unkindness creates invisible wounds, how much more so must an outburst of rage? There's an invisible presence in the world, manifest in other people, in animals, birds and trees, in every form of life and in the very air we breathe. It requires our patient attentiveness and our love; it knows when we transmit the vibrations of rage and it quietly registers hurt.

Shame and sorrow often follow in anger's wake. Maybe that's why the rabbis instruct us to avoid trying to pacify our friends in the moment of their fury, not because we might end up bearing the brunt of it, but because of the shame they will ultimately feel, so that the fewer people who witness their outburst of temper the better.[19] Yet shame awakens humility and sorrow often leads to apology and restored relationships.

But what if there is no 'after the anger'? There's always the danger that anger may become habituated, penetrating the mind and slowly conquering domain upon domain of activity until we are angry at work, angry in the traffic, angry in the shop queue and angry at home. Our inner life becomes a desert, the sun too close, the earth too hot underfoot, the air shimmering with fire. The oases, where we might have found relief and restoration, prove one after another to be chimera; when we arrive there the landscape turns out to be the same as it always was. Or our world becomes a tundra; we grow distant from everyone and everything, the cold surface of our existence hiding fires deep underneath, while we walk across a frozen plateau frightened that they will break through.

Perhaps, in such situations, it would be good if they did. Maybe there's even something redemptive about anger, if and only if it's understood as the manifestation of frustration and hurt and if we pay attention to the pain gathered up beneath it. For anger is at least comprehensible. But once we enter the path of cold, dispassionate cruelty we pass beyond justifications. Sheer, wanton cruelty, – that I find both terrifying and incomprehensible. What created that?

In the Desert

And Moses lifted up his hand, and with his rod he struck
the rock twice . . . And the Lord spoke to Moses and Aaron,
'Because you did not believe in me to sanctify me in the eyes
of the people of Israel, therefore you shall not bring this
congregation into the land which I have given them'.

Numbers 20:11–12

Did Moses really deserve to die just because he hit a rock? Couldn't God, whose almost perfect servant Moses had been for these thirty-nine long years, muster sufficient patience to suffer this single act of frustration?

That's the classic way of formulating the question. But I understand it differently now. I no longer believe that the issue is whether what Moses did was so terrible that he deserved God's harsh judgment. What if God didn't punish Moses because he struck the rock when he should have spoken to it? What if that isn't the reason why Moses had to die but it's rather the other way round? If Moses hadn't felt that he was dying he would never have struck the rock in the first place. He would have known exactly which rock to talk to and how; he would have spoken to it gently; he would have trusted completely in the advent of the water and it would have flowed forth pure and cool, dissolving all the anguish in his mind. But for just this once Moses simply couldn't do it. The reason is that the desert had entered inside him and dried up all his words. All he had left was his frustration and his hopelessness. If death means going nowhere, then he felt that here in this barren and dessicated wasteland he was destined to die.

The remarkable thing about Moses is not that his patience finally ran out, but rather that he kept it for so long. All that wandering in the wilderness would have got the better of me after a single week. Some people love the desert. They see in it a great testimony to the tenacity of life, the scaly resourcefulness of snakes and the thorny armament of bushes in the absence of water. I find the desert terrifying. The external landscape, burnt shrubs, tufts of dehydrated grass, rocks and sand, corroborates the fear of an arid inner world with no rivers, no rainfall, no wells, no sources of water at all. Or maybe the wilderness itself is the reification of internal hopelessness. That's another reason, besides the obvious causes, why I dread global warming. It feels as if someone has skewered the heart of the world on the end of a long knife and is moving it slowly but incontrovertibly nearer and nearer to the fire.

In such circumstances the only salvation is to talk to the rock; so long as there is faith that beneath the rock lies water, so long as there is a rock with which it's possible to talk, the inner world hasn't yet turned entirely into a desert. The spring can still be drawn forth from beneath the boulders to produce clear, sweet water. Then hope and faith will return, with life and beauty and joy. God, we pray, bring forth water from the rock or else we'll die.

But the parched silence of the internal desert is overwhelming. I try to talk to you, inner people of my mind, life long companions of the spirit. How is it that none of you has a single word to say? Why won't you speak to me, down there in the country of my ribcage from where I need to catch your voices reassuring me, saying 'We're still there! Can't you hear us speaking with you constantly, like the sound of water trickling over stones?' But in this desert the inner world feels dead. That's the cause of this great drought. The place is mortal. Its pulverised emptiness articulates a single thought: 'You'll never reach the land of wells and waters. You've lost your way forever; you shall perish here.'

I sometimes wonder about this visceral, primitive fear of drought. It was a recurrent reality of the ancient world; time and again the Bible testifies to its terrors. It's an increasing feature of modern life as well, as across the globe we uproot the protective canopy of trees. History bears witness, also, to mass murders by starvation and dehydration, as when thousands were taken in the Nazi Holocaust from the town of Izbica and shunted backwards and forwards along the railway tracks in sealed and scorching cattle trucks before being dumped on the plain and left, the dying amidst the corpses, until every last person was dead.

Our inner deserts are terrifying too, the rocks a manifestation of our hopelessness and despair, the absence of water a witness to the sterility of our thoughts. Here is the wilderness of desiccated consciousness where nothing can be found except the fossils of ossified hopes. Everyone has a desert somewhere beyond the fertile lands, behind the mountains far within.

What do we do when we enter such terrain? The Psalmist understood, and prayed: 'O God . . . my soul thirsts for you, my flesh longs for you in a dry and thirsty land, where no water is.'[20] If only we knew which rock to talk to. But maybe there really is no water anywhere, at any depth, beneath these stones. I wish I could hear the sound of birds; if a bird were to sing I could watch in which direction it flew away to drink and follow it to the water. If I could only see a hedgehog or a squirrel, if I could walk in the wet grass on the hill above a river, if I could watch the movement of the filtered light beneath the branches of the beech trees, then I would live.

I know that if I were to speak to the rock the waters would flow from beneath it. Nearby there would be joyful voices and once again I would become life's partner in the consciousness of creation. But right now I'm simply unable to do so; I haven't got the patience or endurance any more. I don't even know which is the requisite rock. One after another I stare at them in frustration and the desert grows longer and broader, unending in every direction, and I know that I'll never escape it before I die.

'Because you didn't believe in me to sanctify me', said God to Moses.[21] That's the moment the desert consumes us, not because an unmerciful God has chosen to mete out the ultimate punishment, but because of the law of cause and effect, because there's nothing left in which we believe and therefore we're already dying inwardly here and now.

Sometimes the vial of faith is empty. The problem is probably not intellectual. It's unlikely that the thought of some theological contradiction is preventing us from affirming some essential principle. It's the living faith that's gone, faith in our own vitality, faith in other people, faith in the bond of consciousness uniting all that lives, faith in God. There simply isn't anything left to sanctify. One turns, and all around is desert. One doesn't even know which rock to talk to and, lost in the unbounded, sterile wilderness, one understands with the instinctive realisation of an animal that existence is not the joy of living but the long, slow process of dying.

The Choice

A person is where his thoughts are.

The Ba'al Shem Tov [22]

'Bear free and patient thoughts': I often think about the advice which Edgar, disguised as a wandering beggar, gives his aged and unhappy father by the cliffs at Dover.[23] For the hardest of all regions to govern is our own mind.

There are many people who would never contemplate, and who could never conceivably be imagined, committing such a mad excess as to hurl themselves repeatedly against a wall, beating their head against it over and again, throwing themselves at the plaster and brick, smashing their brains upon it like an impassioned sea against the immovable cliffs. Of course, the effort would be hopeless anyway. But just that is the goad, the tormenting and infuriating point, that there's nothing to be done, that all this impetuous violence is without object, for the maddening thought which drives us lies within. But precisely there inside, in the invisible domain of the inner world of the skull, thought flings itself, turbulent and helpless, frustrated and furious, again and again against the bone horizons of the brain. This happens in far more minds, of people purportedly far more sane, than we would probably want to imagine.

Because we do not usually distinguish the 'I' which thinks from the present experience of our immediate thoughts, we are rendered helpless. We have no place outside of our torment from which to resist its possession over us. Thus we become the victims of our own consciousness. This is a disaster, for what most determines who we are, whether we are happy or unhappy, whether we make others happy or unhappy, is the quality of that very consciousness, which we have abandoned to our mood and which now is pounded, shipwrecked and rudderless, by the thrashing tide of itself.

Yet the rhythm of our thoughts in the brain, the way they beat against its boundaries, their flavour, their sweetness or bitterness, determines, indeed constitutes, the most intimate content of who we are. And, as the ancient teaching indicates, how we treat others is predicated instinctively on our feelings about our own self: 'You shall love your neighbour as yourself; I am the Lord', commands the Torah.[24] The question is invariably asked: 'But what about the person who doesn't love him or herself?' The point is well made. The quality of our consciousness determines not only how we feel to ourselves, but, almost inevitably, how we behave towards others.

Is there anything we can do about it, or are we indeed victims? Are we simply and ineluctably the way we are, just as we might describe a horse or a dog as having a kind and obedient, or, alternatively, a wild and wilful temperament? In the western world we generally spend too little time trying to educate and explore our own consciousness, not its contents, not its knowledge, not the information it has at its disposal, but its quality and essence. 'Control my thoughts? Why should I?' one part of us, aided and abetted by certain strands of modern liberal thinking, asks. 'These are my thoughts, my needs, my wishes, my desires. Why shouldn't I feel them? Haven't I a right to be me? Isn't that what freedom means?' It's possible to spend one's whole life feeding and indulging the mind in such a manner. But what we are offering it in so doing is the very bait with which our consciousness is liable to be trapped. We ourselves will then become the most helpless of its victims.

At one level the mind is easily engaged and entertained; we have only to change the scene before it, read a book, switch on the television, meet up with a friend, go for a walk. Maybe that's what led T. S. Eliot to his damning line 'Distracted from distraction by distraction'.[25] This is harsh. When we have to bear frustration, injustice, and pain, even to hold a conversation may require a major effort and the task of moving our mind to think of something other than the sores to which it returns like the tongue of an animal to an itching wound requires both courage and persistence.

But there are other levels of mind, though recalcitrant and difficult to access without sustained self discipline. Yet their existence is sufficient to teach us that we need not be the victim of our habitual patterns of thought. We realise, sometimes only momentarily, that we have the possibility of choice and we glimpse a fresh vista of inner freedom. For the mind has more profound and purer layers, as the centre of the lake is deeper than its edges, and, as the water there is not static but moves with the currents of the streams which feed it, so that lake itself is only a part of the great flow of water, rising as evaporation, falling as rain, descending in rivers and waterfalls, passing through ponds and pools, gathering in great reservoirs and seas. Consciousness, mind in its true depth, is part of a current broader and more limitless than this. It is clearer, purer, freer and more luminous than we experience it in the swift and often jarring interactions of cramped and unreflective days.

There are critical opportunities when we become aware that we have a choice. These may be the most ordinary of moments, in the traffic queue or round the table. We realise, even in the very motion of responding, that it's not inevitable that we should become angry, that we could in fact have taken a step backwards and not simply reacted, that another avenue, one demanding greater self knowledge and discipline, had been, and always is, open before us. We could have been moved, not by the overpowering impulse to answer or strike back, but by the wisdom of that compassion which sees in every situation not only the self and its impetuosity, but also the other and his or her need for understanding and acceptance.

Equally, these moments of awareness may occur in the most challenging of circumstances, in which to overcome the natural response of fear and hopelessness requires extreme self-mastery and courage. Thus Viktor Frankl wrote, only months after his liberation from Auschwitz: 'The experiences of camp life show that man does have a choice of action. There were enough examples, often of a heroic nature, which proved that apathy could be overcome, irritability suppressed. Man can preserve a vestige of spiritual freedom, of independence of mind, even in such terrible conditions of psychic and physical stress.'[26]

'As a person's thoughts are, there he is', taught the Ba'al Shem Tov.[27] The disciple of his disciple, Rabbi Levi Yitzhak of Berdichev, reputedly once greeted the members of his community in the following manner after the morning prayers: 'Welcome back from the market,' he said to one, 'Welcome home from Lvov,' he said to another. 'What do you mean?' they replied. 'We've been here all the time.' 'But not your thoughts,' he allegedly responded.

Admittedly, Jewish teaching doesn't regard thought as equivalent to action. To think an act is not to have committed it. On the contrary, the person who experiences the desire to do something wrong but restrains himself from so doing is to be praised. Far from deserving condemnation for having performed the act in his mind, such a person should be respected because he has, in the words of the second-century sage Ben Zoma, 'overcome his inclination' and found the secret of true strength.[28] What matters in the realm of ethics is what we actually do.

But it can't be denied that our thoughts form the quality of our consciousness, the essence of who we are. 'A great general principle is equanimity,' opens the ethical will of the Ba'al Shem Tov, focussing us immediately on the task of controlling and directing our thoughts.[29] It should be a matter of indifference to us, he continues, whether we are praised or blamed, held in high regard or looked down upon as a fool. What is important is only that we should cleave to God and do what is compassionate and just. This higher purpose should humble us and make us immune to irrelevant evaluations. It's easier said than done.

We fail to control our moods and responses at our peril; the rewards of mastering them are great. For our mind is a doorway into that greater consciousness whose presence fills all being. In the words of the contemporary Jewish philosopher and mystic Arthur Green, 'Behind this veil of separate and often competitive and struggling individualism lies another reality, one in which all souls are One soul, totally open and present to one another as they come to know that the boundaries that separate them are but illusion.'[30]

This insight may be the secret behind acquiring the ability to 'bear free and patient thoughts'.

CHAPTER EIGHT

Grief

Safi

If there are no dogs in Heaven, then when
I die I want to go where they went.

Will Rogers [1]

Safi, our beloved family dog, passed peacefully away at the dignified age of fifteen. He used to sleep under the bed; every morning I miss the sight of his protruding nose. I miss his bark and the lick of his tongue, his constant companionship and his unconditional love. His death also brings, like every loss, the realisation that a part of my own life is over.

I don't think either Yiddish or Hebrew contain a special word for 'rabbi's dog'. The more's the pity, because Safi was the perfect role model for the job. He probably attended Synagogue more often than virtually any other dog who ever lived; he welcomed countless people at the door of the rabbi's house, slept under the table through hundreds of classes, listened in on innumerable confidential conversations and begged a shocking quantity of biscuits from *bnei mitzvah* pupils. He also did security duty at the synagogue and would gladly, had we allowed it, have been counted in the *minyan*, the prayer quorum of ten.

He acted as therapist to the rabbi on innumerable occasions, understanding the wisdom of silence and the effect of a good lick or a long walk. He welcomed each of our children home from hospital; they'd never, until he died, known life without him. He'd been at the heart of our family since the day, almost fifteen years earlier, when Sandra, a congregant whose son found him lost in the street, brought him to us. We hadn't wanted a boy dog and we didn't want a black dog. But in the event it was the dog who made the decisions; it took him less than a minute to penetrate our hearts. I bless Sandra's memory for her kindness and recall her telling me, 'You'll have to take responsibility for that dog for the rest of his life.' It wasn't hard.

Of course, everyone knows that dogs don't live as long as people. For a decade I'd secretly been counting the years. Until Safi was eight he was as swift as the squirrels, to their occasional detriment. Then he began to slow down. When he was eleven, he started to suffer from arthritis. Every year when we returned from our summer holiday in Scotland I would worry that this was Safi's last. But, albeit with a limp, he walked, swam and even ran through several more summers with the help of pills, tonics and unlimited affection. 'It's the love that's keeping him going,' said a friend as she watched him struggle down the stairs. But sadly there comes a point when one wonders whether that love is becoming selfish.

We knew eighteen months ago that this time was not far off. When he had cancer, they told us at the animal hospital that if we were lucky Safi would have one more good year. He did. But I had to carry him up and down the stairs, which, of course, I was glad to do. Still, he enjoyed his food, short walks, our company, and bossing around the new puppy we had acquired on veterinary advice, to cheer his, and our own, spirits. But it became obvious that his limbs were hurting badly; medication could no longer reduce the pain. We could see how hard he found it even to lie down. Then one night he fell into our garden pond, where fortunately I found him moments later. The thought of him slowly drowning there unable to clamber out or to summon us to his aid was too much to contemplate. Sorrowfully and unwillingly, the family agreed that the time had come when, to the best of our understanding, Safi was deriving little joy from life and suffering a great deal. Our wonderful vet Geoffrey helped him gently to his place in the world beyond.

People had often asked me what to do when their pet died. Now it was our turn. We took Safi for a last meander, letting him nose around the trees outside the house, then the children gave him little bits of favourite food. We prayed with him before he died, because all of us belong to the totality of life, embraced by the one God. Afterwards we came home and looked at photographs. We gave a donation to guide dogs in Israel, in his memory.

The house felt empty. Safi's brush lay in the bathroom for a long time. We think of him whenever we walk past his favourite haunts, like the place along the brook where he loved to swing from the rope above the water, whining like a maniac and oblivious to the world.

Yes – there are millions of incomparably worse things happening all around us, and none of us has the right to be selfish.

But love begins at home, and if we don't love the members of our own household, including the animals for which we are responsible, then we're unlikely to bring much love into the wider world either. And dogs bring a great deal of love and affection with them. In fact, if one punctuates *kelev*, the Hebrew word for dog, a little differently it reads as *ke-lev*, which means 'like the heart'.

Dying

Do not cast us off in our old age;
Do not forsake us with the ebbing of our strength.[2]

The elderly woman was clearly dying; only her face showed above the covers. It was several days since she'd been able to get out of bed. By now even talking was an effort and her words were slurred, so I sat by the bed and simply held her hand. Suddenly she lifted her head and shoulders off the pillows and called out distinctly, 'I need my suitcases!' Her brother came in, said in a kind but firm manner, 'You're not going anywhere,' and reassured himself that she was comfortable before leaving the room. I experienced the moment as a lost opportunity. What vision of imminent departure had spurred that sick and suffering lady to make such a valiant effort? Why did none of us even ask her?

It's impossible that there shouldn't sometimes be missed openings in the face of death. One reason is that, however strong the bond or deep the love, however fierce the desire to accompany a beloved relative to the very end, the paths of the living and the dying must inevitably part. Their emotional and spiritual journeys are not the same. However much they share the worry, sorrow, incomprehension, gratitude and love and the relief of days of reprieve, different preoccupations are almost bound to intervene and begin to separate them long before death.

Close relatives, especially partners, who share the same home, the same bed and the daily planning of their time, know that they are going to have to live on in their loneliness. They may experience bewilderment, frustration, guilt, but above all immense sadness as the reality of irretrievable loss sometimes creeps, sometimes rushes ever nearer. But they also have to entertain realities which the person they love is not going to have to experience. What will it feel like to continue alone? How will they manage the children? Will they earn enough money? To whom, if anyone, will they now be able to turn? I remember a conversation with a man who described to me afterwards how he would sit in the living

198

room on his own at night after spending all day with his dying wife at the hospital, deliberately imagining to himself that it was all over, so that he could prepare himself for the loneliness to come.

The person who is dying is drawn inescapably into the whirlpool of loss. He or she may well have to confront fear, anger and regret, as well as anguish and sheer sorrow. Yet not everything which he or she faces will necessarily be exclusively painful. I've witnessed the most heartfelt and courageous expressions of love and gratitude. If there's time and if the suffering caused by the illness is not utterly overwhelming, there may emerge another phenomenon as well. There may be something nascent in a dying person, an intuitive awareness of the call to make inner preparations the nature of which may remain indistinct but which are nevertheless experienced as profoundly engaging. There is a different quality of light on the horizon of consciousness; the soul is secretly preoccupied with something new. Even in dying there may be a kind of discovery.

In all sorts of ways the family may call out 'Come back!' 'Eat something,' says the sick man's daughter, but today the spoon hovers rejected outside the closed lips. Relatives compare notes: 'Yesterday he managed a whole bowl of soup in the afternoon and a biscuit soaked in tea before he slept. But today he's scarcely swallowed a thing. Go on, you try; he always listens to you. Tell him he's got to keep up his strength.' Every painful, pitiful endeavour is motivated by love, perhaps by fear and frustration as well. Love is strong; it has the power to draw us through the valley of the shadow of death. But when what is present is no longer only the shadow, there are ways in which even love is compelled to yield.

In the Talmudic account of the death of Rabbi Judah the Prince, his maidservant climbs onto the roof and says: 'Those on high want Rabbi [Judah] and those below want him. May it be God's will that those below prove stronger than those on high.' But when she realises how much he must be suffering she changes her prayer, saying, 'May it be God's will that those on high prove stronger'. Still his colleagues continue to pray, so she takes a pitcher and throws it down from the roof. It smashes, shocking the rabbis into silence, and Rabbi Judah is able to die.[3]

At some point the living have to let go. But what might this letting go be like for the person who is about to die? On top of every other kind of pain, he or she may well experience guilt. People sometimes feel they're letting their family down. If they have young children, they may be tormented by the thought that they're abandoning them and that their surviving partner will now have to raise them all alone. If their own parents are still alive, they may worry that they are bringing upon them a terrible and unnatural grief. Rationally, they may know that their illness is a tragedy and that they are in no way to blame. Yet at the same time there may be a surreptitious sense of failure. Family and friends have encouraged them to fight and they have done so with tenacity and courage through calm hours and through cruel. But the illness has proved implacable.

A young man once said to me: 'If only I'd fought harder, if only I'd thought more positive thoughts, I'd have beaten this thing.' It was heart-rending to hear that valiant and generous man utter those words but, however much we tried, neither I nor others could free him from such feelings. Some struggles can't be won at this level because they are not in the end that kind of battle. They are part of a journey determined by causes greater than our own intentions and we have no choice but to follow. I tried to convince this young father, still in his thirties, that his courage, calm and constant proactive love and concern for others were in fact a great triumph. But he only half heard me. I fear that what he felt was: 'So what, if death's going to have the last word?'

Yet even through such pain, another voice can sometimes be intuited. Somewhere within the soul it speaks about wholeness and peace, about meeting long dead loved-ones again, and about the onward journey. It's a voice which is hard to heed because feelings of attachment to this world tend to obscure it. But I've heard enough people allude to it to believe that what it says is 'Prepare for me'.

What kind of preparations are entailed? They are not only those suggested by the kind friend who wisely and sensitively reminds the dying person to speak to the lawyer and make sure that his or her affairs are in order; not only even those which involve the saying of farewells, the sharing of love and gratitude and the endeavour to sort out the entangled threads of difficult relationships and lay unresolved differences to rest. Nor again are they exclusively the preparations suggested by the liturgy of confession: 'God, I know that my life and death are in your hands. May it be your will to heal me with a perfect healing but if it has been determined by you that death is my portion, I accept it from your hands with love. May my death be an atonement for all my sins.'[4] Yet all these levels of preparation are of inestimable value and require valiance and magnanimity.

Who, then, is the inner speaker whose voice says, 'Prepare for me'? I don't think it's some image of death incarnate with long, bony fingers, though no doubt such apparitions haunt our moments of fear. But in this case, I believe, the speaker is life, life from depths and dimensions which may previously have been unknown. Such life may speak with a voice, even a music, which we might never have heard before.

I remember talking to a lady who told me that she had been advised to read only positively-focussed books and to think only positive thoughts. One might have imagined that this would have encouraged her, which, to a degree, it did. But what she also communicated to me was the sense that these directives were chaining her spirit down and alienating her from an internal process which she had to be allowed to nourish. A dialogue was taking place within her between life and her own soul. She couldn't have articulated its contents, but she had to be permitted to pay heed to and foster it nonetheless, even if, or precisely because, it included, and transcended, her own dying.

I recall listening to a man talking about his dreams a week or so before he died. There was a shore beyond which lay alluring islands where he longed to travel. The sands there were beautiful and the light fell on them appealingly. Perhaps it was the recollection of his words which made me think that it was not merely confusion which made that dying woman raise herself from her pillows and call out loudly for her suitcases.

Maybe part of what pertains to dying is the disengagement of the ties of the spirit from the bonds of the heart. It's a journey which may offer, beyond the utter renunciation it entails, a strange and unimaginable fulfilment.

A person has to be allowed to prepare.

The Table

The lady had died an hour ago and I was called to the hospital room. My attention was immediately drawn to the lighted candle on the little bedside table by her head. Next to it were just three other items, a book of Psalms, a ring and a box for sharps – the used capsules, needles and other items necessary in caring for the sick. Since then I've often thought about the contents of that table. For those few modest objects encompassed the whole of human life, the ring for love, the psalms for faith, the sharps for our mortality and the candle for the spirit.

There's no end to what separates us; we're summoned all the time to perpetuate divisions. We argue about anything and kill for nothing. But love, faith, mortality and spirit, these are common to us all. If there is such a thing as shared humanity it's here that we must seek it. A ring, a flame, a book and a box full of sharps, these are ordinary, everyday things; but in our struggle against prejudice and conflict they are our most elementary, and essential, teachers.

I remember the night when my grandfather died. Someone showed me his ring; it looked desolate, parted from his finger. When my grandmother later chose to wear it next to her own, the proximity of those two identical plain gold bands seemed only to heighten their aloneness.

My grandparents became engaged before the First World War. But my grandfather enlisted and was sent to serve as a military chaplain at Verdun. They were finally married on *Lag Be'Omer* in May 1917, when, despairing of waiting for the easy victory the Germans had long been promised by their leaders, my grandfather obtained the briefest of furloughs. Throughout those four terrible years of war, and through the difficult months afterwards when they were separated by the new borders between Germany and Poland, they wrote to each other every single day. The Nazis destroyed the entire correspondence; this is the only one of all their material losses which I ever heard my grandparents lament.

I doubt if that wedding ring had ever previously been removed from my grandfather's finger except once, after *Kristallnacht* in 1938, when he was taken to Dachau and interned. It was my grandmother, who, through her courage and devotion, obtained his release and saved the lives of the family. I attribute that, too, to the power of the love represented by those rings.

There are other objects which similarly encapsulate the blessings, and responsibilities, of enduring love. I sometimes ask the teenagers I teach if they have any possessions of great sentimental value. A girl mentions a broach given to her by her grandmother, who received it from her own mother when she was little. Another says she's been promised her great-aunt's Sabbath candlesticks when she has a family of her own. I hear from a woman about to get married how a necklace is taken out of a dust covered container and placed into her hands: 'My late wife wore this. I kept it for the day when my son would bring home his bride.' It's the tenacity of love which makes these objects so precious.

Next to the ring was a box for sharps, an essential piece of equipment to ensure the safe disposal of the needles through which the painkillers and other medications necessary to the comfort of a very sick person are administered. Such boxes, and the pills and syringes which surround those fortunate enough to be well cared for when they die, remind us that we have nothing so deeply in common as our frailty and mortality. Having served on the chaplaincy of a hospice where those of all faiths and none are welcomed equally, I've seen many times how dying makes our differences secondary and unites us all in a single bond of compassion. Who is not in need of tenderness and the gifts of patience and acceptance when he or she is dying?

I've witnessed great gentleness. We were travelling home from America with Mossy who was just ten months old. The steward on the night flight told us he had a child of the same age and offered to soothe our baby by rubbing his feet. I can still picture that tall man with his large hands reaching down to take off our son's socks and carefully massage the soles of his feet. After that, Mossy slept, far better than his parents, throughout the night.

I've listened to nurses speaking to the dying: 'Mr. Johnson, I just want to tell you what we're doing. We're going to give you a small injection in your right arm to help relieve the pain. It won't hurt; you might feel a pin prick but that's all. Then we're going to lift your head to smooth the pillow and make sure that you're comfortable. Is that all right? We're so sorry to have to disturb you.' The patient seemed to be in a coma, but maybe he could still hear, and anyway, human dignity demands that a person be informed about what's being done to him, especially when he's completely at the mercy of others. Gently the nurses raised the man's head and shoulders and adjusted the pillows. At that moment I believe everyone in the room experienced a similar feeling; our fear of dying was momentarily assuaged in the presence of such compassionate competence.

Yet there also exist people who delight in devising the means to kill with as much pain as possible. Some who bear the name of human seem to rejoice in murder, cheering when a bus is blown to pieces or when an entire family dies in a cafe. Others kill anonymously, from the air, as if the inability to see them makes the victims less disfigured and the perpetrators less responsible. Cruelty is age old. One summer we visited Chillingham Castle near the Scottish border. The dungeon contained a display of mediaeval instruments of torture. When we came out, Mossy, who'd turned green, commented that he'd known for a long time that people killed each other, but he couldn't understand why they would want to squander so much ingenuity in devising such cunning methods to inflict pain.

Death, meanwhile, awaits us all. One would have thought it would teach us compassion. The prophet Isaiah, angry with the empty fasting with which the people around him deluded themselves that they were doing something worthwhile on the Day of Atonement, enjoined them to feed the hungry, clothe the naked and 'not hide yourselves from your own flesh'.[5] Surely he should have said to them: 'Don't hide from the flesh of your fellow human beings'? But just that is his point: your flesh and their flesh, your humanity and their humanity, are the same. We are one in our need for compassion.

Between the ring and the box was a small book of Psalms. I still remember when my grandfather first taught me about the Psalms: 'The whole of life is here,' he told me. 'Pain, anguish, anger, gratitude and joy, the entirety of human experience.' Years later I inherited his best loved copy which I treasure to this day.

There isn't a person who, over the course of a lifetime, doesn't have cause to cry out to God. 'The night the crisis came,' the boy's father told me months later, 'I sat by the bed and said the first words of the *Shema* over and over again. There was nothing else I could do; I held onto the words like a lifeline.' His son had meningitis. In the morning he was better.

For some people the cry is directed consciously and explicitly to God. Some of us cry out to whom we know not, to the world, to the universal life which fills heaven and earth, to the human heart. Sometimes we cry out simply because we have to, driven by the instinctive need to give the spirit words, and we don't know or even consciously care on what, if anything, our anger, hope or loneliness may find a hold and cling.

A woman waiting for chemotherapy asked me, 'Can we say a Psalm together?' As we read, I saw how her perspective was transformed and her eyes relaxed, as if she was seeing a different world: 'Yes,' she said, 'the hills, the trees; I have my favourite tree at the back of the garden. I picture all that beauty to myself and I feel better.'

'It's an outrage,' said another woman after her husband had died in his forties following ten years of struggle with a debilitating illness. 'I refuse to make peace; I will never be reconciled.' Then I thought of the words of the Psalm, 'I am dumb, I do not open my mouth because it is you who did it. Remove your stroke from me; I am consumed by the blow of your hand.'⁶

Everyone needs a language for the spirit. There are many liturgies, drawing on Gospel and Qur'an, on poetry and stories, photographs and memories. But the Psalms and Jewish prayers are my language and the language of my ancestors. Like a river bearing water from its source, those prayers carry the spirituality of an entire people, while at the same time their melodies are as immediate as the smells of a spring evening and the colours of the autumn leaves. They fill the soul as the tide floods the beach, and, like the tiny creatures delivered from the prisons of their rock-pools, we are redeemed and borne away to join a greater world.

Sometimes we call out for the living waters and think that the tide will never come. At other times we forget to call, until the memory of how a greater life once carried us returns to us in our dreams.

The flame of the candle is the life of the spirit. The light burnt peacefully on that small table; the place where a person dies may be filled for many hours afterwards by a deep and unique tranquillity. But the flame also looked frail, as if in testament to the power of death and the shock of its arrival.

There are candles for all ages and stages of life. According to Talmudic legend, a flame illumines the womb; by its light the unborn child can see the entire world and is taught the whole Torah.[7] Candles are often lit at a circumcision, a memorial from the days of the Roman persecutions when the performance of this rite was forbidden. Children count the birthday candles on their cake and make a secret wish when they blow them out. The traditional greeting when writing a letter to a scholar is *Neiro Yair*, may his light shine. When a person dies, a candle is placed by his head, and each year on the *Yahrzeit*, the anniversary of the day of the death, a candle is lit. My-mother-in-law was once staying with us when she had *Yahrzeit* for her own mother. Late that evening I went to sit next to the light and I watched the small flame leap and flicker while the shadows danced across the dark room and my mother-in-law talked of her memories.

The mystics refer to the *Or Haganuz*, the hidden light, with which God first dispelled the darkness and which originally illumined all the earth until, to protect it from the profanity of sin, God concealed it. Each individual existence may be considered a fragment of that light, separated and exiled from its source, to which it testifies in life and to where in death it returns.

A ring, a book, a candle and a box of sharps, four everyday items; I can still see them there on that small bedside table. Such ordinary things as these form the map of our humanity and set the compass of our vision.

My Father

My father died in April.

'He's with Safi,' said Kadya. Then, remembering how the poor dog had been afflicted with terrible arthritis and how my father had struggled in his last months to manage even the short distance from one room to the next, until finally even that became too much for him, she added, 'And where they are now they'll both be able to walk properly again.'

My father died in springtime, in the middle of the night. We all realised some hours before it happened that this would be the last day of his life. The wonderful nurse, who had a special intuition for the needs and feelings of dying people, said he thought that it would happen between four and five in the morning. But, after my father's long struggles, the end came swiftly; he took only two or three more laboured breaths and was gone. Isca, who had cared for him wonderfully through all the years of his illness, was with him. Some hours later I curled up on the floor beneath the bed where he lay dead and thought about him and, in spite of myself, heard the birds singing as the morning grew bright. Their music seemed especially beautiful to me. At once I felt guilty that I should be able to enjoy those simple, cheerful sounds of dawn when he was dead. My father hadn't wanted to die; he fought to live, he stretched out his hands to us to raise him up, he begged us to help him even when he had no more strength to stand or even sit. He longed for just one more view of the garden he loved. Now I was alive and he was not and still the birds continued to sing and the sound of it was beautiful, and I appreciated it and was conscious that I was appreciating it and was glad to be alive and my father, who had always led the way, held my hand, pulled me on my bike, taken me to university, given me lifts to work, wasn't there any more to enjoy it. Yet at the same time I also knew that he would have been happy about that very bird song and that he had wanted his children to love and make the most of life. This was his gift to us. 'Never waste your opportunities,' he used to say, 'Only you can take them.' But at that half lit moment the proximity between life and death was too great.

In the same places where I encounter my father's presence, I meet his absence also.

My tool box sits neglected on my study floor; I'd meant to put up more shelves for the piles of books which lay untidily on their sides. In the flat in Jerusalem where the family lived for over sixty years, my aunts faithfully kept my father's tools; once when I was visiting I even used his pliers to make a necklace of copper stars for a friend and they told me with great pride that those were my father's things. My father was their hero; he was their success story. He was the member of the family who, after they'd fled Germany and lost everything, managed, through seven assiduous years at night school, to gain an education and make good. That flat in Jerusalem has been disbanded now; my father and his two remaining sisters went to their graves within a single year.

My father taught me everything I know about sawing, drilling, painting, soldering and repairing. I never pick up a hammer or a saw without thinking of his rules, 'Never buy cheap tools; it isn't worth it'; 'Always treat tools with respect and never leave them lying on their working face'. The unused planks of timber still lean against the wall of my study; my father would have advised me what to do. The brackets needed to be fixed to a plasterboard wall with a cavity behind it: how does one make a proper job of that?

Sometimes in the morning when I awake I feel as if my father has been calling to me from another world. For a moment images of him stick behind my eyes. I can't remember what he said, but I know that I've visited a world, or that in my sleep a realm has been revealed, from which he's talking to me. Even as the alarmclock calls me back into the bright light and obligations of the day I hear his fading speech. I don't know what my father's saying, or whether the domain from which he speaks is simply an inner country of the heart or soul and has no objective existence anywhere, or if what clings to me before the daylight wipes it from my consciousness is the shadow or refracted image of a world which is more real and more enduring than the one which we who call ourselves the living currently inhabit day by day. I remember what it was like to be with my father in the morning. I remember how when I was seven or eight I used to bounce out of bed as soon as I heard him in the bathroom and as he shaved I'd put on my socks, making sure the tops were stretched and level and neatly folded over to show the colours of my school. I loved those moments with my father, watching him at his shaving.

I think of my father in all the melodies of the synagogue and the pages of the prayer book. My father loved his Jewish heritage; from childhood he knew all the words and all the songs by heart. When my brother and I were small he used to show us his old *machzorim*, the prayer books for the festivals, and explain to us how to calculate the dates on which they were printed from the enlarged Hebrew letters in the dedicatory quotation on the bottom of the front page. I couldn't credit it when he said to us a few years ago that those old books, which followed different, lengthier and more complicated rites, were dated and not worth preserving any longer. 'No!' I objected. How could they possibly not be kept! Maybe he was in some way referring to himself, to some feeling that the melodies of his childhood weren't valued any more. I love those books, I would never ever for a single moment willingly agree to part with any one of them. I think of my father whenever I see them, whenever we sing the opening phrase from any of the special melodies of the year. We're bound together in that music. Last New Year's Eve as my mother, my brother and I helped my father through the front door and out onto the porch after the festive meal, we all sung together in the special modality of the High Holidays. When my father was very ill we sung to him too; invariably after the first words he would pick up the tune and take over. When he was very, very ill and could no longer join in with us, we sung to him nevertheless, hoping, believing that he could still hear us from the world far within his consciousness which he inhabited now. One says of the departed, 'May his soul be bound up in the bond of life'; the words and melodies of the prayer book are part of those bonds of life in which my father's soul is bound.

Some of my best moments on earth were when we laughed together. The fact that he was highly skilled in all things mechanical didn't mean that nothing ever went wrong. I remember when he was boiling beetroot in the pressure cooker and the safety valve flew off; a scarlet fountain shot up to the ceiling and dripped back down amidst the steam into gathering pools of bright red juice. We laughed and laughed. Once we were cleaning the soak-away drain in the garage drive and the only way to reach the stinking sludge at the bottom was to siphon off the murky liquid on top. So we inserted a hose pipe and rolled it down the slope to the bottom of the drive, where, once the suction process had begun, gravity would carry the foul water. But someone had to get the pressure going, so my father turned to me and said: 'Who's going to suck on that hose, you or me?' And once, when we were moving bookshelves down the stairs and at a critical corner a very heavy unit got stuck and refused to budge, we simply put it down and laughed.

My father was sparing with unsolicited advice; perhaps that's why I remember so clearly what he did have to say. Once, when I was fifteen or sixteen, he came up to my room at night and asked me whether I still said the *Shema* meditation before I went to sleep. I was careless about it at the time and his question was well placed. But I have never been negligent since. One night he reminded me, perhaps in order to underline why he and my mother had made such a special effort to give me a good education, that everything can be taken from a person except the contents of their mind. I've never forgotten that lesson either.

In the last weeks of his illness my father called out many times. Most often he wanted Isca, but he also asked frequently for his two sisters Hella and Eva. Eva died in 1943, a young girl, probably from the consequences of diphtheria. Hella died only six weeks before my father. His third sister Steffi, who was several years younger than the others, died last summer, three of the four siblings passing away within a single year. The sisters lie close to one another on the Mount of Olives, overlooking the walls of Jerusalem's Old City.

My father never spoke to us about dying. He was in any case not a person who readily expressed his feelings. But of dying he said not a word. Only, twice while I was with him he awoke from his uneasy sleep with a sudden start and said the words of the daily *Amidah* prayer, familiar to him since childhood, 'God keeps faith with those who sleep in the dust', before lying back down exhausted. What can one say? My father now lies in that ubiquitous dust. God, we trust, has indeed kept faith with him. God, of course, does it on an infinitely greater scale, but Isca, my brother and I, we three too, are all keeping faith in our hearts.

Grief

I had only said, 'It made me think of you when we saw those beautiful rivers; I stood there and imagined how you used to go fishing with your dad.' I hadn't meant to make him cry. But I must have taken his mind right back to the times when his father would go out with him across the Mersey down to the lake in North Wales where they spent those tranquil days they had both so often described to me. I don't remember for sure but I suppose this must have been after the onset of his illness, when his movement was already impaired and his father was once again his mainstay. 'The shadows of the willows in the water, the peace,' he said to me, adding quickly, 'I would always put any fish I caught straight back into the water.'

He was crying while in his typical, self-deprecating way he played a mock violin with his hands and laughed at himself for those tears. I don't know whether his sorrow was for his father who had died several years before, or if it was for the whole vanished world that he was weeping; the lake, the beauty, his own lost mobility, his parents, an existence to which the only point of re-entry was memory and its frequent accompaniment, grief.

The memorial chamber to the Holocaust in the Liebeskind Museum in Berlin is remarkable. Only a few people are allowed to enter at any one time. As I remember it, the space inside is almost entirely dark; the walls present no obvious geometrical shape, the roof is extremely high and the floor has been sunk so that one stands beneath the threshold of normal life which, with the closing of the door, becomes absolutely inaccessible. One can just make out a feeble source of light far above, but the smooth walls offer no hope of any grip and there can be no thought of scaling them. Only, in one corner a ladder has been fixed. But a moment's examination shows that the lowest step is high above the grasp of the tallest person, or even of a person standing on someone else's shoulders. That ladder expresses the delusory nature of hope. From this place there can be no escape. From now on, life outside persists in memory only.

Grief is nothing like that. Its prison walls are made of tremulous air. Everything in the outside world can be seen and touched; the shops, the street, the room, the mug of tea, the photographs, they are all right there, exactly as they were before. But a strange, invisible layer clings to the heart and wraps itself around the mind. Though not impermeable, this curtain alters whatever passes through it; inside is a different atmospheric pressure. Sounds echo and clang. The most ordinary physical sensations feel strange. One stands up and tries to walk; it is as if gravity itself has become unreliable. Time doesn't function in the way it used to do. The semi-silent humming of the air is filled with the vibrations of a tremendous shock; the ordinary daylight makes no sense, this simply cannot be. Inside the invisible membrane the waves of sight and sound founder in slow motion. But the hours remain implacable and the calendar irreversible; the world refuses to be tugged back to where it ought to be. *Baruch dayyan emet*, reads the traditional formula with which we receive our grief, 'Blessed be the true judge'. What it really means is, 'What choice do we have? What else can we do except acknowledge that what is, is?'

I've kept company innumerable times with people who are grieving and quietly respect the inadequacy of words. Somewhere between the well intentioned speaker and the bewildered, mourning heart their flight so often goes astray and they fall to the floor like little dying birds. But affection and compassion are adept at crossing silence and are always understood.

Three or four times in my life I've been overtaken by unexpected and overwhelming grief, pain and sorrow quite disproportionate to the events which immediately provoked them, yet the whole of my life tumbled into them nevertheless. Endings recall grief, the close of a phase of time, the collapse of a relationship, and somewhere behind it all the resurgent pain of a basic, primitive loss, the sore of something spliced away which will never entirely heal, a separation set in the deep hinterland of my life when my mother died when I was small. It seemed as if she was a journey away, down which the night train had taken me headlong and perforce, about which there was neither choice nor the possibility of return. That is why I am suspicious of any parting, and anxious before all goodbyes.

Grief

The instinctive knowledge that the loss is irreversible, that what we love so much is entirely irretrievable, clings to the pain of grief pushing apart the wounded edges of the heart. Scenes of all kinds surrounded me, for which I desperately yearned. Here was the sea, the late afternoon sunshine, the children running from the water out onto the sand and back again into the waves. Here was my mother, with my grandparents, that last winter when we were all together in the snow, in that cold hotel where they came into my room and taught me to say my prayers in bed at night. Here were the trees on a misty English autumn morning. The spectacle changed, but the longing I felt to be there and not here, not here, definitely not here where everything was irrevocably gone – that pain remained the same.

Children must feel hopeless like this when the classroom swallows up the summer and a year is as long as forever. All our life long the child in us continues to rebel and beat against the walls. But they are not susceptible to will power or to force; they are made of time and time, in this dimension, is inflexible. It will never come again; it's gone for evermore. The old Lear could not have put it with a more devastating simplicity as he fruitlessly watched the dead Cordelia's lips for signs of the intake of breath:

> No, no, no life!
> Why should a dog, a horse, a rat, have life,
> And thou no breath at all? Thou'lt come no more,
> Never, never, never, never, never! [8]

Every never is an entire world, and every life has many.

I feel for those whose sorrows are not passing, the woman whose husband has died far too young, the mother whose child has been killed. In their hearts their loved ones sit at the table and talk, walk across the traverse of the field, call out 'Here I am'. But they aren't there; they never ever shall be.

Like Daggers in the Heart

'Tell me, because you must know lots of people who're grieving like us, will life ever become bearable again?'

The view through the window onto the gay array of daffodils belies the absurdity of grief. The loss of their daughter has pitched this family from heaven into hell in a moment. The car hit her and she was killed instantly. There are no explanations; it was one of those accidents which can only be attributed to the fact that we live in a world in which automobiles exist.

The house is as beautiful as it always was. The sunshine falls brightly through the big windows onto the sofas and rugs. Only, she's dead; she won't be coming home, she won't walk through the door and, flinging her jacket across the bannisters, call out 'Hello, mum, it's me'.

'My heart feels as if it's being stabbed by twisted knives,' says her mother. 'I don't want to go on living. Every hour is a separate eternity, let alone an entire day. I can't bear being here when my child is dead. The future is desolate; the thought of it is intolerable. Everyone else seems to be able to find some way to distract themselves, but not me. I can't bear it.' She raised her hands to hide her face and sobbed.

Any theology which fails to listen to this cry of pain, just listen, without rebuff, without avoidance, without deflection, without explanations, is an insult to the human heart.

'She was brilliant. She was never any trouble to us. She'd always done so well; she flew through all her exams and now she was on the threshold of her dreams. She wanted to travel, she wanted to work; above all she wanted to help other people. She was so good to us; she was more like a friend than a child. Why did she have to die? Why did she have to be in just that place at just that time? Why did it have to be her?'

The words cease and the silence resumes, the same silence which has absorbed the sorrow of millions and millions of mothers.

When a child dies, the loss lies not only behind the family but in front of them, waiting at every turn of the page on the calendar, at every festival, on the date which would have been his birthday and at the marking of each new stage of life; when all the other children are trying on their uniforms for school, when her friends are busy applying to university, when everyone else's sons and daughters are getting married, when grandchildren ought to have been born. As Jacob said of Joseph, presumed dead: 'I shall go down to the grave in mourning for my son'.[9] When old age comes and parents need support, their child isn't there. The death of a child not only tears apart the present, it rips up the future.

Meanwhile ordinary life goes on. Time proceeds as time always has. The people who gathered round when the tragedy occurred go back to their everyday lives. The circles around their kitchen tables are intact, except for those who've also crossed into this parallel world which travels on the same buses, shops in the same supermarkets, sits in the same cafes, but hurts unremittingly.

'It's so awful. The house feels so empty. She used to bring all her friends here, she was so popular, they'd arrange these wonderful parties. We used to read the same books. Even if she was away travelling we'd phone each other virtually every day.'

It's possible that those who lose their children in a war or a national disaster are sometimes helped by the existence of a context; the death carries the aura of sacrifice. Or at least there's an address for anger, the government, the enemy, the terrorists. For those whose children die in a freak accident, as a result of negligence or someone's stupidity or from an inexplicable illness there may only be the incomprehensibility, the absurdity of it all. A child's suicide brings an even greater burden of helplessness and torment. Entering the room which used to be his, daring to open the cupboard and sort through his clothes, how can anyone bear it? The mother sits on the carpet and weeps: Throw everything in a black plastic bag, or go out quickly and shut the door; how can anybody deal with this? If only that moment had never happened. If only it hadn't been allowed to exist. If only it would prove to be some fiction, a nightmare from which it would be possible to awake. But there's no point entertaining such thoughts; they merely yield more pain and even God is powerless to repeal time.

'Tell me, because you must see a lot of people like us, will life ever be meaningful again?'

I'm reluctant to respond to that question even though my answer is a tentative 'yes'. It's all too soon for them and I worry lest what I say should prove the cause of even greater hurt. What if they should feel, 'But we could never do that?'

I've met people whose lives, after the death of a child, have a powerful sense of purpose. In every case that direction is itself an expression of grief, at once impelled by it and a means of changing its focus. A new narrative emerges out of this wretched, unchosen transformation of their existence. Faced with the cruel pointlessness of death, people seek ways to impart meaning. Their loss becomes the impetus to something new. My friend from Holon has joined with other bereaved Israeli and Palestinian parents and works tirelessly for peace. My friend who lives in the next suburb has created a charity to help disabled children enjoy a sport her daughter used to love. But for neither of them, nor for any of the countless others, does the pain go away. It changes, it may at times be less intense, but it never entirely departs.

Is life ever bearable again? Yes, probably it will be, though not all of the time. For time doesn't really bring healing; that's not the whole of the truth. Time changes grief, but the loss remains, implacable, and the life of the mourners is irrevocably transformed.

The sun shines on the daffodils in the garden as if nothing had happened. The mother weeps. Hope might as well be a million miles away. How much pain, wretched, unavoidable pain, lies in the pathway ahead.

Then All Judgments are Made Sweet

> *... The world was created by the word of God. His word is the very essence of the world. It is just that humans use the world in a negative manner, and thereby destroy the world ... When someone employs the world for good purposes – for Torah and service – the world itself helps him ...* [10]

I deeply admire those people who take their fortunes with courage and good grace and struggle to turn suffering into acceptance, even love. They are our greatest teachers.

I first met Miss W. when I was a teenager in the voluntary service programme at school. She lived in a house in Kilburn which had been converted into six flats, all occupied by elderly ladies in various states of ill health. At first I used to be afraid of her. She'd ask me about the woman who lived in the flat next door whom she couldn't stand and I'd have to pretend that I hadn't been to see her, wasn't going to see her and would never have anything to do with her for the rest of her life. She was always feeling persecuted. She made wonderful cakes and biscuits, but when she offered them to me she'd remark that they'd probably been poisoned; I could never tell if she was trying to be funny, but her tone was far from humorous. 'Go on,' she would say, 'You eat them first.' She was in fact an excellent baker and the offerings were delicious. 'The very best butter,' she would say, and the thought of it would lead her away from the miserable present and off into the Gloucestershire farmland of her childhood, how she would hide in the wild grass to play truant from school, how the schoolmaster came to tell her parents that her brother was gifted, how he went away to Canada and they'd scarcely heard from him since, how she too got itchy feet and came to London. She was the cook at a fire station in the war. 'There wasn't anything substantial in those rations, but I'd always manage to turn out something for the men,' she'd say, and I'm sure she did. Over the years the sharp remarks and the bitter undertone disappeared. She moved to new lodgings and found her equanimity; only the memories and the wisdom remained. I used to love to go and see her then. 'Put nothing first,' she would say, 'Because everything comes first.' 'I know all there is to know about religion' she would tell me, and in a way she did, because she knew the part which no amount of formal learning can access.

I think of my gentle friend in Israel, a poet and artist, whose son was killed by a bomb. Alongside other Israeli and Palestinian parents who've lost a child in the relentless violence of the Middle East, he devotes his life to working for reconciliation. 'You have to reclaim the story,' he told me as we sat together in a cafe in Jerusalem, referring to the book *Retelling Violent Death* whose author he had recently met.[11] He didn't explain further, but I think what he meant was that those who suffer like him must try not to let the manner of their loved one's death entirely dictate how they're to be remembered. Memory must also focus on the life and gifts of the person. Otherwise the family becomes possessed by the circumstances of the death and ever more relentlessly trapped in the endless recapitulation of the trauma. How then can one possibly live a loving and worthwhile life? Yet that's exactly what my friend is doing. I've been with him in many situations; I've witnessed the way he speaks to people, his constant kindness even to strangers in the street.

I think, too, of the family and friends of Miriam Hyman, who was killed in the London bombings in July 2005. 'Miriam brings out the best in people,' wrote her sister Esther, 'I use the present tense because she is continuing to bring out the best in people,' even after she was killed. One of her friends wrote of 'her generosity, humility and kindness', before describing how only a few days earlier she had met Miriam at 4.30 in the morning at Primrose Hill to witness the dawn as it spread across the sleeping city. We must 'keep her name alive and use it to make someone else's world better – something Miriam would always do', testified another friend, adding that Miriam had been 'the person who made me see clearly'.[12]

Miriam was an artist who brought together her gifts for making friendship and creating beauty by giving paintings to the people she loved. Her family established a trust in her memory to support a charity which trains doctors to restore sight to the blind. They felt that the best way to perpetuate her values was to give others the chance to appreciate the colour and beauty she had so much enjoyed.

Almost a year after the tragedy I sat in the garden with Miriam's parents and we spoke about the approaching memorial service. 'There's a kind of acceptance which is beyond understanding,' said her mother. 'We can't comprehend suffering; but we can find acceptance. I believe that beyond everything lies a great reservoir of compassion.'

According to Jewish teaching, when bad things happen we must try to accept what has occurred. Traditionally, such tragedies are often understood as an expression of God's *din*, God's judgment. We can't be expected to explain them and have no choice but to endeavour to bear our fortunes bravely. We are called upon to try to do so, if we possibly can, without the complete destruction of our faith in life and love. This faith may well be broken, but it's not impossible that it might, if our heart and soul have the strength to nurture it, regrow from the roots.

The Jewish mystics described this struggle as *hamtakkat hadinim*, making the judgments sweet. Writing in 1942, after losing his only son, his daughter-in-law and her family in the Nazi bombardment of Warsaw at the outset of the war and subsequently spending two and a half years in the ghetto, Rabbi Kalonymus Kalman Shapira described how God's presence could be heard in the lowing of cows, the chirping of birds and the sounds of daily life. Lest his hearers should be misled into thinking that he was referring to the spiritual opportunities of the past and to a world which now existed in memory only, he continued, '[When such a consciousness is achieved,] it follows that all evil is transmuted into good. This must follow since even these utterances are part of the world as we find it; their vital energy is rooted in the voice of God in the Torah.' For all utterance has its origin in God's voice as it is heard in the Torah and in creation; only, in the complex process of emanation it is sometimes possible that, through human misconduct, it materialises in an evil form. But, if we are capable of connecting everything back to its source in God, then even the most terrible events 'are all sublimated to the voice of Torah, and all evil is transmuted into sweetness'.[13]

This passes beyond my comprehension, especially when I consider at what time and under what conditions these words were writtten. But I can nevertheless testify that I've been privileged to meet and speak with men and women who are capable of living their lives at such a level.

We do such people an injustice by imagining that their achievements are simply a gift of temperament, as if acceptance had come to them without struggle and patience, without the sharpness of pain. This cannot be so. The hurt doesn't go away. When I said to one such person how much I admired his attitude but how painful and terrible it must all remain, he replied simply, 'There are things which I don't speak about; there are places I don't go'.

Those people are true peacemakers. They testify to an ennobling quality at the core of existence. It really does exist, this capacity to welcome life's joys, to transform life's tragedies and to perceive, not simply in the realms beyond but in those within, a world of beauty and compassion in spite of everything.

What Matters

We're standing in a huddle in the cemetery, reading the inscription on the stone: name, date of birth, date of death, quotation, 'Forever in the hearts of his wife, daughters, family and friends, Shalom'. Beyond are the ranks of tombstones, the rows of trees at the edge of the field, the rim of the overcast sky. But for the moment the wider horizon isn't important; our hearts are entirely absorbed in being here, among the mourners. Our thoughts are interlocked like living pieces of a half-completed jigsaw to piece together an image of the world of this dead man whom we all loved.

Everything, every memory, every word, every detail, matters. Nobody can fully understand the intricacy of the bonds which link together the living and the dead. So what can a few words say, carved on a piece of stone? Almost invariably the family struggle to compose them, searching for apt expressions, desperate to capture the essence of the person in a few apposite phrases, careful to leave no one out, anxious to avoid any conflict. If they want to include too many people, or choose too long a quotation, the words simply won't fit on the stone. What do a hundred letters amount to, with which to commemorate an entire life? Aware of this paucity, we fill the gaps between the chosen words with reminiscence: 'He had a gift for putting everyone at their ease'; 'His sense of humour could drive you mad!'

The cantor is chanting the memorial prayer. We listen with deep concentration, as if we were making an offering of all our memories, as if we were attentive to an inner ear which still harboured the sound of his voice. But no one can reconstitute the dead. Every life is inexpressible. The sum of all our knowledge even of those we love the most is merely fragmentary; it amounts to no more than a small fraction of the people they actually were. How do we know what other lives they touched? 'I've received such beautiful letters,' says his wife. 'People came to visit who knew my father thirty years ago and they told such wonderful stories,' says his daughter. Our own memories of one single other person are generally too many and too complicated for us to be able to recall them. Only a small proportion ever revisit the conscious mind, while all the rest remain locked in reclusive cells impossible to access. 'It's two whole years since she died and I wish I could visualise her as she looked before she got ill. But the picture simply refuses to come; I just can't make it happen.' Yet the image is somewhere there, sealed in a chamber of the heart to which the consciousness has, for the present, no key.

We endeavour to remember. Love and homage lead us to reconfigure the life of the dead person. We try to find the courage to share our memories with his parents, wife, children, defying the absurd but persistent notion that if we mention him to those he loved we will, somehow, be killing him all over again. The minds of even distant mourners are filled with far more associations than they ever choose to tell.

Here around the grave a web of tenderness has drawn our hearts together. It captures us in this precious moment and sanctifies it, uniting the living and the dead. This bond encompasses the passion of a first kiss, the cradling of a baby, a story by a pillow, the stillness of standing quietly together by the river after thirty years of marriage. Just now, this love is at the centre of all our worlds. Nothing else exists as truly and nothing can gainsay it.

What, then, does death undo, if so much of the person who once lived next to us lives on inside us still, imparting to our lives an often undetected, unacknowledged momentum which now travels on through us and through our deeds until we die?

I look up towards the horizon and everything changes. We whose thoughts are interwoven are merely a tiny knot of people surrounded by rank on rank of graves. At the edge of the cemetery the rows of tall trees lift the gaze to the white sky. Beyond is nothing for millions of miles. So what can there be which really matters? Endless space annihilates us; we're swallowed up in insensible eternity.

Infinity nullifies us; nothingness obliterates us. In less than a hundred years there will be no trace or memory of what once was us. Maybe in five hundred years a shard of our kitchenware will still remain, a plastic bowl we threw away which refused to biodegrade. Soon the universe will hold no record of the fact that we ever existed. At death we exit this parenthesis of time, this pleat in the void, where we have eaten, slept and loved. For a while other occupants hold memories of us, we survive in their mortality. But in the vast eternal present of infinity our annihilation already is.

Yet no matter and no spirit is ever utterly destroyed. There is only transformation, not nullification. Atom by atom we are picked apart and dissolved and, at that very same time and through that very process, transmuted into the great otherness to which we ultimately belong.

Broken Heart

Nothing is more whole than a broken heart

Rebbe Menachem Mendel of Kotsk [14]

How much is too much to bear? I was sitting on a stool opposite a frail old lady whose son had been killed in a car crash. She was little and bent with sobbing and she clung to my fingers. 'Why did it have to happen to him?' she asked over and over again. To hold her hands, to face the silence, to know that there was nothing to say, to still my tongue from reaching for platitudes, was almost unbearable. How then must it have felt for her? People do die of a broken heart.

But Jewish tradition also holds great praise for the broken hearted. 'God does not reject the broken and crushed heart,' says the Psalmist.[15] For this very reason the cantor who leads the prayers on behalf of the community over the High Holidays should be at least thirty years old, because 'then his heart is broken'; such a person has lived long enough to be familiar with life's pain and troubles. His or her heart is full of them, and it is the heart which God desires in prayer.[16] The elderly rabbi Rebbe Moshe Mordechai Heschel, who was famous for his piety, was once asked why his supplications were always accepted in heaven. He explained that over the course of his life he had listened to a multitude of sorrows and that each one of them had affected him deeply:

> Since I have heard and listened to a great many Jews with their problems and anguish, there are a great many holes in my heart. I'm an old Jew and when I start to pray I take my heart and place if before God. He sees this broken heart, so many holes, so many splits, so He has compassion for my heart and that is why He listens to me.[17]

Among the favourite sayings of that most incisive of all the Hasidic teachers, Rebbe Menachem Mendel of Kotsk, is the paradoxical aphorism '*Eyn shalem milev shavur* – Nothing is more whole than a broken heart'. The unbroken, unopened heart cannot really feel. It has insufficient experience to comprehend to their depths either the anguish of compassion or the surging music of joy. 'The Lord will open your hearts and the hearts of your children, so that you will love . . . ' teaches the Torah.[18] What do we know of God if we don't love? And if we love, how can we be protected against pain? Hence the heart which is truly human is the heart which is full of holes.

But sometimes the pain is too great. Such terrible things happen to people that it's almost inconceivable how they manage to get up from the floor without collapsing in dizziness, eat without vomiting or bear the agony of their consciousness for one full minute longer. The popular saying, 'God never sends people suffering beyond what they are capable of bearing', may have been intended to inspire courage. Perhaps it is occasionally helpful, in a similar way to how hearing a pedestrian yell, 'You'll never make it,' might fuel a cyclist with the necessary determination to reach the top of the steep hill, if only to prove the speaker wrong. But the words are trite and false. When one considers their sufferings, it's hard to understand how some people continue to live another day or walk a further step.

I think of those parents in Beslan in Russia who rushed to the school when they learnt that it had been seized by gunmen, then watched as other families embraced their escaping children, hoping in desperation that their own seven- or twelve-year-old would run fleeing from behind the building, or at least be carried out alive. 'There's a moment of amnesia in the first seconds of waking up,' someone who'd recently lost his brother told me, 'but then it all comes rushing back and you realise.' Facts have no mercy. Swiftly they repossess the mind and there's nowhere for the consciousness to hide. That's what drives a person to the ultimate and only recourse; that's what makes a person want to die.

What can we say? There are times when all we can do in simple solidarity with what the heart is forced to suffer is bear witness in loving silence. That's what God supposedly does; 'I am with you in suffering,' says God, according to the Psalmist.[19] But God is immortal and God's home is infinity, so how can God really understand the capacity for hurt in the heart of a mortal, the huge pain born in this tiny, fragile, transient organ of flesh? How can God know what it's like to lose someone you love forever? We human beings should understand better; we have to face the fact that one day it will be us, grieving, hurting, dying.

Yet the Torah insists that God does understand. *Vayeda*, says the Torah about God's response to the slavery of the Children of Israel in Egypt, 'God knew': 'The children of Israel groaned under their labour and cried out . . . God heard . . . God saw . . . and God knew.'[20] *Vayeda*, the Torah says, employing the very same word it uses to describe the intimacy of man and woman. But in this particular instance that normally transitive verb lacks an object. So what did God know? The Torah doesn't tell us. There's no describing this being at one in pain, let alone what it might possibly mean to God.

I've often wondered what has the power to stop the aching heart drowning in the whirlpool of the wretched, spinning world.

No Incurable Wounds

Elena Kozhina was a little girl when her family fled Leningrad during the cold and hunger of the Nazi siege. She remembered how in the village in the steppes where they found shelter, her sister fell desperately ill. Her mother held her dying daughter aloft in her arms, crying 'My little bird! My little bird, don't fly away!' But the girl was already dead.[21]

Once, many months later, after the village had been liberated and Elena was free to wander the landscape in search of food and to enjoy the sanctuary of solitude, her mother woke her up in the black of night and insisted that she come outside to look. She knew and loved the steppe by day, but in the dark its vastness astonished her:

> Where did it come from – such freedom, such bliss? The steppe was scarred all around by the war that had just passed over it . . . Yet here it was, overflowing with nocturnal joy.
>
> . . . From our cramped and meagre life, which fit into a tiny circle of light from the broiler lamp, we had suddenly stepped into this deeply and fully breathing world, so generous to us that one could not avoid believing, walking down this road, that there were no incurable wounds or unfullfillable dreams.[22]

I've treasured this passage in my heart ever since I first discovered it. I, too, believe in the power of wonder. I believe, too, that it derives primarily from the impact upon us of nature, night and day, mountain and plain. I believe that the sea can sing to us and its waters be still with us, that the trees can speak to us and their leaves and branches dance with us. Or maybe it is we who are moved by them to singing, or to silence. But the effect is the same and the secret of this great communion lies in the immense vitality of the natural world, in the depths of the heart, in the resonance of the soul and in the power of beauty to bring solace to pain.

Yet how, after all she has suffered, can Elena Kozhina possibly say that there are 'no incurable wounds'? Perhaps such feelings apply only

227

to a very young person, fresh enough on her path through life to find healing. For precisely the problem with the heart is that, when we do come home to it, it proves to have a pitiless memory. Here are garnered the records of all the depredations of time from the very first losses of childhood; here we register the implications of mortality. Whatever love we've experienced haunts us here together with all the hurts we've ever received. Even when we are young, our heart is not only the place where we feel joy but also where we fathom the inevitabilities of sorrow. That is why the man dying in the London hospital desperately wanted the nurses to help him search the world and find the girl who had rejected his first love, in spite of fifty years of happy marriage to another woman. His broken heart had healed, and was, in some remote depth long covered by scar tissue, still broken.

But Elena may be right nonetheless: there are no incurable wounds. For when the heart wakes we experience neither anger, nor envy, nor greed, but an overwhelming tenderness for life. Even our pain becomes a kind of gentleness; it cries out not for revenge but for deeper loving. We exist, at such moments, in the warmth and illumination of a more embracing truth; we feel as if we were at the heart of life itself, registering with deep appreciation its beauty, its delicacy, its susceptibility to hurt. Touched by mortality and eternity at once, we love life and, knowing that we will one day die, love it all the more.

Maybe this is why the kabbalists refer to the heart as both the domain of *Tiferet*, beauty, and *Emet*, truth. Here we live as feeling what the mind can only know as thought; we understand intuitively what's loving and what's wounding in even the smallest of actions and encounters. Yet here, at the same time, we experience exuberant joy and silent awe before the wonder of life's unfathomable energy and the glory of its innumerable forms.

The heart is the place where truth and beauty meet. That's what makes it at once so perilously vulnerable and so utterly indomitable.

CHAPTER NINE

Onwards!

A Conversation with Kadya

A few days before he died, my father opened his eyes and smiled at his youngest grandchildren Kadya and Danny, a huge, beaming, mischievous smile.

He'd been ill for years and very sick for several weeks. His strength was now fast failing and we'd brought the children to say farewell. It was Friday night and we sung the blessings around his bed. Those prayers lay safe and sound in his soul, treasured since childhood, too deep to be lost to the attrition of age, too familiar for his weakening memory to forget. Many times in these difficult weeks when he'd not wanted, or been unable, to speak, the traditional melodies of the liturgy had stirred his spirit and he'd sung them with us, taking over the lead, knowing all the words by heart. Now he was far weaker, yet still we watched his lips for any signs of participation and were cheered when we saw them move, most of all when he said a clear 'Amen'.

Isca sustained and coordinated his care with great devotion, seeking and obtaining the best possible nursing help; thus he was drawn from a mood of almost unremitting agitation to a state of predominant quietness and pain-free calm. Those final weeks brought us all together and we shared special moments of grace and presence with my father. These were, in a unique and penetrating way, holy moments and we will remember them not only with sorrow but also with profound respect and a humble heart.

My father had recognised and smiled warmly at all the other grandchildren. Now it was Danny and Kadya's turn. He opened his eyes and looked at them with a huge, beaming, mischievous, conspiratorial smile and said 'Hello'. It's not up to me to speak for my sweet-natured nephew Danny, but it had never struck me before that my father and Kadya had so much in common. I suddenly realised from where that loyal, cheeky, affectionate Kadya must have inherited some of the key features of her irrepressible spirit. In that smile was the complicity of kindred adventurers; they would be thick as thieves, they would steal the chocolates, they would dare their parents' wrath, they would be rascals together and afterwards they would laugh it all off and plan to do it again. It was, in Nicky's words, 'pure and simple love'. It was a visible moment in the transmission of love from one generation to the next.

The next morning Kadya asked me how my father was. She knew we wouldn't have him with us for much longer. We talked about what was going to happen and where, afterwards, he would be. Then she remembered his great smile.

He was giving you his love, I told her. Soon he won't be with us; he's passing you his love so that you can carry it for him. In that way he'll continue to live in all our hearts, including yours. I reminded her of how her name *Kad-ya*, means 'God's jug'; he's filling that jug with his love, I told her, for you to have and share and give to others throughout your life. That's where he's going to be.

'Onward!' the Sailors Cry

Let a man remember all the days of his life
That he is carried towards death.
Though he travels slowly each day of his journey
And even imagines himself at rest,
He is like a man standing still upon a ship
Who yet is driven on the wings of the wind.

Moses ibn Ezra[1]

'"Onward!" the sailors cry.' This line from the popular Scottish Ballad about Bonnie Prince Charlie, *The Skye Boat Song*, will not leave my mind.

I am on an ineluctable journey across the sea. The wind is in the rigging of my ribs, my heart is tugged at like a sail. The helplessness of this adventure has laid me open.

I wish my youngest child would not grow up so quickly. I want her to stay little for a very, very long time, so that we can still pick her up and cuddle her, so that she can play in the garden with her toys. I don't want time to dissipate her ignorance too fast, or squander her rascally eagerness. But no one can protect her from the knowledge. It's not as if it were in some other place, so that somehow it might be kept from her. Her mortality is inside her, unexplored in her rambunctious consciousness, growing with her, waiting. She is carried on the same sea.

'"Onward!" the sailors cry.' I am caught between fear and wonder; a raw tenderness is exposed inside me towards all the life around me, to which I'm bound by this affinity of fleeing time – people, seals, sea birds, breaking waves.

The elderly man struggled to stand up when he heard the *Shema Kolenu* prayer. These melodies, Passover, High Holidays, are the rhythm of his life, his tide, the longitude and latitude of his days. 'Hear our voice, Lord our God, have mercy upon us and pity us. Do not forsake us when our strength comes to an end.' I could feel the tears in his words again when he said the blessing after I had given him the scented Etrog to smell which I brought to his bedside in the hospital. Now, thank God, he is a little stronger.

This is our uttermost helplessness, before the unknown moment when the horizon ends and the invisible world receives us for evermore.

There are times when I try not to think about it. But the sea still sings in my heart like the sound of the waves, though far from the ocean, in the recesses of an old conch shell.

' "Onward!" the sailors cry.' What can one do? I only hope that death won't find me half unused, that when it unpacks me it won't mock me for my stinginess on the journey: 'Why did he keep so much back in his heart? What did he fancy he was saving it all for? Look at that soul! It's hardly even been touched!'

The coast line behind me is beautiful in the sun, the mountains, woodlands and bays. Twice I have been on the shores of childhood, for myself, and now with my children. I am very lucky. Maybe I'll go there once more with my grandchildren, watching the happiness of life's beginnings with the sand castles and moats, while listening in spite of myself, subconsciously, intently, for how the heart first absorbs the knowledge of its own undoing.

Earlier the sun seemed overhead but now it has passed midday. The sea is majestic in the long light. Grey, pale blue and shimmering white dance on its surface, until far away in a faint line the ocean vanishes into the invisible.

Love and wonder are our great resources for the living of this present. Maybe fear and apprehension will not ruin them, but rather this strange kinship will nourish them, this bond of life in the mystery of being.

Where the Love Goes

This song of mine will wind its music around you, my love,
*   like the fond arms of love.*
This song of mine will touch your forehead like a kiss
*   of blessing . . .*
It will be like the faithful star overhead when dark night
*   is over your road . . .*
And when my voice is silent in death, my song will
*   speak in your living heart.*

Rabindranath Tagore: The Crescent Moon [2]

To a friend whose parents both died within a year

You parted from your parents with great love. You left nothing important unsaid. When worry and grief drove you down to the depths of your heart, what you found there was gratitude, amidst the anguish and the sorrow. You and they both knew how much you loved each other and when you wept it was a testament not only to pain but to the generosity of life.

When people gather at such times they recognise and understand; they felt the closeness of your love for one another and were touched and humbled. 'We're privileged to have so much love about us,' your parents said. But it was they themselves who created it.

They're dead now, but their love hasn't gone away. It's said of babies that when they're born they bring their loving with them. When people die they don't take it back again to the grave. Their loving lives; it's their gift to us, in the immensity of life.

Your parents are present in you and in your children. People like your family are the salt of the earth, you'll all do anything to help anyone. I told your parents how you turned up that time at my house with flowers from the garden and raspberries from your allotment. 'How are your parents?' my wife and I asked you. In their old age the love they gave you came back home and you cared for them with constant, attentive affection.

233

They'll be there many years in the future when, humbled by her beauty, your grandson folds the veil over the face of his bride. He'll remember how his parents talked about their own grandparents, recalling how they used to sit together holding hands, looking out at the trees. That was what they most wanted from life, each other, the trees, and peace. Thus they passed on to their children the most important heritage of all; they taught their family how to love. In the night, when love's distillation enters another womb, they will be there too, as a future generation they never met prepares to pass this knowledge on to the unborn.

'Love is strong as death': those words from *The Song of Songs* testify not only to love's heartache but to love's tenacity.[3] I was once at the bedside of a young woman who was dying. 'My children won't remember me,' she said. 'They'll be too small when I die and they won't recall a single thing about me. They'll grow up knowing nothing about their mother.' She turned her face away from me and cried. She knew she'd be dead within weeks.

I waited quietly while she wept, then told her I thought her words didn't encompass the whole of the truth. 'They will remember you', I said. 'It's true, they may have to look at pictures to visualise your face. But you'll always be their mother in their hearts and minds. Your love will grow with them and within them. Maybe it won't happen for a long time, maybe your presence will be dormant in them for many years, but a day will come when they'll be curious about you. They'll want to find out everything they can; they'll be glad whenever they encounter people who used to be your friends. They'll want to understand who you were and what you did, where you went and how you met their father. They'll miss you and they'll wonder what it would have been like to know you. You'll be a living presence inside them; they'll recognise that it's also you in them who nourishes their capacity to live and learn and love.'

But aren't the dead destined to be forgotten? 'He shall never return to his home and his place shall know him no more,' says Job wryly in his anguish of spirit.[4] 'It's decreed that the dead be forgotten from the heart,' notes the Bible commentator Rashi, rephrasing a rabbinical adage.[5] If the living are not to be so crippled by memories that they're left in a state of perpetual mourning, how else are they supposed to manage, unless they forget?

The issue, though, may be more complicated. Time may not necessarily be experienced as transporting the dead ever farther away from us because, where the dead are, time doesn't exist. Time, therefore, is incapable of dividing us any further from them. Hence the past is not exclusively past; it also exists in the dimension of an eternal present which refuses to recede.

The crucial difference may in fact be that the living remain bound to the future. That's part of the misery of mourning, being compelled by the dawn to get out of bed and carry on with life's inanities while the heart is still in love with a person who's no longer there. Each day is a tearing apart. The presence of the dead in our inner world is only a reminder of their absence. Listen, feel their absence around the empty house. Wouldn't it be easier if they simply went away, forgotten forever from the heart?

Maybe that's part of the reality of mourning, suffering the sadness of the slow transposition of the love of those who have died from the past into the future. Behind us they stand next to us, bringing us memories often framed in sorrow. Beyond us, they belong to life.

They've died. If they, and we, were lucky, they died at peace. Life came to them like an ocean to a rock pool, like a river to a water drop; they were taken away. They're comprehended in the single consciousness of life; they are no more, and are in everything.

Becoming

. . . und hört im Herzen auf zu sein.
. . . and ceases in the heart to be.

Rainer Maria Rilke: Der Panther [6]

Everything travels, everything is transformed; nothing remains as it was. We are in a constant state of imperceptible reformulation. The limbs and organs of our bodies are no longer composed of the same cells as they were when we were children or when we first loved. Innumerable preoccupations, anxieties, hopes, surprises, shocks and disappointments have penetrated the heart in the interim, deepening it, hurting it, disturbing it, awakening it and inevitably changing who we are.

Yet even those many years of growth and attrition are only the temporary, local phases of an incomparably greater becoming, a short sojourn on the journey of all the specific elements which compose us and, reconfigured by us, travel on to impact other lives. For everything which now shapes me has traversed many forms and shared in many lives; its passage through me is no more than a brief, intermediate stage in its unending migration. There's nothing I call mine, my home, my body, my blood, my heart, my soul, which will not one day be absorbed into some other, greater context. The very word 'mine', which we use to signify the permanence and safety of unequivocal belonging, 'It's mine, not yours', 'It's mine and I own it', points paradoxically to an irresistible impermanence.

'For dust thou art and unto dust shalt thou return,' says God to Adam, explaining the meaning of his mystifying punishment, death. [7] 'A king may go a progress through the guts of the beggar,' declaims Hamlet in more lurid terms. [8] Yet the exchange of elements from one form of matter to another begins not with dying but at the moment of conception. Breathing, drinking, eating; listening, touching, feeling; I am in a constant state of interchange with everything which nourishes

236

me at every level of existence and there is nothing I take from it which I shan't return to it at some moment of life's choosing. For all things continue to exist. Only I, this self and this conceptualisation of it as a discrete and definite entity, this configuration of a particular con-stellation of matter, thoughts and feelings as 'me', only this will cease to exist. But whatever has formed me and however I in turn have shaped it, the residue of my words and actions, the invisible impact of my feelings and my state of consciousness on everything around me, will travel onwards through innumerable pathways of cause and effect.

There is no definable moment at which the journey begins. Which of us can point to the origins of the love that created us? The extent of our emotional vision is many generations too short. No single encounter is an absolute fresh start; no feeling is engendered independently of the innumerable relationships which brought us to this passion, or this dejection, at this moment. Furthermore, clusters of sentiment, once formed, are all but indivisible. It's impossible to say with precision, 'I owe this aspect of my capacity for loving to my grandmother and that facet to the dark haired girl who was the first to pitch me into the depths of my own heart'. Hundreds of years of emotional history are reformulated in a second in our lives.

When, two years ago, I went to my parents' house to ask for their blessing before the Day of Atonement, my father, who was frail and often cried during poignant moments of ritual, wept as he placed his hands on my head. I cried too. Kadya, whom I drew into the circle of my father's benediction, clung to me and watched. 'Why was grandpa crying?' she asked me afterwards. I don't think I ever offered her an answer. But I still sometimes reflect on her question, forming in my mind an analogy with prayer, with those ancient liturgies which have remained intact for centuries because worshippers intuitively recognise that it's not the semantic signification of the words but their measure and melody which gives them meaning, the burden of spirit which they carry from generation to generation and from soul to soul. Similarly, we bear in our hearts the memories and vestiges of friendships, romances, happy marriages and relationships thwarted by circumstance or mis-understanding, the joy and pain of which have never entirely dissolved and which, in strange combinations and new interactions, come to fruition once again in our lives. Nor is there a moment when we do not pass ourselves on to others, known or unknown; even solitude is a form of communion with an inarticulate world which perceives and responds to us by means of ceaseless subliminal currents and invisible energies. The very trees are cognisant of us as we pass by. Their knowledge, were we able to decipher it, might prove to us both wondrous and disconcerting. We would be humbler creatures if only we could understand how to apprehend it.

Yet I am, despite my transience, responsible. I'm not simply a branch on which birds of passage alight to rest their wings before they fly on. Nothing leaves me as it came; in innumerable ways so complex it would be impossible to describe them, of many of which I'm not even conscious, I shape and form, build and recreate. Therefore I bear responsibility not only for my actions but also for the impact of my presence and absence, the quality of my consciousness, the love I give or fail to manifest. The moral and spiritual quality of my life, which neither I nor any other human being can ever know well enough to judge with complete justice, may be described as the sum of all those transformations, what I have done, action by action and breath by breath, with all the matter, feeling, thought and spirit which has encountered, formed and been transformed by me.

Yet to live from day to day we need more familiar and observable boundaries. 'I want it for my very own!' says the little child, picking up the teddy bear she's just been given for her third birthday. But what is 'my very own'? Are we, always and invariably, so inescapably provisional? None of us could bear it. We have to live on the assumption that life is sufficiently predictable to be pinned down by those possessive adjectives: his, hers, mine. After all, there are laws to enforce respect for property and rules to protect the integrity of persons. They are our barrier against moral chaos. Pronouns and possessive adjectives are our defence against the constant awareness of our own passing and the transitory nature of all things.

Thus we are entitled, even commanded, to consider everything precious, our possessions, our bodies, our thoughts and feelings, especially the privilege of consciousness itself. But we do so out of respect for life, not from any sense of ultimate ownership. For in the end, nothing of it is ours. Even the 'I' itself which appears to hold all these phenomena together in an illusion of semi-permanence is only a temporary creation, a partially fictive identity imposed upon the constant flow of life unto itself. This movement will redistribute the atoms of my body, the products of my thoughts and efforts, the reactions engendered by my feelings, even my very awareness, the invisible essence which enables me to call myself 'me'. It will return it into the vast, all-present, all-engendering consciousness to which it has always belonged and this 'I' will, in one and the same moment, both cease to breath and be reclaimed by what truly is.

Of all that exists, only the eternal being remains the same. Or rather, the sum of it in its totality remains the same. For it too, through its pervasive and inarrestable presence, participates in our constant becoming. What should we call it, the unnameable, that essence more elusive than the concept of essence, that being upon which the imposition of language is already a form of idolatry? You silence me. Into you I shall dissolve.

Yet, for all that I am mortal and provisional, or precisely because of it, I long to practise not the science of detachment from the world but the art of love. Of course, the two disciplines are interrelated; otherwise selfish desire would overwhelm the tenderness and generosity within the very nature of love. I know that when loss comes I won't be able to teach myself not to weep, though I will tell my heart that in the end the tears must stop, that acceptance is the will of God. I cry because my dog grew old and his beautiful ears couldn't hear and his legs hurt when he climbed down the stairs and a lump was revealed in ex-rays of his lungs and he had to be put to sleep. I cry at the end of every holiday for the glory of the western light on the sea and the happiness of watching my children run across the sand. I cry for my father; often I find myself thinking of him subliminally and as soon as I disengage with the surface preoccupations of my life he's there with me in his living and his dying. I cry, selfishly, because time itself is irrecoverable, because every invaluable second is passing constantly beyond recall, and no amount of philosophy will prevent me from feeling that death is the dissolution of the most precious bonds in all the world.

I know that this is not entirely the case. Everything separates, but nothing perishes. The soul rejoins the ocean, the entirety of all being; only the 'I' is gone forever. I hope this realisation will suffice to redeem me from bitterness and curb in me the futile and ultimately wanton pursuit of what simply cannot be. I would like to prove an accepting man, a person whose heart is moved rather in appreciation for what has been than in anger and regret because of what can be no longer. But, though the bonds of love will cut and wound me, I nonetheless seek to love far more. Time will not need my help in unpicking its ties. That will come inevitably; pain is part of the very love which I embrace.

Meanwhile I both accept my limitations and defy them. For if I could make my dreams come true I would want everything which has travelled through me to continue its voyage touched and moulded by a further love. I would want people, whoever they are, not to feel anxious or aggressed against in my presence but rather to understand that here is someone who means to be kind; I would want the animals to sense that there is no cruelty here; I would want the trees to know 'This person wishes no harm to life'. Meanwhile, of course, I fail to live up to my good intentions.

But beyond all other depths of love, God, I belong to you – God, being, presence, silence which pervades and transcends all forms and all dimensions of this ceaseless, invincible becoming.

Transcendence

'From where shall wisdom be found and which is the place of understanding?' asks Job in the book which carries his name.[9] But the rabbis didn't necessarily read the verse according to that plain meaning; they, especially the mystics, loved puns.

A pun to them was not an artifice but a trapdoor; follow it and secret stairs would lead down to a deeper level of understanding. That's scarcely surprising, since to them the whole apparatus of language, the arrangements of the letters, the semantic meaning of the individual words, syntax, grammar and, especially, context were only a concession to the limitations of the human mind. For the Torah wasn't composed of verbs and nouns but of black fire on white fire, of names of God, of mysteries and combinations of signs and letters incomprehensible to us, all of it a manifestation of the same divine speech, the same sacred energy, by which the world came into being. Why then should it be so extraordinary if the relationships between words are not as we, familiar with the limited discipline of mere human speech, might have averred them to be?

'From where shall wisdom be found and which is the place of understanding?' The mystics understood this verse in a strange and arresting manner. The plain meaning of the Hebrew word *me'ayin* is indeed 'from where?' and the author of *Job* is evidently posing a question: 'Wisdom shall come from where, and what is the place of understanding?' But *me'ayin* can also be translated as 'from nothing', which changes the meaning of the sentence to: 'Wisdom shall come from nothingness'. Though the immediate context refutes this interpretation, a deeper connection invites it: The mystery of the unfathomable 'whence' which is the origin of wisdom points to the indescribable nothing, no thing, existence itself before it receives any form, the very flow of invisible being which fills all consciousness and extends beyond all apprehension. It simply is, and the life of all that is proceeds from it, belongs to it and returns to it in constant, unceasing motion.

Why do we experience such affinity with life? Beyond joy, beyond compassion, beyond the moment of empathic intuition, what is this bond with the very wind, which simplifies all thought into silence within its sound? What is the consciousness at the core of being? The centre for which we search cannot be the mind, nor even the heart. These organs apprehend, they receive and reflect; what fills them lies outside of themselves. What we truly seek is the source of being, pure being, the same being as it flows through all conscious life.

Here is the reality which is both everything and nothing. It is everything; it is God, it is the sum totality of all that is, it comprises life in its entirety, comprehends all forms of existence. Yet it is also nothing, because it constitutes consciousness not only as it is fulfilled in every form, but also as it precedes all forms. It's not yet a bird, causing it to perch and sing, or fly away. It's not yet a fox, walking soundlessly across the woodland floor, pausing, listening, a front paw raised. It's not yet a human being, planning, worrying, imagining, panicking. It pre-exists whatever perceives it; therefore all words are at once too indistinct to describe it and too prescriptive to name it. Call it God, and God and it are at once over-defined, while the syllable God remains just a word, just a sound. Perhaps that's what led the kabbalists to use for God the names *Eyn Sof*, Without End, to point towards what transcends our capacity for description, or *Sod Ha'efshar*, the Secret of the Possible, to indicate that which extends beyond the boundaries of all possible imaginations.

'Nothingness' also expresses the necessary state of the observer. The preoccupied mind does not perceive; thoughts go round and round in circles, unable to escape the gravitational pull of their own origins and implications. But contemplation brings stillness, quiet. Or a sudden perception transforms the mind in wonder and all at once, feeling the world from the heart, we listen in silence and fullness: look at the sea in the long western light. Awe has taken hold of us, reverence before God.

In the actual moment of awareness there can be no attempt to describe the experience; that of itself would already constitute a withdrawal from it, a reformulation of the mind as an observer, an entity supposedly independent from the very source which bestows on it its capacity to perceive. The mind and heart in their greatest moments of apprehension simply are, and, if they are touched by the will towards anything, it is the desire for greater permeability, for less impurity, to be nothing other than participants in what fills and moves them now.

Here, perhaps, lies the significance of another play on words. For the letters, *aleph, yud, nun,* which compose the Hebrew word *ayyin,* 'nothing', are the same as those which form the word *ani,* the pronoun 'I', *aleph, nun, yud.* Only the order of the second and third letters has to be changed. Hence the very spelling epitomises the classic Hasidic idea that the challenge is to transform the I, our self-will, into nothing, for the sake of the service of God. Maybe, then, the nothingness in which wisdom is to be found also includes the human being in such a state of selfless readiness. We've all encountered people who communicate a spirit of deep acceptance, who've attained a good humoured humility in which their portion is to them neither irksome nor constraining but simply an opportunity for service. We recognise in them the qualities which neither learning nor discipline alone can acquire, wisdom and compassionate understanding.

However, to think of nothingness as if it were solely absence would be wrong. Wisdom isn't a void and it doesn't derive from self-abnegation alone. Its source lies in the vast reservoir of life beyond us which the removal of the barriers of self enables us to perceive. Hence the words of the Psalm, 'The beginning of wisdom is the fear of the Lord', for at the heart of wisdom lies the experience of awe and wonder, which is what the Hebrew phrase 'fear of the Lord' really means.[10] The consciousness should be at once focussed and receptive; then respect and reverence for life will fill it as water descends to the place which is low. This leads to a final, albeit more tenuous, play on syllables. For, although the two words are written differently, one with the letter *aleph* and the other with an *ayyin, me'ayyin* may also suggest to the ear the word *ma'ayyan,* a well or spring; the source from which the consciousness receives its capacity to apprehend the grandeur, beauty and infinite vitality of being.

Why should such an experience be the origin of wisdom? Wisdom, though never rooted in ignorance, is not chiefly developed by greater knowledge of the practical facts. After the revolution in information technology it remains as it was before, the fruit of experience and reflection. Even the concentrated mind cannot discover it alone. Mind, heart and spirit know it together; in the moment of apprehension they are reunited as one. But ultimately the source of wisdom lies beyond them too. Only when, like a rock pool at the edge of the sea, the tide of a greater awareness fills the consciousness, does wisdom enter. When that tide withdraws, this knowledge remains for a while, and the consciousness retains its mystery just as the sea-creatures, crabs, anemones and tiny fish are caught in the clefts and crevasses of sand and stone. But wisdom endures and develops only if the tide replenishes the pool again and again.

Wisdom, according to the Kabbalah, overflows into understanding and compassion. It transforms who we are. It frees us from the burdens and limitations of constant reaction. It allows us to reshape our destiny, if not by changing the course of outer events then at least by enabling us to perceive them differently. This may be the meaning of the rabbinical saying, 'Everything is in the hands of heaven, except for the awe of heaven'.[11] Whatever the circumstances, one factor always remains within our grasp, the possibility of altering our attitude. Sometimes there really is nothing more we can do than accept our fate in the calmest and most courageous way we can. But in other situations, inner transformation may lead to outer change as well. For when we see life in a different way, a more refined awareness begins to guide our actions and we participate in the shaping of a different world. We are freed from at least part of the burden of preoccupation with self and can live with deeper understanding and greater compassion.

I Sleep but My Heart is Awake

Ani yeshenah velibbi er
I sleep but my heart is awake [12]

For years I've been haunted by this verse from *The Song of Songs*, 'I sleep but my heart is awake; the voice of my beloved knocks . . . ' It speaks at once of the beauty of love and its mystery, of the power of the spirit to draw us into its embrace and, almost simultaneously, of its ephemerality, its absence at the decisive moment of encounter: 'I opened to my beloved, but my beloved had withdrawn; he was gone.'[13]

It's remarkable how often the meanings of much loved poems and verses change as we grow older, becoming richer as our experience transforms us. Thus, when I became a father and began to explore the significance of the words in the context of my relationship with my children, I discovered in that sentence from *The Song of Songs* a different depth of resonance. This was not only because of the play on the name of our middle child, 'I sleep, but my heart – (in Hebrew *Libbi*) – is awake', on which Nicky and I frequently used to reflect in exhausted resignation while the young lady in question pottered unwearied about the house at midnight, but because the verse carries a series of interpretations which penetrate deeply into the meaning of the bond between the generations and which express both the joy and the vulnerability of parenthood.

Rashi explains that 'my heart is awake' can be understood as a reference to God, who 'neither slumbers nor sleeps'.[14] As so often, Rashi is following the ancient homiletic tradition of Midrash. In this case the passage in question refers the reader to the verse from *Psalms*, 'The rock of my heart and my portion is God'.[15] Thus even when I sleep, my heart, that is my God, is awake to protect me. Like the vast majority of parents, Nicky and I have always done our best to look after our children and try to keep them safe. For as long as it is within our ability we shall certainly continue to do so. But, as all fathers and mothers know, our powers are severely limited. Our children will soon leave home to travel on their own paths through life. Yet even while they remain within our daily care we cannot entirely protect them from illness, accidents, terror and war. We can only teach them to be sensible and entrust them to God's providence, uncertain of what that means, but well aware of the frailty of our own endeavours. Like most parents we would much prefer, if something bad has to happen, that it fall upon us and not upon them, that fate should not strike where life is at its most innocent, most curious and most tender. So we pray that even when they sleep, but especially when they get up and set about their day, when they cross the roads, take the buses and set off on their bikes, God will always be awake to look after our children, and all children, to keep them healthy and safe: 'I sleep, but my heart, my God, is awake . . . '

Drawing on Judaism's mystical tradition, Hasidic teaching understands the verse differently, relating it to a key doctrine about self and selflessness: When the 'I' within us, that is, the part of us composed of the desires, envies, angers and frustrations which comprise our ego, sleeps, then, and only truly then, does our heart fully come awake and we discover that we are part of a vast and breathing world permeated by the presence of God. We too belong to this vibrant, luminous universe and the divine presence, in the course of its ceaseless traverse through all things, flows even through us, vital, conscious, but mortal partners in the infinite life of God. Such moments of awareness are recognised not only by the mind, or even in the heart; we know them with our soul. They form life's most privileged and profound experiences and I hope my children will apprehend them many times. Each is its own revelation, a star perceived through a parting in the canopy of the forest. Together they form a path across the sky by which to navigate in darkness, uncertainty and fear. I wish I had the capacity to make such encounters happen for my children, but I know that this is impossible. All I can do is teach them the ways of the Jewish faith, talk to them about God, take them to beautiful places and trust that they will find that God in the meeting place of their own souls where I am an outsider, for only they and God can enter here: 'My heart is awake; the voice of my beloved knocks . . . '

Onwards!

'I sleep, but . . . ' Since my father died, a new kind of awareness has been preoccupying me. When children are small, they have to rely on parents, family and carers for their most basic needs; they have no choice. In the face of so much evidence about neglect and abuse, and with so many other demands and stimuli to distract them, one has to hope that the adults around them will be worthy of such trust. Only if that trust is lovingly honoured will the child grow up to feel safe, confident and happy. But as children, and, more especially, parents grow older, the balance in the relationship slowly changes. Parents want to feel that they, in turn, can trust their children. This isn't a question of whether they go to bed when they're supposed to, or how long they leave the lights on for reading, or whether they get into trouble at school, or settle down to do their homework, vexing as all those daily tensions sometimes are. The matter is bound up with mortality itself, with time's unassailable control over the passage of generations. It's the way of the world for parents to die: 'I sleep, but my heart is awake'; that is, I will sleep in the dust, but I deeply hope that my children will be alive in this world for many and good years long after I have gone. It therefore matters to me profoundly, as it no doubt does to most parents, to be able to entrust to my children my deepest faith and values and to bequeath to them my love and appreciation for the wonderful gifts of life upon this earth. That is a very deep trust indeed.

I trust my children and pray that this trust, rooted and tended in love, should not be a burden for them, but rather a blessing which supports and guides them everywhere they go.

The Beach At Mull

I stood on the beach at Mull and my heart was full of parting.

It was a wonderful late summer afternoon, the sky rich with clouds yet bright with sunshine, the sea flowing gently into the bay, the waters almost still. The children were turning over stones searching for crabs; from time to time one of them would cry out, 'I've found one; here!' and we'd all go running across to look. It was the last day of the holiday.

Those summers are the measure of my life. Two whole weeks of space, still ten more days, just four days left, one single day remaining to replenish the heart and fill the 'why?' with answers big enough to last for an entire year: What am I doing with my life? Where is it all going? The great excitement of setting off turns to desperation. I never understand; I have no resolution to one single question.

The sea moves with the quiet rhythm of a breath, rising, falling, pushing the water almost noiselessly past the clusters of pebbles in the sand, over the face of a rock, submerging it, revealing it, drowning it until the turning of the tide.

My wife and I had been here many years earlier, before any of the children were born. We remembered the path that petered out half way up the cliff leaving us clinging to the rocks and scrub, the walk to the fossil tree, how our dog Safi, scarcely more than a puppy then, looked longingly at every passing car and begged to be carried at the end of our twenty mile walk. We had watched the birds from the same table and looked out over this same bay. How far away would this summer's visit seem were we to return in ten years, in twenty, or in our late seventies, wearing those dark green capes which old people wear and pushing the stones over with a walking stick, saying, 'Do you remember how the children looked for crabs?' It won't feel far. I hope we will be happy then. I hope, if we live so long, that we will have learnt the arts of being and loving and saying farewell.

A crab is a creature from the past, crustacean with its pink shell, strange pincer claw and swift sideways scuttle. Around the bay, facing the mainland but also the great waters of the open Atlantic Ocean, is Duart Castle. I would have liked to go there to see the view and read about who lived there and when, to imagine the owners watching the grey ships departing in silence and returning in relief in the war of the North Atlantic.

A crab makes the castle seem young. The sea makes everything around it and within it appear younger still, with its great risings and fallings, before there was any human or animal breathing, the constant movement of the waters in and out of the beaches and bays.

In the gentle sunshine of this late summer afternoon it feels as if I could lay my soul upon the sea just as I can put my head on my wife's stomach to be comforted like a child by the intake and release of breath, this permanent reliability of life.

In my mind I'm already dead. I'm recently dead and the children tell their children on this beach how they once came here when they themselves were little and stood on this same watery sand. I'm ten thousand years dead. The tides ebb and flow over this very shore. Is it any consolation, in the face of this vast, annihilating expanse of time, that maybe these same sands and waters will still survive?

One of the children is frightened. I didn't see what happened, but she's running towards me crying.

There is comfort in holding her small hand.

Acknowledgements

In acknowledgement and appreciation of

My father, Adi, who while he lived was always there for me, who
nurtured my love of traditional Judaism, whose loyalty and humility I
deeply respect, and whom I think of over and again since he died;

My mother, Lore, whom I would so much have
liked to have known for longer;

Isca, my mother's younger sister who became my second mother,
without whose love and insight I would never have reached
the point where I could write this book;

Raphael my good, kind and faithful brother, and his family;

Nicky, my wife, without whose love and companionship I
could not imagine my life, and whose help and advice
I seek in everything I undertake;

Our children, Mossy, Libbi and Kadya, whose affection,
spirit and curiosity make every day an adventure;

My aunt Ruth and my cousin Michal, for many
conversations about family history;

The members of the New North London Masorti Synagogue,
my community, for challenging and inspiring me;

David Elliott, for being such an excellent editor, for devising the best
structure for this book and for hitting upon a compelling title;

Michael Joseph, for offering me encouragement when writing
was slow and difficult and for giving me the confidence
that it was all worthwhile;

Bette Rabie for her wisdom, support, kindness and generosity in
her careful readings of several drafts of the manuscript;

All the people, animals, birds and trees who've given me inspiration

And for the gift of life from God.

Notes

Chapter One – Setting Out

1 Shakespeare: *King Lear*, Act 4, Scene 6
2 The Authorised Daily Prayer Book of the United Hebrew Congregations of the Commonwealth, Centenary Edition, (London 1998) p. 1, my translation
3 The opening lines of a poem of uncertain authorship, carrying the acrostic Shemayahu, included in many prayer books, thus *Siddur Otzar Tefillot* (Printed by Avraham Yitzhak Freidman, New York) p. 102, my translation.
4 Boris Pasternak: 'Daybreak', in *Doctor Zhivago* (Translated by Max Hayward and Manya Harari, The Harvill Press, London 1996) p. 496
5 Wilfred Owen, 'Futility', in *The Collected Poems of Wilfred Owen*, edited by C. Day Lewis (Chatto and Windus, London 1974) p. 58
6 Midrash Lamentations Rabbah, Petichta 24
7 Psalm 126:1

Chapter Two – Learning

1 Rebbe Yehudah Aryeh Lev of Gur, *Sefat Emet* on Lech Lecha, year 5632 (Jerusalem 5731 / 1971, page 41b)
2 Rebbe Shneur Zalman of Liadi in *Chummash Peneenei Hahasidut* to Bereshit 12:1 (ed: Sholem Kowalsky, Yitzchok Fajgenbaum and Sh. Ch. Porush, Jerusalem 1987) p. 88.
3 C. P. Cavafy, 'Ithaka', in *Collected Poems* (Translated by Edmund Keeley and Philip Sherrard, edited by George Savidis, The Hogarth Press, London 1984) p. 29
4 See the commentary of Rashi to Deuteronomy 34:4
5 *Fugitive Pieces*, by Anne Michaels, (Bloomsbury, Great Britain 1997) p. 176
6 Maimonides: Laws of the Foundations of Torah 2:2, in *A Maimonides Reader*, edited by Isadore Twersky (Behrman House, New Jersey 1972) p. 45
7 Mishnoh Avot 4:1
8 Babylonian Talmud, Berachot 8b
9 Albert Einstein: 'Strange Is Our Situation Here On earth', in *The World Treasury of Modern Religious Thought*, edited by Jaroslav Pelikan (Little, Brown and Company, Boston, Toronto, London 1990) p. 204

10   Babylonian Talmud, Shabbat 115b
11   From 'The Dash', by Linda Ellis (quoted from the world wide web)
12   The Kestenbaum Edition Tikkun (Mesorah Publications, New York, 2001) p. 246. The footnote follows the Masoretic tradition.
13   Babylonian Talmud, Sanhedrin 64a.
14   Proverbs 23:23
15   Psalm 42:9

Chapter Three – The Heart's Education

1   Gerald Manley Hopkins: 'The Wreck of the Deutschland', in Gerald Manley Hopkins *Poems and Prose*, selected and edited by W. H. Gardner (Penguin Books, England 1976) p. 14
2   William Wordsworth: *The Prelude*, Book 2, lines 250–3, 261 (Penguin Books, 1976)
3   Rupert Brooks: 'The Great Lover', in *The Poetical Works of Rupert Brooke*, ed. Geoffrey Keynes, (Faber and Faber, London 1974), p. 31
4   Song of Songs 3:1
5   Genesis 29:11 and Rashi's commentary there
6   Psalm 118:24
7   Song of Songs 8:6
8   Viktor E. Frankl: *Man's Search For Meaning*, (Washington Square Press, New York 1985) p. 76
9   William Blake, in *Blake: Complete Writings*, edited by Geoffrey Keynes (Oxford University Press, London, Oxford, New York, 1972) p. 161
10 'Parting', by Boris Pasternak, in *Doctor Zhivago*: (Vintage, London 2002) p. 490
11 The Song of Songs 5:2
12 'I Am', by John Clare, in *John Clare: Selected Poems*, ed. J. W Tibble and Anne Tibble (Everyman's Library, Dent, London and Melbourne 1984) p. 297
13 George Eliot: *Middlemarch*, (Penguin Books, London) p. 226.
14 Psalm 139:11–12
15 In Rachel Remen: *My Grandfather's Blessings* (Riverhead Books, New York, 2001) p. 164–5
16 Psalm 104:33

Chapter Four – Becoming a Rabbi

1   Deuteronomy 28:66–67
2   Zohar III 204a, quoted in *The Wisdom of the Zohar*, (The Littman Library Of Jewish Civilisation, Oxford University Press, 1991) Vol II, p. 670
3   The Daily Morning Service: Authorised Daily Prayer Book (Centenary Edition) (Singer's Prayer Book Publication Committee, Great Britain, 1998) p. 15–16

4   William Wordsworth: 'Lines Written above Tintern Abbey'', in *Words-worth and Coleridge: Lyrical Ballads* edited by R. L. Brett and A. R. Jones (Methuen and Co Ltd. London,1968) p. 114

5   Psalm 145:9

6   Micah 6:8

7   Mishnah Avot 1:2

8   Goethe: Faust, Tragödie, Erster Teil, 682–3

9   Genesis 28:12–15

10   Wliiam Blake: 'The Gates Of Paradise'; illustration with caption 'I want! I want!'; in *Blake: Complete Writings*, edited by Geoffrey Keynes, (Oxford University Press, London, Oxford, New York, 1972) p. 766

11   Babylonian Talmud: Niddah 30b

12   *Dying We Live*, edited by Helmut Gollwotzer, Reinhold Schneider and Kaethe Kuhn (Pantheon, New York, 1956)

13   See Rebbe Yehudah Aryeh-Lev of Ger, *Sefer Sefat Emet Al Hatorah Umo'adim* (Jerusalem 5731) Vol. 4 Bemidbar, p. 23, for Shavuot 5633

14   Rebbe Yehudah Aryeh-Lev of Ger, *Sefer Sefat Emet Al Hatorah Umo'adim* (Jerusalem 5731) Vol. 4, Bemidbar, p. 23, for Shavuot 5633

15   Quoted in Samuel H. Dresner: *The World of a Hasidic Master: Levi Yitzhak of Berditchev* (Shapolsky Publishers, New York, 1986) p. 106–7

16   Psalm 19:4

17   Genesis 18:25

18   Exodus 33:13, and Babylonian Talmud, Berachot 7a

19   Thus see Rebbe Yehudah Aryeh Lev of Ger: *Sefer Sefat Emet Al Hatorah Umo'adim* (Jerusalem 5731, 1970/1) Vol 5 Devarim, commentary on Ekev, 5642, p. 42

20   Viktor Frankl: *Man's Search for Meaning* (Washington Square Press, New York 1985) p. 90

21   Jean Sasson: *Mayada Daughter of Iraq: One Woman's Survival in Saddam Hussein's Torture Jail*, (Bantam, Great Britain 2004) p. 240–1

22   *Osip Mandelstam: Selected Poems*, translated by Clarence Brown and W. S. Merwin, (Oxford University Press, London, Melbourne, Toronto 1973) No. 307, p. 78

23   Rebbe Yehudah Aryeh Lev of Ger: *Sefer Sefat Emet Al Hatorah Umo'adim* (Jerusalem 5731, 1970/1) Vol 2 Shemot, commentary to Beshallach, 5631, p. 65

24   Perek Shirah, Chapter 5

25   Perek Shirah, Chapter 3

26   Exodus 15:2

27   Psalm 19:3

28   Aharon Appelfeld: *The Story of a Life* (Penguin Books, London 2006) p. 101–2

29   Maimonides: *The Guide of the Perplexed*, edited by Shlomo Pines (University of Chicago Press, Chicago and London, 1963) Part 3, Chapter 48 (Vol. 2, p. 599)
30   Genesis 9:2

Chapter Five – Conscience

1   Leviticus 19:18
2   Deuteronomy 10:19
3   Genesis 4:9
4   Milton: *Paradise Lost*, Book 1, lines 25–6
5   1 Kings 19:11–13
6   Genesis 4:9–10
7   Leviticus 19:16
8   Mishnah Sanhedrin 4.5
9   Anna Akhmatova, 'Instead of a Preface, Requiem 1935–40', quoted in Anna Applebaum: *Gulag: A History*, (Penguin Books 2004), p. 1
10   Mishnah, Avot 2:20
11   Pastor Martin Niemöller: Speech given on January 6, 1946 to representatives of the Confessing Church in Frankfurt. There exist various versions of this saying, which was apparently adapted to different circumstances by Niemöller himself.
12   Primo Levi: 'Shema' in *Collected Poems* (Faber and Faber, London 1988) p. 9
13   Goethe: 'Harfenspieler', in *Gedichte* (Wilhelm Goldmann Verlag, Munich 1964) p. 110
14   Babylonian Talmud: Berachot 31a
15   Yalkut Shimoni to the Torah, Beshallach 233, et al.
16   Babylonian Talmud: Berachot 5b
17   Primo Levi: 'The Truce', in *If This is a Man and The Truce*, (Abacus (Sphere Books) Great Britain 1987) p. 188
18   Mishnah, Avot 5:13
19   Abraham Joshua Heschel: *Quest for God*, (Crossroad, New York, 1987) p. 5
20   Nelson Mandela, speech in Trafalgar Square, London, for the Campaign to Make Poverty History, February 2005.
21   Targum Yerushalmi to Genesis 4:8
22   Leviticus 19:14
23   Psalm 85:12
24   Genesis 12:2
25   See Babylonian Talmud: Arachin 16b

Chapter Six – The Privilege of Life

1   Psalm 104:18, 20–21
2   Responsum of Rabbi Ezekiel Landau of Prague: *Noda BiYehudah*, Part 2, Yoreh Deah 10
3   Exodus 23:11
4   Job 38:1, 5–6
5   Midrash Kohelet Rabbah 7:13
6   Proverbs 12:10
7   Thus see Babylonian Talmud: Shabbat 128b
8   Exodus 20:10
9   Maimonides: *The Guide of the Perplexed*, ed. Shlomo Pines (University Of Chicago Press, Chicago and London, 1963) Part 3, Chapter 48 (Vol. 2, p. 599)
10 Perek Shirah, Chapter 1 and Chapter 5
11 Dylan Thomas: 'Ferne Hill' in *Deaths and Entrances* (J. M. Dent and Sons Ltd. London 1971) p. 65–66
12 Moses Cordovero, in Daniel C. Matt: *The Essential Kabbalah* (Castle Books, New Jersey 1997) p. 22
13 In *Sippurei Hasidim*, compiled by Shlomo Yosef Zevin (Bet Hillel, Jerusalem, no date of publication given) p. 263
14 Leviticus 9:23–10:3
15 Based on Rashi's commentary to Leviticus 9:23
16 *Chummash Peneenei Hahasidut: Sefer Vayikra*, (edited by Rabbis Sholem B. Kowalski, Yitzchak Fajgenbaum and Sh. Ch. Porush, (Agudath Peneenay Hachassidut, Jerusalem 5745), p. 68–9
17 Leviticus 9:24
18 Leviticus 10:3
19 Alfred Feldman: *One Step Ahead: A Jewish Fugitive in Hitler's Europe* (Southern Illinois University Press, 2001) p. 213
20 Psalm 115:17
21 *Chummash Peneenei Hahasidut: Sefer Bereshit*, (edited by Rabbis Sholem B. Kowalski, Yitzchak Fajgenbaum and Sh. Ch. Porush, (Agudath Peneenay Hachassidut, Jerusalem 5747–1987) p. 11
22 Shakespeare: *King Lear*, Act 3, Scene 6
23 Psalm 51:12
24 Ezekiel 36:26
25 Proverbs 15:1
26 Jeremiah 17:14

Chapter Seven – Struggles

1   Psalm 22:2
2   Babylonian Talmud: Pesachim 115b
3   In Shaul Meizeles: *Eyn Shalem Milev Shavur: Imrot HaRebbe Mikotsk* (Modan, Israel 1988) p. 34
4   *'Bivediduti Hagedolah'* by Rachel in *Shirat Rachel* (Davar, Tel Aviv, 5738) p. 25, my translation
5   Numbers: 5:11–31
6   Shakespeare: *Othello*, Act 3, Scene 4
7   Thus see the homilies in Babylonian Talmud: Sotah 4b–5a
8   Goethe: 'Harfenspieler', *Goethe: Gedichte* (Wilhelm Goldmann Verlag, München, 1964) p. 110
9   Babylonian Talmud: Rosh Hashanah 16b
10 Vasily Grossman: *A Writer at War*, edited and translated by Antony Beevor and Luba Vinogradova (Pimlico, London 2006) p. 192
11 Moses ibn Ezra: 'Hekitzuni Se'ipai', in *Shirat Tor Hazahav BiSefarad* (The Hebrew University, Jerusalem, 5746) p. 88 my translation
12 Deuteronomy 29:9
13 William Shakespeare: *Richard II*, Act 5, Scene 5
14 Targum Yerushalmi to Genesis 4:8
15 The Forgiveness Project: www.theforgivenessproject.com/
16   Mishnah, Yoma 8:9
17 Leviticus 19:17
18 William Blake: 'The Poison Tree', in *Blake: Complete Writings*, edited by Geoffrey Keynes (Oxford University Press, London, Oxford, New York, 1976) p. 165
19 Mishnah, Avot 4:18
20 Psalm 63:2
21 Numbers 20:12
22 'The Ethical Will of the Ba'al Shem Tov' in *Sefer Shivchei Habesht* (Yad Binyamin, Jerusalem 5729 / 1969)
23 Shakespeare, *King Lear*, Act 4, Scene 6
24 Leviticus 19:18
25 T. S. Eliot: *The Four Quartets*: 'Burnt Norton' in *T. S. Eliot: Collected Poems* (Faber and Faber, London and Boston, 1963)
26 Viktor E. Frankl: *Man's Search for Meaning*, (Washington Square Press, USA, 1985) p. 86
27 The Baal Shem Tov on portion Noach, *Amud Hatefilah 56*, in *Sefer Baal Shem Tov*
28 Mishnah: Avot 4:1
29 'The Ethical Will of the Ba'al Shem Tov' in *Sefer Shivchei Habesht* (Yad Binyamin, Jerusalem 5729 / 1969) p. 215
30 Arthur Green: *Seek My Face: A Jewish Mystical Theology* (Jewish Lights, Woodstock, Vermont 2003) p. 25

Notes

Chapter Eight – Grief

1 Will Rogers, see www-hsc.usc.edu/~cypert/dick/inheaven.html
2 Psalm 71:9, but made familiar (in the plural form) in the liturgy for the Day of Atonement
3 Babylonian Talmud: Ketubot 104a
4 The Authorised Daily Prayer Book, Revised Centenary Edition, (Singer's Prayer Book Publication Committee, Great Britain, 1998) p. 811, in my, fairly free, translation.
5 Isaiah 58:7
6 Psalm 39: 10–11
7 Babylonian Talmud: Niddah 30b
8 Shakespeare: *King Lear*, Act 5, Scene 3
9 Genesis 37:35
10 Rabbi Kalonymus Kalman Shapira, in Nehemia Polen: *The Holy Fire: The Teachings of Rabbi Kalonymus Kalman Shapira, the Rebbe of the Warsaw Ghetto*, (Jason Aronson, Northvale, New Jersey, London 1994) p. 131
11 Edward K. Rynearson: *Retelling Violent Death* (Brunner Routledge, Philadelphia, 2001)
12 Website in honour of Miriam Hyman – www.miriam–hyman.com
13 Nehemia Polen: *The Holy Fire: The Teachings of Rabbi Kalonymus Kalman Shapira, the Rebbe of the Warsaw Ghetto*, (Jason Aronson, Northvale, New Jersey, London 1994) p. 132
14 After the title of the book by Shaul Meizeles: *Eyn Shalem Milev Shavur: Imrot HaRebbe Mikotsk* (Modan, Tel Aviv, 1988)
15 Psalm 51:19
16 Mishnah Berurah, note 12, to Shulchan Aruch: Orach Chayyim 581:1
17 *Abraham Joshua Heschel: Prophetic Witness*, by Edward K. Kaplan and Samuel H. Dresner, (Yale University Press, New Haven and London, 1998) p. 17
18 Deuteronomy 30:6
19 Psalm 91:15
20 Exodus 2:23–5
21 Elena Kozhina: *Through the Burning Steppe: A Wartime Memoir*, trans. Vadim Mahmoudov (Duck Editions, London 2000) p. 43–4
22 Ibid. p. 143

Chapter Nine – Onwards

1 Moses Ibn Ezra: 'Yizkor Gever' in *Shirat Hator Hazahav BiSefarad* (Hebrew University, Jerusalem 5746) p. 90, my translation
2 Rabindranath Tagore: 'The Crescent Moon', in *Collected Poems and Plays of Rabindranath Tagore* (Macmillan, London, 1977) p. 84–5
3 *The Song of Songs* 8:6

4   Job 7:10
5   Rashi's commentary to Genesis 37:35
6   Rainer Maria Rilke: 'Der Panther' in *Rilke: Poems*, selected and edited by G. W. McKay (Oxford University Press, Oxford and New York, 1965) p. 47
7   Genesis 3:19
8   Shakespeare: *Hamlet*, Act 4, Scene 2
9   Job 28:12
10 Psalms 111:10
11 Babylonian Talmud: Berachot 33b
12 The Song of Songs 5:2
13 The Song of Songs 5:6
14 Rashi to Song of Songs 5:2, and Psalm 121:4
15 Psalm 73:26